GETTING STARTED IN PERSONAL AND EXECUTIVE COACHING

GETTING STARTED IN PERSONAL AND EXECUTIVE COACHING

How to Create a Thriving Coaching Practice

Stephen G. Fairley
Chris E. Stout

WILEY

John Wiley & Sons, Inc.

Published by John Wiley & Sons, Inc., Hoboken, New Jersey.
Published simultaneously in Canada.

For general information on our other products and services please contact our Customer Care Department within the United States at (800) 762-2974, outside the United States at (317) 572-3993 or fax (317) 572-4002.

Wiley also publishes its books in a variety of electronic formats. Some content that appears in print may not be available in electronic books. For more information about Wiley products, visit our website at www.wiley.com.

Library of Congress Cataloging-in-Publication Data

Fairley, Stephen.
    Getting started in personal and executive coaching : how to create a thriving coaching practice / Stephen Fairley, Chris E. Stout.
      p. cm.
    ISBN 0-471-42624-5 (pbk.)
    1. Personal coaching—Practice.   2. Executive coaching—Practice.   I. Stout, Chris E.
II. Title.
    BF637.P35F35 2003
    650.1—dc22

                                                                          2003014094

Printed in the United States of America

10 9 8 7 6 5 4 3

Contents

Series Preface

Getting Started

As the behavioral health care marketplace grows more challenging, providers are finding it necessary to develop smarter business tactics in order to be successful. We are faced with shifting payment structures, increasing competition, complex funding mechanisms, the bankruptcy of many managed care agencies, and growing malpractice liability risks, all against a backdrop of layoffs and dwindling economic resources. It is times like these that make Wiley's *Getting Started* series of books all the more important.

Many individuals studying in the mental health professions graduate with no idea of how to go about starting their own mental health practice. Alternatively, there are many mental health practitioners who wish to shift the focus of their current practice into other areas. The *Getting Started* series of books provides the information, ideas, tools and strategies providers need to enable their practices to evolve and thrive under any circumstances. This series works to break down the ingredients of a successful mental health practice into more manageable components, and thus more achievable components. It is my goal to bring readers the best of the best in the *Getting Started* series in an effort to help them start, maintain, and expand their successful mental health practices.

The *Getting Started* series is not discipline specific. It is meant for behavioral health care students at all levels of study, as well as providers—undergraduate students, graduate students, and professionals in all the fields of behavioral health care. Current books include *Getting Started in Personal and Executive Coaching* and *Getting Started in Private Practice*. Other titles will focus on various mental health disciplines, including forensic practice, group practice, and marriage and family practice, as well as topics such as integrating technology with your mental health services.

Successful practice in whatever area or specialty takes work; there are no overnight successes. But being successful is quite doable. This series provides the organizing methods most of us never learned in graduate or medical school training, or that were available only by hiring one's own consultant. You will learn what works and what doesn't work without having to make costly missteps first.

Is establishing or growing your practice going to be difficult? To a degree, the likely answer is yes. Of course, it will take some work, but it will likely be well worth the effort. I hope you find the *Getting Started* series to be a helpful set of tools in achieving your professional goals.

Chris E. Stout
Series Editor

Introduction

Getting Started in the Business of Coaching

Is your coaching practice completely full?

Are you getting more referrals than you can really handle?

Do you know exactly when, where, and how to find 10 new clients in the next six months?

Are you making more money than you thought possible in your first years of coaching?

If so, then put this book down! Because someone out there needs it more than you do.

However, if you're like the more than 50 percent of coaches out there with fewer than 10 paying clients and making less than $20,000 a year, then you absolutely need this book. Before we go any further, let me tell you what this book is *not* about:

- It's not about a model of coaching or academic theories.
- It's not about strategies that sound good on paper but haven't actually been tried in real life.
- It's definitely not about fluff, hype, or some ambiguous promise of "Take these five steps and you'll have a full practice in 90 days."

Instead, here's *what you'll find* in this book:

- Straightforward answers to serious questions about how to build, maintain, and sustain a thriving coaching practice
- Hundreds of proven techniques and strategies for finding and landing new business
- Real-world illustrations from top coaches all across the country about their secrets to success
- Fifteen step-by-step strategies for rapidly finding your first 10 paying clients
- Exactly what separates financially unsuccessful coaches from financially successful coaches
- Precisely how much money you will need to launch your coaching business if you're just starting out
- The 10 biggest pitfalls new coaches fall into and how to avoid them
- Loads of practical action steps you can take to quickly apply these ideas and techniques
- The actual nuts-and-bolts of starting and operating a coaching business
- What new coaches can do to significantly increase their chances of success
- The 11 largest markets for coaching you can tap into right now

The ideas, strategies, techniques, and insights in this book are based on research I (Stephen Fairley) conducted with 300 coaches nationwide, one-on-one interviews with top coaches in the field, my personal experience building a thriving executive and business coaching practice in Chicago (www.TodaysLeadership.com), and my success in helping many coaches, consultants, and other small business owners effectively market their services and obtain a higher return on investment from their marketing dollars (www.MYOBforCoaches.com). For information on how you can receive free business coaching, see the last pages of this book.

WHO IS THIS BOOK FOR?

I wrote this book for four groups of people:

- *New coaches just starting out* who are serious about building a thriving coaching practice and are actively looking for ways to successfully accomplish this

- *Experienced coaches* who know how tough it is to find new clients and are desperate for more effective ways to market and sell their services and aren't afraid to try new things
- *Personal coaches and executive business coaches* who want to discover how to expand their services into new markets and rapidly gain a competitive advantage in the field
- *Consultants, psychologists, therapists, and professional speakers* who want to add coaching to their repertoire of services, but don't know the best way to do it and don't have a lot of time for a long learning curve

If you don't fit one of these four categories or you're not really serious about creating a dynamic, successful coaching practice, you will probably find this book a complete waste of your time, and I suggest you would be better off putting it back on the shelf, because even if you read it, the hard-hitting, real-world strategies and illustrations won't be of much use to you.

However, if you do fall into one of those four categories and you are serious about building your business, then I believe there is no better, more comprehensive book available to help you achieve your goal. A rather bold statement? You bet, but it's true.

WHY SHOULD YOU READ THIS BOOK?

Here are some little-known facts about *new* coaches:

- Seventy-three percent of all coaches make less than $10,000 in their first year.
- Only 60 percent of all second-year coaches have managed to find 10 paying clients.
- Less than 11 percent of all coaches make more than $50,000 by their second year in practice.

The news doesn't get much better when talking about coaches in general:

- Even though coaches charge an average of $160 a hour for their services, 53 percent of them make less than $20,000 a year.
- Thirty percent of all coaches are still not able to find 10 paying clients.

- Only 9 percent of coaches make more than $100,000 a year doing coaching.

Here's the bottom line on why should you read this book: Many people are starting out in the field of coaching, spending thousands of dollars and hundreds of hours undergoing coach certification training, launching new ventures with visions of making a lot of money by doing what they love to do, but are quickly confronted by the cold reality of not being able to find new clients or even make a reasonable living. I'm seeing a growing trend of good people leaving the field because of unmet expectations—based on a false pretense and fueled by unrealistic stories of select people becoming financially successful in a few short months. Many coaches are desperate for someone to show them what really works—not based just on their own personal theories about how things *should* work, but based on real-world research about what is working right now and what the top coaches in the field are doing to be successful. You should read this book if you're committed to building your business; you recognize it will take all of your time, energy, and resources to make it a long-term success; and you're looking for solid answers, because that's exactly what you will get in this book. I promise.

Here's the premise of this book: At its core, professional coaching is no different from any other small business. To be successful you must do the things that successful small business owners do—implement a strong marketing plan, use solid sales skills, understand the fundamentals of operating a company, and keep track of your finances. If you want to become a successful coach, you must understand and apply the principles, strategies, and techniques discussed in this book.

> Professional coaching is no different from any other small business. To be successful in coaching, you must become successful at running a small business.

Here's my challenge to you: Take the next 15 minutes, sit down, and go through the questions in the next section. If you can easily and clearly answer all of them, then put this book down and walk away. However, if you can't, then commit to spending the next few weeks working your way through this book and discovering how to apply what's in the book. An initial 15 minutes of your time is all I'm asking for, but it could lead to critical decisions that will determine the long-term success of your coaching business.

THE GETTING STARTED INVENTORY

Before you jump right into this book, we *strongly* encourage you to spend some time carefully going through each of the questions in this inventory. Write down your answers as a record you can refer back to as you go through the book.

I have found that *the results you get from this book will be greatly increased if you first answer these questions.* This is not a test. These questions are designed to give you a perspective on where you currently are with regard to several critical areas of planning, starting, and marketing your coaching business. As you can see, each question is tied to a particular chapter in the book where you can find out more information about a particular topic.

This book was not designed to be just read straight through, as most chapters can stand alone. When a previously covered topic is referenced in a chapter, we have tried to give you the exact chapter you can go to for your convenience. So as you come across a question or topic in this inventory that you find especially interesting, feel free to turn immediately to that chapter.

Remember: *In order to know where you are going, you first have to know where you are.* This inventory will help you quickly discover where you are.

1. What are the major differences between coaching, consulting, and counseling? Can you easily explain them to interested prospects? (See Chapter 1.)
2. What are the three biggest obstacles you will face when trying to market and sell your coaching services (pick one: personal, life, business, or executive coaching)? How can you overcome them? (See Chapter 1.)
3. From an objective point of view, what kind of impression do prospects have when they are first introduced to you and your

services? Is this the exact impression you want them to have, and do you know the most effective ways to shape and mold their feelings and thoughts about your company? (See Chapter 7.)

4. What would you say if a prospect said to you, "Amazing! You're the third person I've met this month who does coaching. I'm interested in hiring a coach, but why should I hire you and not one of the other coaches?" (See Chapter 7.)

5. Describe in as much detail as possible who your ideal primary target is. For example, my ideal primary target is at least 40 years of age, usually college educated, has an annual income of $100,000 or more, works within 20 miles of my home, holds a management or leadership position at work, is constantly looking for new challenges, tends to be a rather driven person when it comes to setting and accomplishing professional goals, has a high commitment level to personal growth, reads a lot of self-help books, and attends two or three development workshops a year. (See Chapter 2.)

6. How are you positioning yourself and your services to your target market in terms of quality, service, pricing, and selection, for the elite or everyday person? (See Chapter 2.)

7. What are the most important parts of a successful business or marketing plan? (We mention 10 in the book.) (See Chapter 6.)

8. Approximately how much money does the average person invest in starting up a new small business? ("None" is not an acceptable response.) Is there a correlation between how much you start out with and how quickly you can become financially successful? (See Chapter 4.)

9. In your first couple of years three basic categories will make up the majority of your expenses: marketing materials, office equipment and supplies, and ongoing sales and marketing efforts. What percentage of your annual financial plan do you anticipate spending on each category? Where are you more likely to receive the highest return on investment (ROI)? (See Chapter 4.)

10. What are the absolute necessities you must have in order to officially launch your coaching business? (And "Nothing but a telephone" is not an acceptable response. See Chapter 5.)

11. How much money do you anticipate investing in your first year of business (including all your start-up costs, initial and ongoing sales and marketing efforts, and all capital expenditures), and what are the top 5 to 10 things you will spend it on? (See Chapter 5.)

12. Name as many of the top industries or areas for coaching as you can. (There are 12 detailed in the book; see Chapter 3.)

13. Pick one of the areas from the preceding step that you would like to focus on and write down several specific marketing strategies you can easily use to find new clients in that area. (We discuss almost 100 different strategies in one chapter alone; see Chapter 3.)

14. Name several strategies you can easily implement to rapidly find your next 10 paying clients. (See Chapter 9.)

15. What are the most common objections you will hear from prospects, and how should you reply? (See Chapter 9.)

16. What would you say if a prospect asked, "What are the specific benefits and results I would receive from using your services?" (See Chapter 10.)

17. What are the biggest, most common marketing mistakes new coaches make? (We list 10 in the book; see Chapter 10.)

18. Identify the top four ways coaches are currently finding clients. (See Chapter 8.)

19. What do you say to people who ask, "What do you do?" (To keep their attention and pique their interest you must be able to do it in one or two clear and compelling sentences; see Chapter 8.)

20. What are some specific techniques you can use to significantly increase the number and quality of referrals you receive from other people? (See Chapter 8.)

21. Name a few simple things you can do to limit your risk of being sued. (See Chapter 11.)

22. What are the most powerful Internet tools coaches are using to find new business and land new clients? (See Chapter 12.)

23. Name a few of the biggest mistakes coaches make about their web sites. (There are 28 mentioned in the book; see Chapter 12.)

24. What strategies and systems are the most successful coaches using right now to significantly increase their revenues? (See Chapter 13.)

25. What do coaches who are making more than $100,000 a year know and do that other coaches don't know or do? (See Chapter 13.)

SUMMARY

Well, how did you do? Were you able to answer every question in a clear, concise, and compelling manner, or were there some areas you found difficult? If you are like the vast majority of coaches, your response is the latter—and that's a good thing, because it means you really thought about each question and the profound impact it has on the short- and long-term success of your coaching business.

Now for the real question: What are you going to do about it? You have probably identified several areas you need to work on, and now you have three choices:

- Ignore your discovery and go back to the old way of doing things.
- Turn to the next chapter and start working through the book step by step.
- Pick a specific area to work on and turn immediately to the applicable chapter.

Here are my recommendations:

Choice 1: Ignore the principles, techniques, and strategies in this book at your own peril and to the detriment of your coaching business. (What did you think I'd say?) Not the best choice.

Choice 2: This is the best option if you are relatively new to the world of coaching, or you have never successfully owned and operated a small business before, or you have started your practice in the past two years.

Choice 3: This is the best alternative for coaches with established practices who are probably applying most of the basic principles, but are looking for more effective ways to grow and sustain their businesses and want strategies that produce better results faster, with less effort.

Whatever your choice, I wish you the best of luck and much success in your business venture. I would love to hear from you periodically as you go through this book as to how it has helped you build, market, and sustain a thriving coaching practice! You can e-mail me at Stephen @TodaysLeadership.com. You can also sign up for a *free* monthly e-zine filled with practical strategies and proven marketing techniques for building your coaching business at our web site, www.MYOBforCoaches .com.

CHAPTER 1

Decisions, Decisions . . . Personal Coaching or Business Coaching?

WHAT KIND OF COACH ARE YOU?
PERSONAL COACHING
    Positives and Negatives of Personal Coaching
    Characteristics of Successful Personal Coaches
    Titles Personal Coaches Use
    Pricing Your Personal Coaching Services
BUSINESS COACHING
    Positives and Negatives of Business Coaching
    Characteristics of a Great Business Coach
    Titles Business Coaches Use
    Pricing Your Business Coaching Services
DISTINGUISHING COACHING FROM OTHER FIELDS FOR MARKETING PURPOSES
IS PERSONAL OR BUSINESS COACHING RIGHT FOR YOU?
SELF-ASSESSMENT INVENTORY
    Recommended Responses
ACTION STEP

What Kind of Coach Are You?

As professional coaching grows in popularity, it will experience an external struggle to define, refine, describe, and distinguish itself from other fields, as well as an internal struggle to create subspecialties. The field of psychology offers a typical model. In the early years, the primary struggle was to differentiate psychology from psychiatry (it struggles with this even today, as most lay people still don't know the difference between a psychologist, a psychiatrist, and a social worker). As time went on, the field began to divide into other specialties, with the first few being experimental, clinical, and academic psychology. Today, the American Psychological Association recognizes over 50 major divisions with many other specialty areas.

Currently, there are two major branches of professional coaching—personal coaching and business coaching—but each is quickly gaining subspecialties. Each division goes by various names. For example, personal coaching is also known as life coaching, success coaching, personal life coaching, and professional coaching. Some of the more popular subspecialties include spiritual coaching, relationship coaching, coactive coaching, Christian coaching, personal development coaching, and career coaching, among others. This book uses the term *personal coaching* to refer to all of them, except where noted. Business coaching is also known as corporate coaching, management coaching, executive coaching, and leadership coaching, to mention a few, but some people define each of these areas as a subspecialty of business coaching. This book uses these terms interchangeably and refers to all of them by the generic term *business coaching*, except where noted. Yes, I do realize there are distinctions and separations between the many areas and even the specific names, but the differences are primarily not in the techniques coaches use, or in their ability, their training, or even their experiences, but in the particular populations served and the problems most commonly encountered during coaching.

In this chapter we will:

- Briefly define the two emerging branches, personal and business coaching, for the purposes of this book.
- Discuss the positives and negatives of both personal and business coaching.

- Provide an overview of the characteristics of successful personal and business coaches.
- List the job titles commonly used by people in each field.
- Inventory the current prices of services and reported average incomes.
- Present a map of how you can distinguish coaching from different fields for the purpose of positioning and marketing yourself.
- Give you a self-assessment inventory to help you determine which field would be a better fit for you given your interests, experiences, and location.

As you read through this chapter, if you have not already decided which area you will focus on, please try to keep an open mind. If you have already decided, now is the time to start making yourself more aware of the potential positives and negatives and to develop a plan for maximizing the former while compensating for the latter. However, make no mistake: What title you give yourself and what field you see yourself in will largely determine what kind of clients you attract to your practice. There are some definite advantages and distinct disadvantages with both personal and business coaching. Let's explore each area in turn.

PERSONAL COACHING

Personal coaches usually work with a wide range of individuals on a host of intrapersonal and interpersonal issues, such as coping with a specific problem or crisis, focusing their energy, achieving their dreams, making career transitions, living a happier, more fulfilled life, overcoming conflict, enhancing their communication skills, specifying and achieving their life goals, and building better relationships, to name a few. Clients may or may not be connected with a business, and their careers or jobs may or may not have anything to do with the focus of the coaching, with the exception of career coaching, which almost always has a professional connection.

POSITIVES AND NEGATIVES OF PERSONAL COACHING

Every field has its positives and negatives. Personal coaching is no different. On the positive side, the target audience for personal coaching is fairly broad. It can include adolescents, college students, working professionals, people in career transitions, couples, business executives, and adults in general. You can focus on people who are in a crisis situation, adults in a midlife transition, couples with relationship difficulties, professionals who want to advance their careers, soccer moms who want more out of life, elderly people who are facing death—the possibilities are only limited by your imagination . . . and a few other things. It's the "few other things" that can make personal coaching a difficult field to be in. Here are the top five negatives of personal coaching:

1. *The market is so big you can have a hard time focusing.*

   One of the biggest mistakes new coaches make is targeting too large a market. In your desire to help all different kinds of people with all different kinds of problems, your lack of resources can quickly become a fatal weakness to your business, because no one has the time, energy, or financial wherewithal to effectively target a vast audience. It's easy to tell when a personal coach has fallen into this trap. Ask them who they help and what kind of problems they commonly coach around. If they list more than three distinct target markets or more than six completely different kinds of problems, it is very likely their business is hurting because they are unfocused. On one personal coaching web site I came across recently, the author listed a few typical clients:

   - Individuals who want to live a bigger life
   - Professionals who desire more from their career
   - Adults who struggle with personal relationships
   - People trying to balance their work and life
   - Adults who have elderly parents and are trying to take care of them
   - People in a midlife transition
   - Women who are going through a divorce

   While their attempts at being comprehensive are laudable, their results are most definitely not. This gives the clear impression that they help everybody, which most prospects interpret as actually helping nobody. Personal coaches have to be very specific about who they help. You must be able to clearly and concisely tell who your target audience is. More about how to do that is found in Chapter 2.

2. *Personal coaching is highly discretionary, so it strongly depends on the economic situation of your target market.*

Simply put, when the economy is good and people feel like they have a lot of extra spending money, personal coaching can be a relatively easy sell, but when the economy is bad and the future is grim, people are focused on surviving the layoffs, not obtaining their dreams. This is a simple principle from psychologist Abraham Maslow, in his "hierarchy of needs" (Figure 1.1). People are most concerned with safety and security needs and can focus on the needs above, like self-esteem, only when the needs below are satisfied. Self-actualization is characterized by being solution-focused and possessing an appreciation for the fullness of life, concern for personal growth and development, and the ability to have peak experiences. Sounds like a great coaching client!

3. *You cannot charge nearly as much for personal coaching as for business coaching.*

Most people do not go into coaching, or any other field, just for the money. Many people are making the transition into coaching from other professional fields where they were very successful, held a 9-to-5 job, and had a steady paycheck and benefits; they have also built up a certain lifestyle they would like to

FIGURE 1.1   Maslow's hierarchy of needs.

maintain. In addition, many people move into coaching because of what it stands for—balance, fulfillment, happiness, self-control, increased freedom, and an inherent promise to have a completely portable business, allowing you to set up and live anywhere you want—even on the beaches of Hawaii. However, self-employment can be a hard taskmaster. There are the regular bills to pay, your lifestyle to maintain, and all the start-up costs of a new business. In order to cover expenses, coaches have to charge what is often seen by the average consumer as an extremely high amount per hour. Yet this same amount in a business setting is viewed as a normal expense.

There are two primary reasons why the average business coach is able to charge significantly more per hour than the average personal coach. First, the number of experienced business coaches is much smaller than the number of personal coaches. The entry bar into the world of business coaching is set much higher than that of the personal coaching world, where literally anyone can set up shop and many people believe they become qualified as soon as they open their doors for business. This problem will only be compounded as thousands of personal coaches enter the field every year. Second, regardless of the economy, individual clients are much less inclined to pay monthly fees of hundreds or thousands of dollars than are companies and organizations that are used to paying high fees to consultants, lawyers, investment bankers, and accounting firms.

4. *With a potential audience so vast, it's hard to find truly effective ways to reach it.*

In some ways, the potential audience for personal coaching is vast, especially if you think you can help everyone with almost any problem (which is not true). However, in order to actually make a living from coaching, the challenge becomes developing a niche that you can effectively target and finding enough people in that niche who can afford your high hourly fees. The typical client of a personal coach has a family income of at least $60,000 to $80,000 per year. That leaves out about 80 percent of the American population, and in many geographical areas of the country, it leaves out almost everyone. People in the upper income brackets (more than $80,000 a year) have many, many products, services, and companies vying for their time, attention, and financial resources. If you wish to be successful in personal coaching, you have to find effective ways to reach people in your target audience. This book will help you do that.

5. *The biggest danger of personal coaching is how easily it can become confused with or used as a replacement for counseling or psychotherapy.*

This one issue has the potential to totally reshape the field of personal coaching and is something you will begin to hear more about in the near future. Here is the situation I believe will quicken the pace of this debate: There is a small but growing number of coaches currently specializing in coaching various forms of mental illness, such as attention deficit disorder (ADD) coaches and coaches who purport to help people through periods of depression, grief, or life transitions. While this may be the attempt of some psychologists or mental health therapists to be creative in packaging their psychological services, I have personally met several "coaches" who have neither the professional training nor experience to help people with serious mental illness, either from a coaching or psychotherapy perspective. Yet they are targeting people with various diagnosable mental disorders such as ADD, depression, and anxiety and implying that they can help them through coaching. I believe this opens them up to all kinds of litigation, lawsuits, and charges of ethical violations. In my personal opinion, it is only a matter of time until someone accuses a personal ADD coach or someone "coaching" a person out of their depression of illegally practicing psychology without a license and initiates a lawsuit. In addition to this overt problem, many psychologists and mental health clinicians charge that regular personal life coaching looks like, sounds like, and has goals similar to those of a clinician's psychotherapy practice. With the field of psychology crushed under the weight of managed care, there are many people in the field considering possible alternative streams of revenue, including consulting and coaching services. I believe within the next two to four years there will be a movement at the state level in several jurisdictions to regulate and restrict the practice of personal coaching through licensure. If psychologists, social workers, and mental health counselors band together, they could try to subsume personal coaching under the rubric of mental health and restrict entry into the personal coaching industry only to individuals with graduate degrees and licensure, much as the field of psychology is regulated today. This has already begun in Colorado, where the state professional licensing board has taken a stance that although business coaching does not fall within the purview of the regulatory board, personal coaching does. While I am not aware of any current litigation activity, it is simply a matter of time. Helping the psychologists' and professional licensing boards' cause would be their well-developed lobbying groups and the persuasive argument that the coaching field could become another source of taxable revenue for cash-hungry states. If you're concerned about this issue, be sure to check out Chapter 11.

CHARACTERISTICS OF SUCCESSFUL PERSONAL COACHES

Given the previous section, you may perceive I believe that every personal coach should have a strong background in psychology or counseling. While this certainly can be helpful, I do not believe it is always necessary or sufficient. Many coaching skills were taken directly from the psychology field, and most modern psychotherapeutic treatments are focused on helping people with some of the same techniques and models that coaching uses. For example, psychologists using the Brief Strategic Model of counseling are highly interactive with their clients, use a strength-based model (versus the pathology-based model of the medical profession), form measurable goals, focus on the future, develop specific strategies for overcoming problems, and often see their clients for only 6 to 16 sessions. Sounds a lot like coaching! However, just as a degree in psychology does not guarantee you'll be a great psychologist, neither does it guarantee you'll be a great coach. I know of many great personal coaches who have no formal background in psychology.

If you are considering becoming a personal coach, be sure you feel comfortable that you either currently meet or are willing to work hard to meet virtually all of these characteristics:

- Are a great listener
- Excel in problem solving

- Enjoy a good challenge
- Have the ability to focus
- Willingly offer clients encouragement and support
- Are able to be clear and concise
- Have the ability to see through the fog to the core issues
- Have a wide variety of life experience
- Are open to different ideas
- Like to brainstorm
- Have extraordinary communication skills
- Can easily build rapport with people
- Have a flexible personality
- Are willing to challenge your clients when needed
- Feel comfortable holding others accountable
- Desire that your clients experience change
- Can offer different perspectives

Although these characteristics will not ensure your success as a personal coach, they certainly will help you service your clients more effectively.

TITLES PERSONAL COACHES USE

There are many variations of the titles coaches give themselves. Some of the more popular ones include:

- Personal coach
- Life coach
- Success coach
- Relationship coach
- Career coach
- Career and personal coach
- Professional coach
- Coactive coach

Generally speaking, the top four titles are more appropriate if you are going to specialize in working with individuals and professionals outside of their company or business. The middle two are more associated with coaching people about their careers and job transitions. The last two are perhaps more flexible in that they are appropriate when working with either individuals or inside an organization or company, depending on who you are trying to target within the organization. There have been coaches who have been successful in landing corporate accounts while calling themselves a personal coach, and vice versa, but my suspicion is that in most of these situations there were many other factors working in their favor, helping their prospects not to be turned off by their title (e.g., a direct referral, an outstanding reputation), and that a beginning coach may not fare as well. Also, as in any field, as coaching develops into a recognized industry more and more people will look to hire a coach who specializes in the area they are most concerned about—their personal life or their professional life.

PRICING YOUR PERSONAL COACHING SERVICES

The hourly fees for personal coaching range from $40 to over $300 per hour, with the average being $132 per hour, according to my survey of 300 coaches nationwide. Living in metropolitan areas seems to correlate with slightly higher hourly rates, possibly because awareness and acceptance of professional coaching has increased over the past couple of years. Eighty percent of personal coaches charge either an hourly or monthly fee.

A staggering 61 percent of full-time personal coaches report making less than $20,000 a year, but 18 percent are making more than $75,000. The average annual income for full-time personal coaches has been estimated to be between $30,000 and $40,000. Chapter 13 goes into detail about what top coaches do to significantly increase their revenues.

BUSINESS COACHING

Business coaches typically work with business professionals, managers, executives, and owners on issues such as leadership development, increasing employee motivation, organizational strategy, building a company, organizational development, change-management issues, career advancement, overcoming sales and marketing challenges, career derailment, succession planning, effective communication skills, time-management issues, team building, and management training.

POSITIVES AND NEGATIVES OF BUSINESS COACHING

Business coaching is a fast-emerging field that combines the best of industrial and organizational psychology, management consulting, organizational development, sports psychology, and business consulting to provide a different paradigm of how people function in an organization and how the organization itself functions. There are as many opportunities for business coaching as the number of businesses that exist in a given community. Many successful executives and business owners are used to working with high-powered professionals who charge high fees and bring particular skills and abilities that help businesses be more successful. They are more willing to recognize when they need outside help and expertise to deal with a specific situation. There are a wide variety of situations that a coach could be called in to deal with, including keeping a good manager from derailing his or her career, helping a new leadership team make the transition smoothly, evaluating the potential of top managers for an upcoming VP opening, succession planning, developing a management training program, mediating conflict between executives and employees, developing a marketing strategy for a new product, keeping a president from burning out and leaving, or helping a CEO create a strategic vision for the company. Most of the issues relate somehow to the interaction between the person and their work.

There are also a number of potential negatives of being a business coach, including these:

1. *You have many more sophisticated competitors.*

    Competition for an executive's time and the company's money for these kinds of services can come from major consulting firms, management training companies, business strategy organizations, well-known consultants, and even law and accounting firms that are adding coaching to their list of services. As a business coach, you are no longer just faced with proving you can do the job; you are up against companies that spend millions of dollars every year marketing and advertising their services. They may have whole professional sales teams that specialize in landing the deal and then another whole team of consultants who just do the work, while you are required to be an expert in all three areas, marketing, sales, and coaching—all at the same time. You have to be faster, smarter, more efficient than, and just as effective as your larger counterparts if you want to build a successful business coaching practice.

2. *The bigger the deal, the bigger the company, and the longer the sales cycle.*

As a business coach, you are most likely to be paid either by the hour or by the project. Only a few coaches are able to obtain the ever-elusive retainer fee, under which a company pays the coach a flat fee for a set number of hours, regardless of whether the company actually uses them. This basically means that if you are not working billable hours, you are not getting paid. In addition, the majority of your time is spent trying to land that first deal with a given company, and you intuitively know that the larger the company, the more likely it will be able to supply you with multiple projects in the future. As such, it is often tempting to target bigger and bigger companies with more and more people, hoping that landing a project with a major company will lead to many more in the future. For some business coaches this strategy works. However, the downside is that the larger the company, the less likely you are to be able to talk to a true decision maker, and the longer you will have to spend on the sales cycle to actually secure your first project. For example, I know a business coach who spent almost two years trying to obtain a coaching project with a major *Fortune* 500 company. He finally had the contract and was slated to begin work on a $70,000 project in less than 30 days through the development office. One morning he received a phone call. The company had just announced a major cutback, and the entire development office had been laid off. Not only was his contract gone, but so was the high-level contact that he had worked so hard to develop for the past two years.

3. *Business can disappear with the next quarter's earnings.*

When the economy is up and businesses are experiencing consistent positive cash flow, they are much more willing to try new things (like a business coach) and think outside of the box (they believe real people change over time, not all at once), and they are more tolerant (they'll work to change a manager's behavior using one-on-one coaching instead of just firing them), but when times are tough and every quarter is a "make it or break it" one, businesses tend to fall back on what they have tried before (regardless of whether they have had much success). You might spend several months working on getting your first coaching project with a company and be almost there when suddenly two or three of its "for sure" deals fall apart, and all your hard work goes down in flames in a single meeting. If none of their industry peers are using business coaches to solve their problems, businesses don't want to be known as being out in left field. It's okay to try something that everyone else is doing and fail at it. After all, everyone else tried it too. But if you try something that no one else is doing and it fails—then you risk looking foolish to your peers, which no business owner or executive wants to experience.

4. *Consultants and coaches are often the last people hired and the first people fired.*

Even though companies are willing to hire outside help to resolve an issue, they are likely to do everything they can to solve the problem using internal resources first, and they are likely to wait way too long before they reach out for help. I have talked with many companies whose problems could have been helped if they had simply called in a coach or consultant a year or two earlier. This directly relates to the next potential downside.

5. *It is more difficult to find corporate coaching work that is developmental rather than remedial.*

Business coaches are not usually called in help some manager achieve a dream. More than likely, they are called in to deal with a specific problem in the form of a derailed executive, a damaged image, or a distressed CEO. It is difficult to find ongoing projects that are truly developmental—"Bill is a good manager and we want to groom him to take over the next opening for a vice president. Can you help?" The more typical assignment is, "Frank is going to get fired if he doesn't change. You have 60 days to turn him around or he's gone." In spite of all the research that strongly indicates that companies that develop their people are financially stronger, real training and development is not commonplace in today's companies, and it is one of the first areas companies cut back on in an economic downturn.

CHARACTERISTICS OF A GREAT BUSINESS COACH

There is a fair amount of overlap in the personal characteristics of good business coaches and personal coaches, including:

- Exceptional problem-solving skills
- Great listening ability
- Advanced communication skills
- Ability to focus on the core issues
- Willingness to challenge and confront a client when necessary
- Broad life experience

Some other characteristics of good business coaches also include:

- Solid knowledge of how a typical business runs and the organizational structure
- Results-driven personality
- Avoidance of exclusive language (for example, psychobabble or consultant language)
- Winsome interpersonal skills
- Strong belief that they can create opportunities for positive change and growth within the confines of a business or large organization
- A tough skin and a willingness to deal with conflict when it arises
- Willingness to stand up for personal values and beliefs
- Broad background in business, preferably at the level at which they want to coach (If you want to coach CEOs, it is immensely helpful to have been a CEO, though not absolutely necessary.)
- Experience building and maintaining a significant number of mid- to high-level contacts within the business community, especially in their target market
- Basic knowledge about a number of business areas: finances, marketing, sales, leadership, management skills, and customer relations
- Comfort in speaking the language of business and knowledge of the lingo; for example:

  - CEO: Chief Executive Officer
  - COO: Chief Operating Officer

Tim Ursiny, PhD, RCC, CBC
President and Founder
Advantage Coaching & Training
Wheaton, Illinois
DrTim@Advantagecoaching.com
www.AdvantageCoaching.com
(800) 657-5904

Advantage Coaching & Training is a very successful executive, business, and personal coaching practice. Tim Ursiny is a prominent member of the Worldwide Association of Business Coaches and the author of the book, *The Coward's Guide to Conflict* (Sourcebooks, 2003).

How did you first get started in coaching?

Well, I had just started my consulting practice prior to attending a Carlson Learning conference when someone introduced herself to me as a coach. I was intrigued and did some research, and when I found out what coaching was all about, I said, "This is it." From there, I went to a coach training seminar and starting building my coaching practice. Today, we primarily do executive coaching, coach training through the Worldwide Association of Business Coaches, corporate training, and some personal coaching.

You have an interesting twist on a traditional way of getting new clients. Tell us about it.

Like many coaches I find a lot of my clients from giving presentations, but what I have found is that while talking about coaching doesn't work, showing people what coaching is can be really powerful. So I always make it a point to give a 5- to 10-minute live coaching demonstration during my presentation. I usually ask someone from the audience who has a specific situation they would like to be coached on to come up to the front, and I coach them on that issue right on the spot. Based on my experience, when we don't do a live coaching demonstration we don't get clients. When we show people the power of coaching is when the clients come.

(Continued)

You have been doing coaching for several years now, and as you look back, what is one piece of advice you would have for a new coach just starting out?

Simply this, do not believe what other coaches tell you about how easy it is in this business. It takes a lot of hard work, effort, and time.

When most people talk about client loyalty, they mean the loyalty their clients have for them, but you take a different perspective. What is that, and how has that helped you to succeed?

I firmly believe in client loyalty—my loyalty to my clients. I'm incredibly loyal to my clients. One of my largest, long-term clients was the training division of Arthur Anderson, and as you can expect, all that business was gone when Anderson went through the big accounting scandal with Enron. What many people don't know is that as a company, Anderson treated their employees very well and many people had been at Anderson their whole career and were devastated by the situation and all the layoffs that ensued. However, when we found out they were closing down the entire training division, we went to our former clients and offered free coaching to all Anderson employees and free groups to help them deal with the aftermath. The unexpected benefit was that now, many of these same people who left have landed at other companies and are now calling us in for more coaching. I'm intensely loyal to my clients. They know that no matter the problem or situation they can call me because I've got their back.

You have been very successful in the corporate arena. What are a couple of mistakes you made early on in your practice that coaches should avoid?

One of my first big appointments was with an HR director of a *Fortune* 100 company. I had barely walked in before she said, "Okay, what's your pitch?" Immediately, the tension in the room became intense and I stuttered trying to determine how to prove the value of my services to her. The appointment went downhill from there. As I analyzed what went wrong in that meeting I realized that I felt pressured to have a pitch, when in truth, I didn't have one. When I walk into a cold appointment there is no way for me to know if they could benefit from my services until I know more about them. Now, when I go into companies I don't use PowerPoint or fancy slides, I just ask questions and really listen to their responses. I don't try to sell them on coaching; I look for a way to coach them, with their permission, on the spot. This is how I show the value in what I do.

- CFO: Chief Financial Officer
- ROI: Return on investment
- EBIDTA: Earnings before interest, depreciation, taxes and amortization
- P&L statement: Profit and loss statement
- Knowledge of how to read business statements and documents

This is not to say that if you do not fit all of these categories you cannot be successful as a business coach, but simply to point out that, broadly speaking, there are several differences between business and personal coaches, and the barriers to entry are higher for business coaching than for personal coaching.

TITLES BUSINESS COACHES USE

Business coaches use a number of titles, including these:

- Executive coach
- Business coach
- Leadership coach
- Professional coach
- Corporate coach
- Consultant
- Business success coach
- Marketing or sales coach
- President or CEO
- Psychologist or organizational psychologist

The most common are the top two, but I don't believe there is a distinct advantage to using one of these titles over any of the rest. Your title should tend to be more descriptive of your primary target audience. Two words of caution regarding the last title, *psychologist* or *organizational psychologist:* First, *psychologist* is a protected title, and it can be used only by qualified people. Second, even though some people disagree with me, I strongly recommend that if you are a psychologist who coaches and wants to primarily target businesses, you consider not using your professional title, for two reasons. First, every psychologist has experienced the negative reaction they receive at a party or networking event as soon as they mention their profession. Unfortunately, there is still a stigma in the business community that psychologists only work with sick or unhealthy people. Using that title can push good prospects away from you because of their concern about being stigmatized or pathologized. Second, use of your title while providing coaching or consulting services can increase your legal liability, as someone may misconstrue that you are performing your services under your psychologist's license and hence hold you to all the rules and regulations that accompany that title. If you have a doctorate degree in psychology or any other field, I would recommend including the PhD, MD, or DBA on your business card for credibility, but don't emphasize the field you obtained it in. Remember, business owners don't want to hire an academician or a doctor, they want a practitioner. Emphasizing your practical, hands-on business experience over your educational credentials and certifications will help you achieve better results when converting prospects to clients.

You have another decision to make when it comes to listing your titles—should you put your official corporate title on your marketing literature? As the owner and operator of your business, you probably also hold the title of president, CEO, partner, or director. I would make the argument that if you want to do business inside corporations or with mid- to high-level professionals and executives, you probably should use your corporate title either in place of or in addition to your coaching title, for the distinct reason that owners and executives like to know they are talking with someone of equal stature. Presidents don't waste their time with salespeople, and CEOs only want to spend time with other executives of equal business stature.

PRICING YOUR BUSINESS COACHING SERVICES

There is a huge range for how much business coaches charge, from a low of $50 an hour to more than $700 per hour. The average amount is $198 per hour, with 51 percent of business coaches charging $140 to $260 per hour. Factors that contribute to a higher per-hour rate include living in or near a major metropolitan area and having more professional coaching experience. In fact, hourly rates seem to increase over the average amount by $20 to $30 per hour for every two years of experience. While the hourly rate may seem like a lot, especially in comparison with personal coaches, remember the challenges business coaches face in both finding and keeping work. Most seem to work within two structures on a monthly fee basis, just like personal coaches, and on a per-project basis. A very small percentage of business coaches are able to move their practices entirely to a monthly retainer fee basis.

Twenty-seven percent of full-time business coaches report making less than $20,000 a year, but 36 percent of them are making more than $75,000 annually. The average annual revenue of a business coach is estimated to be $70,000 to $80,000. Chapter 13 goes into detail about what top coaches do to significantly increase their revenues.

DISTINGUISHING COACHING FROM OTHER FIELDS FOR MARKETING PURPOSES

I anticipate this will be the most controversial part of this book, because here I'm going to detail how professional coaching differs from other professional fields. There are good people who will totally agree with me on these distinctions and good people who totally disagree. I'm very comfortable with this, because I put this section in here not to prove a point, but to give you a way to answer your critics and educate your prospects and clients about what you do and how it is different from other professional services. Part of your goal in marketing is to position yourself, and you cannot effectively do that in the minds of your prospects until you have told them how you are different from the 100 other professionals who offer services. You will also encounter the occasional person who really doesn't know what coaching is, and it's always good to have a clear, concise answer ready. With that caveat, let's begin.

The major areas you will most likely be asked to distinguish coaching from are consulting, mentoring, managing, training or teaching, facilitating, and counseling or psychotherapy. Figure 1.2 shows a chart I created to help visualize the areas where these fields differ and where they overlap. As you can see, the four quadrants are distinguished by the client being more of the expert versus you, the service provider, being more of the expert and whether you, as the provider, are more likely to ask questions or give answers in the process of providing your particular service. Certainly, there are notable exceptions in every category, but this chart is solely for the purpose of illustration, not a comprehensive definition. For example, under the "Therapist or counselor" area, there are many therapists who are very directive and provide a lot of direct answers to questions during therapy. Likewise, there are therapists who

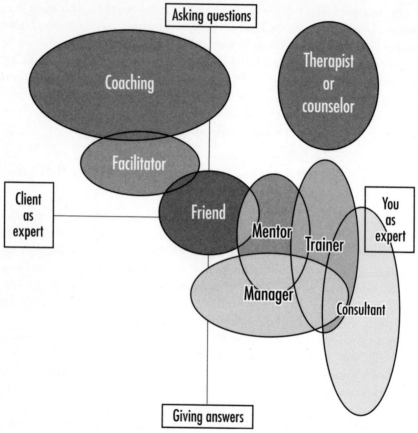

FIGURE 1.2   Relationship of coaching to other fields.
(Copyright © 2003 by Stephen Fairley. All rights reserved.)

view clients as being more the experts in their own lives, and consider that the therapist is only there as a guide or mentor. There are also consultants who take a very coachlike approach and ask a lot of questions, especially in the initial design stages. The perspective I'm presenting is that most consultants are hired because they are seen as experts in a particular area and they are there to provide an expert solution to a problem. Yet there are many coaches who have a specific area of expertise and may slide in and out of the consulting role. In fact, most business coaches would fall into that category.

In each of these areas there is some amount of overlap, which I'm not going to discuss. Instead, I'm going to tell you of a few specific ways I have used to help prospects I meet quickly differentiate coaching from other fields. The best way I know to do this is to focus on the extremes of each field. When asked by a prospect, this is how I would define and distinguish these fields:

Coaching.   Coaching is a one-to-one interactive relationship that helps people identify and accomplish their personal and professional goals faster than they could on their own.

Consulting.   Consulting is more about being viewed as the expert. Consultants are the ones who give you direct answers to specific problems. It's about having all the right answers. As a coach, I come in as a partner to you and your business. It's about asking all the right questions. You are the expert in your business, not me. Also, the end product of most consulting is a report. Once the report is finished, so is the consulting relationship. In coaching, the assessment is only the beginning of the relationship, because as your coach I will also walk alongside you as you implement the plan. The end product then becomes a dynamic relationship that helps you achieve bigger goals faster. [Please note that I recognize that many coaches and consultants believe the two terms are interchangeable and one may actually be a subset of the other. If you do coaching and consulting, it may not make sense for you to emphasize the differences, but for coaches who only do coaching, it can be helpful to distinguish coaching from consulting.]

Mentoring.   There are three major ways mentoring differs from coaching. First, mentoring is usually free. Coaching is not. Second, mentoring is typically done on an informal and as-needed basis. Coaching is a formal relationship and uses a semistructured format. Third, you probably don't set up specific goals and measurable results as part of a mentoring relationship, but in coaching you do.

Managing.   The biggest differences between managing and coaching are in respect to authority, permission, and trust. A manager has a great deal of authority over the employee, a coach has none. A manager does not need to ask permission of an employee to make changes and can require that person to comply with those changes or risk being fired. Coaching is not a one up–one down relationship. It is a partnership of equals. And there is no guarantee that managers have the best interests of their employees at heart. Optimistically, we would like to believe they do, but we all know of situations where they obviously did not. Coaches do not have a hidden agenda, and their primary concern is the welfare of their clients. Coaching relationships are built on a mutual foundation of trust and partnership.

Training or teaching. The typical training is defined by holding an event and the transmission of knowledge. In coaching, we are focused on developing a relationship, not delivering an event, and while there may be some exchange of knowledge in a coaching relationship, the primary purpose is to help you identify and achieve your personal and professional goals. Coaching is not a one up–one down relationship; it is a partnership of equals in which your personal growth and development are the most important measurements of success.

Facilitating. Facilitation usually involves several people or groups of people where the facilitator maintains an objective stance and has no other purpose than to assist those people in clearly communicating with each other and reaching a common agreement. While a coach is also an objective person, coaches do not maintain an objective stance. They are actively involved in the relationship with a clear purpose and goal—to help you identify and achieve your personal and professional goals faster than you could by yourself.

Counseling or psychotherapy. The primary differences between coaching and counseling or therapy are the people who are served and the problems confronted. In counseling, the person is seen as broken, bruised, and in need of healing. In coaching, people are viewed as creative, resourceful, and whole. Typical problems most therapists deal with are depression, anxiety, and severe relationship difficulties. In coaching, we don't fix broken people; we help healthy people perform at a higher level. One way to think of this is to imagine a scale starting at 0 and extending to both +10 and −10 [Figure 1.3]. If 0 is normal or average, however you define it, then counseling takes people who are at −10 and moves them closer to 0—back to normalcy. Coaching starts with people who are at 0, or often at 4 or 5, and helps them to move closer to +10. Does that make sense?

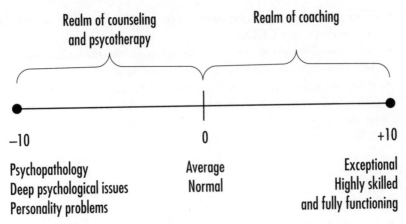

FIGURE 1.3   Relationship of the realm of coaching to the realm of counseling and psychotherapy.

IS PERSONAL OR BUSINESS COACHING RIGHT FOR YOU?

If you are reading this book, you most likely have already decided if you want to be a personal or business coach. However, some of you may not really be sure you have made the best decision, or truly have not decided at all yet, or sincerely believe you can play in both fields at the same time. While a few people can do both personal coaching and business coaching well, the majority of successful coaches specialize in one or the other. In researching the field of coaching for this book, I found that most people who say they do both personal and business coaching really do 80 to 90 percent personal coaching, and may have one or two clients that they consider business coaching clients. The reason for this stems largely from the fact that the way you market your coaching practice to prospects depends to a great extent on which field you see yourself in—personal or business coaching. You ask, "How will my decision about which field I'm in affect me and my coaching business?" Let me name a few specific areas where I believe this decision will affect you, along with some illustrative examples:

- The title you give your company
- Your personal job title (life coach or personal coach versus business coach, president, or CEO)

- Who you see as your primary target audience (adults in general versus corporate CEOs)
- Who you develop strategic partnerships with (the owner of a fitness center versus your local investment banker)
- Who you obtain your coach training and certification from
- What kind of marketing materials you decide to use (just business cards versus a professionally designed web site and brochure)
- What kind of books and magazines you choose to read (personal development books versus the *Wall Street Journal* and *Fortune* magazine)
- The kinds of assessment tools you offer clients (simple self-report inventories versus sophisticated 360-degree feedback)
- Whether you develop formal proposals for clients
- How much you charge for your coaching services ($132 per hour versus $198 on average)
- Where you look for and find prospects (giving free seminars at the public library versus networking in exclusive groups)
- What kinds of issues and challenges you typically work with clients on (living a balanced life versus leadership development)
- How you describe what you do to prospects
- What kind of sales and marketing activities you participate in
- The kinds of coaching packages you create

Table 1.1 shows a few more differences between personal and business coaches, based on the results of my 2002–2003 survey.

SELF-ASSESSMENT INVENTORY

If you are still unclear or unsure, at any level, about your decision to focus on personal coaching or business coaching or try to do some of both, the following questionnaire may help you clarify your thinking.

1. How many years of direct, professional business experience do you have?
   - ☐ 0 to 4
   - ☐ 5 to 10
   - ☐ 11 to 15

TABLE 1.1   Differences between Business Coaches and Personal Coaches

Category	Business Coaches	Personal Coaches
Gender	64% female, 36% male	76% female, 24% male
Population of local area	Average of 1–3 million	Average of less than 1 million
Length of time coaching	39% less than 2 years 29% 2–5 years 32% more than 5 years	61% less than 2 years 20% 2–5 years 19% more than 5 years
Full or part-time practice	68% full-time 32% part-time	60% full-time 40% part-time
Length of time coaching per client	53% coach a client more than 6 months	29% coach a client more than 6 months
Amount charged per hour	Mean = $198 Median = $170	Mean = $132 Median = $100
Work with a coach they have hired	61% yes	68% yes
Number of coaches in company	51% are solo practitioners	78% are solo practitioners

□   16 to 20
□   20+

2. On a scale of 1 to 10, how comfortable do you feel speaking the language of business?

1   2   3   4   5   6   7   8   9   10
Not very   *Somewhat*   *Very*

3. What is the highest level of management experience you have personally held in any company of any size?
□ I have never held a management position in any company.
□ Frontline manager to upper-level manager.

    ☐ Executive position (including vice president, director, regional general manager).

    ☐ C-level position (CEO, CFO, COO, president, or owner).

4. How many years of management or leadership experience do you have in any company?
   - ☐ 0 to 5
   - ☐ 6 to 10
   - ☐ 11 to 15
   - ☐ 16 to 20
   - ☐ 20+

5. In the company where you had a leadership position, how many employees were there?
   - ☐ I was the sole owner and employee.
   - ☐ 2 to 20 employees.
   - ☐ 20 to 100 employees.
   - ☐ 100 to 1,000 employees.
   - ☐ 1,000 to 10,000 employees.
   - ☐ 10,000 or more employees.

6. Have you been recognized by others as having a certain area of expertise related to business, such as strategic planning, financials, customer relations, marketing, sales, or plant operations?
   - ☐ Yes
   - ☐ No

7. Based on your knowledge and understanding of the kinds of issues most business coaches encounter, how interested and comfortable are you in coaching around those areas?

       1   2   3   4   5   6   7   8   9   10
     Not very   *Somewhat*   *Very*

8. Based on your knowledge of the kinds of issues most personal coaches encounter, how interesting does that seem to you?

       1   2   3   4   5   6   7   8   9   10
     Not very   *Somewhat*   *Very*

9. How comfortable are you in actively marketing and selling your coaching services?

1   2   3   4   5   6   7   8   9   10

Not very   *Somewhat*   *Very*

10. Approximately how many people live within 30 miles of you?
    - ☐ Less than 50,000 (rural area)
    - ☐ 50,000 to 300,000 (small city to large city or suburban area)
    - ☐ 300,000 to 1 million (large city or suburban area to metropolitan area)
    - ☐ More than 1 million (major metropolitan area)

RECOMMENDED RESPONSES

1. Business coaches are likely to have had several years more professional business experience than the typical personal coach. They draw on this experience to quickly build rapport with their target prospects.
2. To be successful in the business world, you need to be very comfortable speaking the language of business. If you don't have the experience or the common language, it will be much more difficult to build a solid relationship with prospects. However, you can build your business vocabulary by reading business books, subscribing to *Executive Book Summary* (www.summary.com), taking a couple of MBA classes, and reading the *Wall Street Journal, Fortune, Forbes, Fast Company, Entrepreneur,* and *Inc.*
3–5. Most thriving business coaches have had executive-level or ownership experience in companies of the size they are targeting. For example, a business coach targeting mid-sized companies has usually had successful leadership experience in a different mid-sized company. Their earlier success in business allows them to build a strong case as to why a business owner or executive should pay them to coach a company.
6. While I do not personally believe coaching is all about being the expert or the best authority on a particular area, such as marketing, finances, or sales, there is plenty of evidence that business coaches who have a particular area of expertise build their practices significantly faster and are much more financially successful

than coaches who do not have a particular area of expertise. They often use this expertise to gain an initial foothold into a company.

7. The top seven issues most commonly encountered by business coaches are leadership development, strategic focus, communication skills, marketing products or services, sales coaching, organizational development, and change-management issues, in that order. Could you hold an in-depth and interesting conversation with a business professional on any of these topics at any time?

8. The top seven issues most commonly encountered by personal coaches are living a balanced life, keeping one's focus, career transition issues, a specific crisis, work-related issues, relationship challenges, and spiritual difficulties.

9. In general, business coaches have to be more active in marketing and selling their coaching services due to increased sources of strong, sophisticated competition. While there are very few direct competitors to personal coaching, except other personal coaches, business coaches face competition from *Fortune* 500 consulting firms, large law and accounting firms, marketing and sales agencies, large management consulting firms, national leadership training companies, specialized training seminars, and the like. Unless you start your practice with a large number of direct referral sources already in place or a ready-made contract with your previous employer, it is extremely difficult to build a financially successful business coaching practice without actively marketing and selling your services.

10. Strictly from a demographic standpoint, you will have a very difficult time making a living coaching if you live in a rural area, unless you employ very creative and innovative marketing strategies to limit the downsides of a limited target population (such as a comprehensive Internet marketing campaign like that used by one of the coaches interviewed in this book). The larger the population is in your geographical location the larger your potential target market is. Regardless of what you have read or heard about coaches finding many new clients by simply setting up a web site, it does not happen for 99 percent of coaches. The vast majority of your clients will come from the population in

38

your surrounding area, especially if you are doing business coaching. Of all the business coaches I know about, have talked to, and have interviewed, I can easily count all the really successful ones who live in a geographical area with less than 100,000 people—so it's not impossible, just highly unlikely. Be sure to take this into account when making your decision of who to target and how you are going to target them.

ACTION STEP

Use an Internet search engine (I personally like www.google .com) to search for three topics:

- Coaching
- Business coach
- Personal coach

Write down the domain names of the top 5 to 10 web sites under each category (e.g., www.TodaysLeadership.com), and read through the sites. Note how each person or company describes who they work with (individuals, professionals, companies, other) and the titles they give themselves. What correlations do you notice?

CHAPTER 2

Target Your Market or Waste Your Time

DEFINITION OF MARKETING

Marketing is simply telling people what you do—over, and over, and over again. Throughout the next few chapters we will go into great detail about the tools and techniques you will need to effectively market your coaching business and make your sales easier. In this chapter we will:

- Discuss the importance of identifying your target market—who you want to sell your services to
- Give you detailed information about how to develop an ideal target market profile
- Introduce you to the Target Market Identification Inventory, which can help you examine the important questions to ask when deciding on a good target
- Walk you through the process of developing a profile of your ideal target market

WHY TARGETING YOUR MARKET IS CRITICAL TO SUCCESS

According to the Small Business Administration, the biggest reason for failure among small businesses is *undercapitalization*—starting out with insufficient money to sustain your business during the start-up phase. A closely related reason is failure to generate sufficient revenues by finding new clients. Success in business hinges on accurately identifying the best target market for you and your services. Without a clear idea of who you are targeting, you will find yourself haphazardly targeting all kinds of people, businesses, and industries—and, in most cases, wasting your time, energy, and precious resources pursuing "opportunities" that rarely result in actual business.

Whether you are coaching full-time or just starting out part-time, you have very limited amounts of time, energy, and financial resources, and you must allocate them strategically to produce the best chances of success. In business, this is often referred to as *return on investment* (ROI)—the return you receive for the investment you make. A positive ROI can happen only if you create a clear image of who is most likely to buy your services, based on several criteria. Once you clearly define who this is, do not make the mistake of actively going after people who are outside of your target market. Success depends on *focus*. Focus your energies on identifying, meeting, cultivating relationships with, and obtaining business from members of your target market.

> Success depends on focus.
> Focus depends on energy.
> Find your energy, create your focus, and success will follow.

The first step in marketing is developing a comprehensive picture of your target market, covered in the next section.

CREATING A TARGET MARKET PROFILE

There are a number of ways to categorize or segment your target market. You may not believe that some of these areas make any difference, but try to define as many of them as you can. Following are the most important categories, along with several examples.

CONSIDERATIONS WHEN TARGETING INDIVIDUAL PEOPLE AND PROFESSIONALS

Age: 25 to 35; 45 to 55; over 65

Gender: 60% female, 40% male

Level of education: College degree; professional degree

Geographical location: Rural setting; urban setting; northeast; southwest; within 15 miles of your location

Annual income level: $50,000 to $100,000; over $100,000; high-networth individuals

Ethnicity: Caucasian; African American; Asian; Hispanic; other

Profession: White collar; banker; lawyer; college student; homemaker; salesperson; unemployed

Industry: Accounting; manufacturing; professional services; high-tech; telecom

Job title or position: President; vice president; project manager; owner; partner; none

Psychological needs: Desires job security; wants prestige; has a high level of energy; wants a constant stream of new challenges; has a conquering spirit; feels frustrated by lack of time; feels angry about the lack of a life outside of work; wants to create a more satisfying relationship

Personal interests: Is a lifelong student of personal growth; is trying for a job promotion; regularly reads business and financial magazines; enjoys traveling and outdoor activities; enjoys self-improvement seminars; is highly spiritual; is trying to retire in the next 10 years

CONSIDERATIONS WHEN TARGETING ENTREPRENEURS AND SMALL BUSINESSES

Annual revenue: $100,000 to $1 million; $5 million to $20 million; $20 million to $50 million

Number of employees: 1; 2 to 4; 15 to 25; 25 to 50; 50 to 100

Number of managers: Several first-time managers; owner does all the managing; two frontline managers who supervise 40 people

Number of years in business: 3 to 5; 6 to 10; 11 to 20

Title or position: Owner; partner; CEO; president; vice president; manager

Industry: Accounting, Manufacturing, Professional Services, high-tech; telecom

Kinds of services or products: Business to business or business to consumer

Sales cycle: Usually shorter with one or two decision makers — the owner or partners

Speed of growth: Growing 35 percent annually compared to the industry average of 10 percent; hiring large amounts of people; just received infusion of cash from investors

Geographical location: Southeast; western suburbs of Chicago; within five to seven miles of your business

Common organizational challenges: Struggling in the economic downturn; needing to find new clients now; experiencing the negative effects of a layoff; bringing on a new partner; experiencing conflict between key executives; having difficulty motivating employees; needing to find and keep top talent; having a chaotic environment; lacking processes; lacking a human resource department; lacking organizational focus; going in too many directions with too few resources; lacking a rainmaker due to departure or burnout

CONSIDERATIONS WHEN TARGETING BUSINESSES AND CORPORATIONS

Annual revenue: $30 million to $50 million; $50 million to $500 million; $500 million to $1 billion; more than $1 billion

Number of employees: 100 to 500; 500 to 1000; 1000 to 10,000; more than 10,000

Title or position: CEO; partner; vice president; senior director; division manager; account executive; project manager; sales department head

Industry: Accounting; manufacturing; professional services; high-tech; telecom

Sales cycle: Can be shorter with one decision maker—the owner; usually much longer with multiple levels of decision makers including a board, outside investors, or many divisions or departments

Kinds of services or products: Business to business or business to consumer

Common organizational challenges: Struggling in the economic downturn; needing to develop new managers; experiencing the negative effects of a layoff; restructuring top-level management; bringing on a new CEO or president; resolving conflicts between team members; finding and keeping top people; transferring technical people into management positions

WHICH MARKET SHOULD YOU TARGET?

Now that we have laid out several different ways in which you can categorize your market, let's talk about which of these markets may be best for you. As a general rule, an individual coach or even a small group of coaches will have great difficulty successfully targeting more than two

Sandra Johnson, RCC
President
Sandra Johnson & Associates
Minneapolis, Minnesota
sfjohnson@visi.com
(952) 937-8687

Sandra Johnson is an Executive Coach and the author of the upcoming book *Corporate Cults*.

You got started in coaching like a lot of people, landing your first big project from a former employer. Tell us your story.

I came across an interesting article about this new field called "professional coaching," and as I read it, everything it said sounded a lot like what I was doing every day as a leader at my company, Marriott. When I read that article, I was the general manager of a hotel with responsibility for the entire business unit, and I also served on several boards and task forces within the company. Although I enjoyed my job, I realized I was spending 80 percent of my time doing 20 percent of what I love! The idea that I could combine leadership with coaching seemed like a phenomenal idea so I signed up for the Coach Training Institute. I hadn't been out of school long when Marriott called me to do some projects. They turned out really well and my business has taken off from there.

Do you have any tips for new coaches just starting out?

- Build your practice at the point where you have experience. If you have experience within education, start there; in manufacturing, then start there.
- Expect to work long hours at first, but don't expect to replace your full salary within a year.
- Becoming a coach is becoming an entrepreneur. Make sure you want to become an entrepreneur before you try to become a coach.
- Coaching really is a business. You have to do finances, marketing, sales, and strategic planning. If you are not good at that you must

outsource it to someone who is. You have to have the full package to be successful in running any business; coaching is no exception.

- For business coaches, ask yourself, "What else do I have to offer besides coaching," because it often takes more than that to get in the door. You have to have a niche and clearly understand where your prospects are coming from.

What do you believe coaching is going to look like in three to five years?

I believe we will see more standardization in designations. I hope by then a set of core competencies will have been established. I also think we'll see a stronger division between niches. Business coaches will flock together, as will personal coaches.

to three markets at the same time. It is much better to focus 60 to 70 percent of your time on one market, 20 to 30 percent on your secondary market, and whatever time you have left that cannot be put to better use on the first two markets, spent targeting a third market. When trying to identify the target market that's right for you, look at three areas: your experience, level of interest, and geographical location. The more these three areas overlap, the better chance you have of finding an ideal target market (Figure 2.1).

Level of interest. Energy, enthusiasm, and passion are contagious. You must be able to consistently display all three when talking to or about your target market. If you are not truly interested in a particular population, you will not be successful in convincing them to purchase your services.

Personal and professional experience. You will find it much easier to attract clients with whom you have something in common—having work experience in a specific industry, holding a certain position in a company, being in a particular life stage, or living a particular lifestyle. Think about all of the life experiences you have had and find ways to capitalize on them. People are attracted to others with whom they have things in common and to others who project the life they

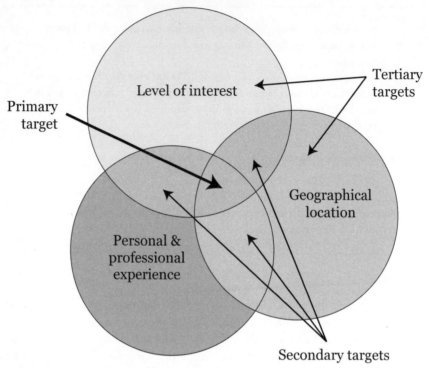

FIGURE 2.1 Overlapping areas of experience, interest, and location define primary, secondary, and tertiary target markets. *(Copyright © 2003 by Stephen Fairley. All rights reserved.)*

want to live. Do not believe the myth that you can be all things to all people. You will succeed only in confusing your true target market. You will build your business faster if you focus on the areas in which you have either personal or professional experience. For example, even though the monetary rewards are much higher, not everyone can or should go into business or corporate coaching because they do not have the personal or professional experience in a business setting.

Geographical location. One of the aspects I love best about coaching is its portability. You can literally coach people around the globe from anywhere. There are no true geographical limitations. That being said, the overwhelming majority of coaches find most of their clients within 30 miles of their home base, because it takes multiple contacts before a person will decide to purchase coaching, and the greatest likelihood of making multiple contacts comes from being in close physical proximity. Although some coaches tout the effectiveness of their web sites or e-zines in attracting clients, there are two realities you must appreciate: First, it truly takes an extraordinary amount of time and money to attract enough people through Internet advertising (which is what a web site is) to make a sustainable business; second, unless those coaches live in low-population areas, they are missing 80 percent of their possible business if they minimize or ignore the people directly around them.

TARGET MARKET IDENTIFICATION INVENTORY

The Target Market Identification Inventory was designed to help you think through the critical questions when determining which market or markets would be a good fit for you.

1. What are the specific areas where you have the most interest in coaching? Try to envision coaching a specific type of person, industry, position, life stage, or issue—do you feel energized or drained?
2. Consider people in the target market you already have in mind, and briefly list all the personal and professional experience you have in common with them in the following areas:

   - Experience as a customer or client in that market
   - Experience with friends or family members who are in that market
   - Experience as an employee in that market
   - Experience as a manager in that market
   - Experience as an executive, owner, or leader in that market

3. How long have you been targeting that specific market?
   ☐ Just started
   ☐ 3 to 6 months
   ☐ 7 to 12 months
   ☐ 1 to 2 years
   ☐ More than 2 years

4. What have the actual results been in terms of level of interest expressed, number of free coaching sessions given, new clients gained, projects started, and revenues generated?

5. How satisfying has your experience with the sales process been when trying to target that market in terms of meeting a person in your ideal market, gaining their attention and generating interest in coaching, making the initial appointments, giving a free coaching session, developing proposals, waiting out the time they take to make a decision, and closing the deal?

1   2   3   4   5   6   7   8   9   10

Not at all   *Somewhat*   *Very*

6. How satisfying has your actual coaching experience been with that target market?

1   2   3   4   5   6   7   8   9   10

Not at all   *Somewhat*   *Very*

7. What *personal* experience do you believe makes you the best qualified to coach people in that market?

8. What *professional* experience do you believe makes you the best qualified to coach people in that market?

9. On a scale of 1 to 10, how comfortable and confident are you when it comes to selling your services to that target market?

1   2   3   4   5   6   7   8   9   10

Not at all   *Somewhat; getting used to it*   *Very; even enjoy it*

10. How long can your business survive on your existing cash reserves and current incoming revenues?
    - ☐ It's on a month-by-month basis.
    - ☐ 3 to 6 months.
    - ☐ 7 to 12 months.
    - ☐ More than 1 year.

11. Approximately how many people live within a 30-mile radius of your practice?

☐ I live in a rural area and know almost everyone around me.

☐ I live near or in a suburb of a small city (50,000 to 250,000 people).

☐ I live in a decent-sized city of at least 250,000 to 1 million people.

☐ I live in a metropolitan area (1 million to 5 million people within 15 to 20 miles).

☐ I live in a major metropolitan area (5 million to 20 million or more people within 15 to 20 miles).

12. How many individual people or companies who are directly in your primary target market live within a 30- to 40-minute drive of your location?
    ☐ Only a handful.
    ☐ Probably a little more than 100 or so.
    ☐ At least several hundred.
    ☐ More than a few thousand.
    ☐ Too many to count.
    ☐ I honestly have no idea.

13. Describe your life stage and what you anticipate the effect will be on your target market.

RECOMMENDED RESPONSES

1. Try to be as specific as possible; instead of "adults" perhaps your target is "professionals in career transition." Also, do not neglect the areas that give you a strategic advantage over your competition. Maybe you speak a foreign language, or your significant other is an executive in a particular company, or you were the CEO of a midsized manufacturing company. List only areas that truly interest you and that you are passionate and enthusiastic about. Be careful about misleading motives like: you heard the money was better in this area or a conference speaker said other coaches are being successful in that industry.

2. Make an accurate assessment of what specific experience you have had from various perspectives within that target audience.

The more broad and deep your experience, the better you will be able to relate to and sell to that market.

3. Assuming you are doing the right things (is that too big an assumption?), you should begin to notice some level of interest from your target market within three to six months. If you have been targeting that market for more than 12 months without noticeable results, you should either strongly consider that you are targeting the wrong market for yourself and your services and immediately start looking elsewhere, or take a serious look at revamping all your marketing efforts.

4. Perhaps you have spent the majority of your time targeting a specific market and have had some results but are unsure as to what to do next. Take a serious look at the actual results you have achieved in that market in terms of how many new clients you have gained in the past six months. (You should be able to land one to three clients per month if you are working full time in your business.) Is the revenue you are currently generating from your sales and marketing efforts worth your time, energy, and resources? Is there another market that would provide a better return on investment for you?

5. Different markets have different sales cycles, but every market has one. Start tracking how long your market takes at each stage. How long does it take on average to get your foot in the door? After you propose coaching as a solution to their problem, how long does it take for them to make a decision? Is this whole process satisfying or frustrating to you? Are you able to handle the level of frustration you're experiencing, or has it affected your ability, energy, and desire to work with that market? The general principle to remember is: The larger the company, the bigger the typical project, the higher the fee, and the longer the sales cycle.

6. After you get over the initial excitement that someone is paying you money to coach them, do you find working with that target market to be fun, exciting, and enjoyable in such a way that just thinking about your next coaching session brings you a certain energy? Do you find yourself periodically thinking how you can add value to their sessions by sending them an article you read or

giving them a great book they might enjoy? If not, perhaps your passion is elsewhere with a different target market. You will be a much better coach and attract many more clients if you coach people and problems around your passion.

7–8. If you don't truly believe you are the best-qualified person to coach your target market, then how do you ever hope to convince your prospects? Be very specific when answering these questions. Why? Because I can guarantee you that your prospects will ask you these questions, and you must have believable answers and be able to tell them in a clear, concise, and confident manner why you are the best-qualified person to coach them.

9. If you circled a number below 5 you have some work to do, because like it or not, as a small business owner you are the primary salesperson, and if you want to make money doing coaching you either have to sell your services or pay someone to do it for you. Whether you read books, go to sales seminars, or hire a sales coach, you need to become more comfortable selling. The other thing you can do is increase your marketing efforts, because the more effective your marketing materials are, the less time and energy you have to spend selling. Remember that!

10. The biggest reason for small business failure is lack of initial start-up funding. As a professional service business, you should try to have at least 12 to 18 months of capital available to cover your business expenses, in addition to your personal living expenses. If you have less than six months of funding available to support your company, based on your cash reserves and incoming revenues, you should immediately try to increase that. Some of your options may include taking out a loan, redistributing your personal finances, lowering your fees, adding additional easy-to-sell services, decreasing your overhead, or refocusing on targeting individuals rather than companies because the average sales cycle for a company is significantly longer than for an individual. Individuals will usually make the decision within a couple of weeks. Small companies can usually make a decision in one to three months, but midsized to large companies can spend six months to two years before they make a final decision and offer you a project. You can't afford to wait that long if you're low on

cash and revenues. I do not recommend canceling or simply post-poning all your marketing strategies if you are low on cash. Marketing your company leads to sales, and sales lead to revenues. Cutting your marketing budget can lead into a downward spiral that ends in the loss of your business.

11. If you live in a rural area, or a small city of less than 100,000 people, you may be better off targeting individuals and professionals rather than businesses. In those areas relationships are everything. Work hard to increase your networking opportunities. Think outside the box when it comes to attending different kinds of networking events, as they are probably limited in number. Also, consider developing and implementing a strong Internet marketing strategy, including a well-designed web site and e-mail campaigns to people and small businesses outside your area.

12. Do not overgeneralize here. Try to be realistic. Only a small percentage of your target market will purchase your services. Those are the people who need, want, and can afford them. If you have incredible sales and marketing skills you may be able to land more than 5 percent of your target population as clients, so if your target population is too small, you may either have to redefine it to include a larger group or find ways to expand your geographical reach (this can be a daunting task). Obviously, the greater the number of potential targets in your immediate geographical location, the greater your chances of success. If you checked the last response ("I honestly have no idea"), then it's time to do some serious research before you go any further. Use the Internet, your local chamber of commerce, and your research librarian for initial help.

13. For better or worse, your life stage will play a large part in determining how successful you will be in targeting a specific market. Few senior-level executives will listen to 30-year-old whiz kids regardless of how much education they have. Targeting parents will probably not work unless you have been a parent yourself. Be realistic in how this will affect your target market—"My life stage has nothing to do with my coaching" is simply a naïve response.

ACTION STEP: PROFILING YOUR IDEAL TARGET MARKET

We have talked about why you need to identify your target market, how to target your market, and what important questions to answer about your market. Now is the time for you to write down a profile for your ideal target market. Go through each of the following sections and carefully describe your answers in as much detail as possible. If you cannot fully answer a question, do some research on the Internet or at your local library, interview some friends or colleagues who are in that target market, or talk to an industry trade association. If you have more than one target market, do this separately for each one.

As you go through some of these sections you may question whether it is necessary to discuss every one. I would argue that every section is important, because you often never know the exact thing that pushes an undecided prospect toward giving your services a try. Perhaps it was because your brochure spoke to the needs of executives in the midst of a career transition that they immediately identified with or the phrase you used to describe your life coaching services spoke directly to their greatest challenge in life. The point is that the more information you have about a certain target the easier you can identify their primary concerns and challenges, which makes your job that much easier when it comes to talking to that target at meetings, through your brochure, in an e-mail, or on your web site. Different areas have different levels of importance, but in the end, every little bit helps.

Marketing to Individuals, Entrepreneurs, or Small Businesses

Age range?

Gender?

Level of education?

Geographical location?

Annual income level?

Ethnic group?

Professions or occupations?

Industry?

Job title or position?

Psychological needs?

Personal interests

When do they buy?

How do they buy your kinds of service?

What do they perceive they are buying?

Why should they buy from you?

Marketing to Entrepreneurs or Small, Midsized, and Large Businesses

Annual revenues?

Number of employees?

Number of managers?

Number of years in business?

Position of person you are targeting?

Industry?

Kinds of services or products?

Sales cycle and speed of decision making?

Geographical location?

How fast are they growing?

What are their typical challenges, issues, or problems?

How do *they* talk about their challenges or issues?

What specific words or phrases are they likely to use to describe their problem?

What kind of personality do they likely have?

What other kinds of professional services do they buy?

Who do they have regular contact with?

Who are they likely to turn to when making a difficult decision?

What kinds of people or businesses do they trust?

Preferred style of communication (e-mail, phone, in person)?

When do they buy?

How do they buy your kinds of service?

What do they perceive they are buying?

Why should they buy from you?

SUMMARY

In this chapter we have focused on the critical first step in your marketing—identifying your ideal target market. Without a comprehensive picture of your ideal market there is no point in going further, because the whole purpose of your coaching services is to solve your clients' problems, and if you don't know who those clients are, you will never be able to identify their primary problems and challenges. Be sure to spend sufficient time developing and refining a profile of your ideal target market.

CHAPTER 3

The 12 Largest Markets Where Coaches Are Making Money Right Now

Successful coaches know where to look for clients. They look for opportunities where others see only obstacles. They target only their market when others track every person that passes by. In this chapter we will cover:

- The top 12 largest markets that successful business and personal coaches target
- The greatest challenges each of these markets face
- The positives and negatives of working with each market
- Specific marketing strategies you can use to effectively reach each market
- Eight key questions to ask to determine which particular target markets are the best for you

Though it may seem at first that many of these markets are designed more for business coaching, 30 percent of personal coaches also work with a number of business professionals, executives, and other people with career-related issues, just as many business coaches work with their clients on life issues. The targets are similar—personal coaches just reach out to clients in different ways and work on different issues.

There are several ways to segment the largest coaching markets:

- By the size of the company: start-ups, small businesses, midsized firms, and large companies
- By industry: professional service firms and technology firms
- By position and department in the company: sales, new managers, senior managers, business owners, and general managers

SEGMENTATION BY SIZE OF THE COMPANY

Business development is similar to human development. There are different stages and cycles associated with each, and each stage presents unique challenges and opportunities. For example, many start-ups are characterized by chaotic and unfocused environments. As the company grows past 15 to 20 employees, it is forced to adapt its behavior in order to successfully move forward. Growing a company from its first million in sales to past the $30-million mark takes a certain level of leadership and organizational skills that differ from the skills it takes to launch a new business. Many companies experience turmoil when trying to handle the massive growth spurts they encounter on the way to becoming a successful mid-sized company, not unlike the period of adolescence. Regardless of what stage a company is in, it requires a different set of leadership skills and organizational abilities. Leaders must learn new skills, managers must change their behaviors, top talent with particular skill sets must be hired and retained, and the company culture must adapt.

This section will give you an overview of the different ways to think about your target audience based on the size or developmental stage of a company. I have included three subsections for each segment: positives of working with this group, negatives, and basic marketing strategies. You will notice there are often more negatives than positives presented. This was done intentionally because many people focus only on the positives of a target market and, to their detriment, overlook the negatives. I wanted to help you see that for every upside there is a potential downside. I strongly encourage you to closely examine the reasons you have for targeting a particular population, as well as how you are going to cope with the potential difficulties you will encounter.

START-UPS AND ENTREPRENEURS

Start-ups are one of the top hot spots for coaching right now. They are typically owned and operated by one or two people, are in their first three years of business, and have less than $500,000 in annual revenues. New businesses have many needs that a great coach can fulfill: directing organizational development, focusing the time and energy of the entrepreneur, being a sounding board for wise decision making, providing a realistic assessment of situations, lending objectivity, and creating a supportive atmosphere, just to name a few. There are between 250,000 and 500,000 small-business start-ups every year in the United States, depending on who you ask and how you define a "small business," while thousands more are incorporated (which generally requires a greater level of sophistication and dedication on the part of the owner than just hanging up a shingle). Some of the best and worst reasons why you should consider targeting start-ups and entrepreneurs follow.

Positives
- More and more people every year are choosing to start their own businesses rather than work for someone else. This trend always increases during an economic downturn because large companies

lay off thousands of qualified, experienced workers, some of whom decide they never want to be laid off again.
- Start-ups definitely have a need for coaching. Entrepreneurs need the focus a good coach can bring, along with assistance in developing their vision and making their action plan more concrete.
- People who start their own companies are generally more likely to take the risk that a coach can help them speed up their development.
- Change can often happen in large steps and in a relatively short period of time, and if you can help entrepreneurs build their business you may end up with a paying client for life.
- Entrepreneurs usually bring a lot of energy and enthusiasm to the coaching relationship. They can be wonderful clients to work with—if you are the right kind of person and use the right kind of coaching.
- If you don't have a lot of direct business experience, but want to work with business people, coaching entrepreneurs can be a good transition. Just be honest about your personal experience or lack of it.

Negatives
- Entrepreneurs are often idea rich and cash poor.
- Entrepreneurs have great visions, but often have no idea how to get there, which can be very frustrating.
- Because entrepreneurs are risk takers, they may expect you to become a risk taker with them (which may translate into waiting to get paid until they land their first big deal, taking a straight contingency fee, or accepting stock in their company versus being paid real money).
- Because change can happen relatively quickly, the coaching relationship is often short-lived (a typical engagement can be two to four months), especially if the goals are very limited.
- If you don't have a thick skin, an ability to take a person telling you exactly what they think of you and your ideas, a willingness to be challenged, a very flexible personality, a love of brainstorming, and a willingness to hold your clients accountable, coaching entrepreneurs probably is not for you.
- There does tend to be a big difference between entrepreneurs who have been typical frontline to midlevel employees versus those who

have been in positions of power and authority (senior manager or vice president and above), especially in midsized to large corporations. The former are much more likely to fall into the negative stereotypes discussed in this section. The latter have often experienced the need for and benefits of using outside experts, partners, and consultants in their corporate experience, and are likely to be more willing to pay for your coaching services and appreciate the value you bring.

Basic Marketing Strategies

- One of the difficult parts about targeting clients in this market is knowing where and how to locate them. Most entrepreneurs are too busy to spend much time at traditional networking events, and their businesses are often too small to justify belonging to any major networking groups.
- Here are a few places where I have found entrepreneurs: through local chambers of commerce, through accountants who specialize in working with small businesses, via financial advisors who work with small-business owners, by buying a direct-mail list of newly incorporated companies, through a direct referral from one of their friends or family members, and through specialty network groups—such as those designed specifically for entrepreneurs or that are industry specific.
- Present yourself as a professional and a coach who specializes in working with start-ups and small businesses.
- Be ready to present a list of testimonials and references from other entrepreneurs and small business owners you have helped.
- Find a way to quantify your coaching results; for example, "For every $1,000 an entrepreneur invests in my coaching they decrease their time to market by three months," or "I use coaching to help entrepreneurs increase their sales by 20 percent in 90 days."
- Focus on tangible results: "I can show you how to increase your effectiveness by 15 percent while working less hours."
- Offer dynamic seminars and practical workshops designed to attract entrepreneurs and start-ups.
- Talk about the hot buttons that virtually all entrepreneurs face: no time, no money, not enough resources, lack of action steps and sales skills, marketing on a small budget, poor accountability, setting and completing specific goals.

- Be more flexible with payment terms; allow clients to extend payments over a longer period of time.
- Develop and test several creative, catchy programs: "The three-month business-building program for entrepreneurs," or "Focus your energy and jump-start your business in 90 days."
- Offer a low-cost (under $300) product or service that can act as a teaser introduction to your services.
- Find or create a niche and market to the niche. For example, helping entrepreneurs write business plans, develop marketing plans to get their products to market faster, or implement effective sales strategies for small businesses.

Six Types of Entrepreneurs

Because of the current success coaches are having with entrepreneurs, I have included some extra information about them, not found in the other sections. The typical owner and operator of a start-up usually falls into one of six areas. Being aware of these patterns and typical challenges will aid you in connecting with entrepreneurs and quickly identifying the areas where they may need the most coaching.

- *Technicians.* These professionals have a long history in their field and recently either left, retired from, or were let go by a midsized to large company and want to continue doing what they have been doing, whether that's computer consulting, graphic design, developing web sites, advertising, or writing. They know the need is out there and they are very good at what they do, so why not start up a company doing what they love? However, they certainly didn't expect it to be this hard to attract new clients.

Typical challenges:
- They have no natural aptitude or interest in either marketing or sales.
- They may not have very good interpersonal skills.
- They prefer working alone or on a small team with other technicians.
- They don't understand how to build or run a business.
- They can be quite good at convincing people one on one that their ideas are good, but not enough so that people believe they should either pay for them or give them money.

- They focus on features and services, instead of results and benefits

Coaching points:
- Help them focus on the benefits and results of their services or products.
- Help them develop their interpersonal skills, specifically their communication skills.
- Help them feel more comfortable about sales.
- Give them an understanding of what marketing and sales are, and how they are different.
- Move them forward in their understanding that every small business owner is a salesperson.
- Help them find a way to either be more comfortable with the sales role or find a way to outsource it to someone who is.
- Encourage them to join a group of business owners who are not technicians.
- Push them out of their comfort zone.
- Help them take their vision and make it a reality.
- Keep them focused on the main thing and not get sidetracked by their many ideas.

- *Dissatisfied employees.* These folks are currently employed in a 9-to-5 job, but want to make more money or create a better future for themselves and gradually make the transition out of their full-time career.

Typical challenges:
- They don't have enough time, energy, or resources to make their dream happen.
- They are reticent to take the plunge and leave the security of their full-time job.
- They may realize halfway through that they only want to play on the side, without taking on all the responsibilities of owning a small business.
- They can become paralyzed by anxiety about their job.
- They are used to having a lot of resources at their fingertips and expect the same in their small business.

Coaching points:
- Help them structure their week to allot a certain percentage of their time to developing their idea or small business.
- Help them set deadlines for accomplishing particular goals or tasks (write a business plan in the next three months; find one paying client in the next 30 days).
- Assist them in discovering whether they truly want to have a side company.
- Help them improve their time-management skills.
- Help them find ways to build extra reserves into their lives.
- Be careful about how hard and fast you push them. Follow their pace, not your own.

- *Educated service professionals.* These white-collar professionals usually have a professional degree (PhD, MD, JD, DDS, DVM), have worked for many years attaining their education, and are either starting off in their new career or frustrated with the slow growth rate of their current position. Working with these people can be challenging because of their technical training. They are the consummate professionals.

Typical challenges:
- They are too focused on their trade or profession instead of running their business.
- When business gets tough (too many clients or not enough clients), they may stick their head in the sand and totally ignore running their business.
- They will grill you all about your professional qualifications.
- They like to use their personal name as their business name (which I believe is a handicap in some fields when it comes to trying to sell to larger clients).
- They can be difficult clients to obtain unless you have a lot of academic qualifications, experience, and training (it also helps to have a degree in their specific field).
- They can be arrogant at times—to you and to their own clients.
- They may have a heavy debt load from graduate school that precludes them from doing many things.

- They may want to pay you only what they charge someone else (because to pay you more would mean that they were worth less than you).
- They are highly intelligent people who usually know very little about marketing, sales, or operating a small business.
- They will only work with someone they believe is close to their intellectual equal.
- They usually want a strong combination of both coaching and consulting, rather than just coaching.
- They often will use buzzwords or particular terms and language that only another professional in their field would recognize.
- They have sensitive egos.
- They may involve you in a long sales cycle to get them to commit to entering a coaching relationship with you.
- They see themselves as intelligent professionals and may have a difficult time outsourcing anything (even important business areas that they have no experience or interest in).
- They can be very resistant to the idea of growth (just want to do it themselves).
- They may focus either too much on interpersonal skills (think psychologists) or not enough on interpersonal skills (think lawyers and accountants).

Coaching points:
- They need to have a solid understanding of the sales process.
- They need to have a solid understanding of the marketing process.
- If they are new to the field, they need to understand the basics of business finance.
- Help them spend more of their time talking to qualified prospects instead of "tire kickers."
- Help them get networked with other professionals in different fields.
- Move them out of their comfort zone when networking.
- Help them work on developing a good audio logo. (They usually answer the question, "What do you do?" with their professional title: "I'm a psychologist" or "I'm a lawyer.")

- Push them to set specific goals and adopt solid action plans, and hold them accountable for the results they obtain.
- Keep in mind that while they want to work with other professionals of similar stature, they often want part of that relationship to be a friendship or mentorship.
- Show them specific ways that your coaching is helping them move faster, save money by making fewer mistakes, or use their time more efficiently.
- Ask them up front to commit a certain amount of time and money every month to building their business. If they are unwilling to do this, don't waste your time working with them.

- *Serial entrepreneurs.* These people have probably started and abandoned a new business every year for the past decade. They are looking for a way to make it big, and they start each new business with unbridled enthusiasm and endless energy, but they quickly move on when the road becomes too difficult or the start-up costs too much money.

Typical challenges:
- They have too many ideas and jump from idea to idea.
- They may walk away from a good idea if it looks too difficult.
- They lack commitment to the coaching process.
- They may have unrealistic expectations for the speed of change.
- They may have a difficult time envisioning how you could help them, because they are the party with all the great ideas.
- They require a lot of energy and enthusiasm from their coach.
- They are usually either great at the 10,000-foot level (a great visionary) or great at the 1-inch level (a great technician), but usually not both, and usually not at the 3-foot level (where the rubber meets the road).
- They are always ready to move on to the latest and greatest idea without following through on their previous great idea.
- They are constantly changing or improving their ideas.
- They are often low on cash unless they have already been successful at creating and selling something.
- They love to talk about ideas, but get anxious when anyone pushes them about creating a specific plan.

- They are weak on follow-through.
- They are high to very high risk takers.
- They are looking for ways to leverage their time, energy, and resources.
- They could get pulled into a scam in their eagerness to find the next big thing.

Coaching points:
- Help them decrease the chaos in their life.
- Help them institute solid procedures for making business decisions.
- Show a great deal of enthusiasm for them personally, and make it clear that this will not change even if you don't like their ideas.
- Push them to write down a specific plan of action and exit plan if things don't go the way they wish.
- Give them a solid assessment of their strengths and weaknesses (growth areas).
- Be a sounding board for their constant inflow of ideas.
- Help them focus, focus, focus!
- Talk about ideas with them, but end every session with specific action steps.
- Hold them accountable.
- Generally, serial entrepreneurs are either great technicians or great salespeople. If they are great technicians, coach around increasing their communication and interpersonal skills. If they are great salespeople, help them ask better questions instead of talking too much.
- Help them find out if there is really a market need for their ideas.

- *Artists.* These folks are often also dissatisfied employees who keep their day job primarily to pay the bills and allow them to pursue their real love—their art. This may be writing, painting, sculpting, trying to make independent films, graphic design, or another such trade.

Typical challenges:
- They have no extra money.
- They are willing to hang on by a thread forever.
- They are tenacious.

- They often don't know about sales or marketing and don't care to know about sales or marketing.
- They don't see what they are doing as a business; it's a hobby that makes them money.
- They believe many people simply misunderstand them, their intentions, or their product.
- They are very frustrated by their job.

Coaching points:
- Help them to see that if they want more than a hobby from their art, they must look at their hobby as a legitimate business and operate it like one.
- Teach them the importance of sales, marketing, and finances, then help them outsource this to someone they can rely on.
- Work with them only if you believe in what they are doing.
- Set specific goals for your coaching; otherwise it will become unfocused.
- Consider setting a specific time frame within which you will help them, then renegotiate at the end of that time.
- Recognize your tolerance levels, and end the relationship when you become too frustrated to help.
- Do not set unrealistic expectations for the coaching; it may be long and produce little in terms of tangible results.

- *Inventors.* These people have a continual influx of great ideas, many of which could solve various problems faced by businesses or consumers. However, many of their ideas never make it off the drawing board. They are looking for someone who believes in them and can help one of their ideas come to life.

Typical challenges:
- They do not take constructive criticism well, especially about their ideas.
- They may want or crave a lot of praise for how great their ideas are.
- They see their creative abilities more as a hobby than as a business.

- They have many, many ideas, most of which will never leave the drawing table.
- They are often unfocused and jump from invention to invention.
- They can be enticed into a scam by someone who promises them a lot of money (or promises to make them famous) for their inventions.
- They like to hang out with other inventors and technical people.
- They often lack interpersonal skills.

Coaching points:
- Help them determine if they truly want to create a business or are simply satisfied with maintaining their hobby.
- Help them realize that it is very difficult to start a business with a single product (even though this has been done before).
- Work carefully with them to increase their social skills and communication ability.
- Help them focus on one idea or invention at a time.
- Help them improve their time-management skills.

SMALL BUSINESSES

Coaching in the small business market is really exploding! This is undoubtedly one of the hottest markets for coaching right now—especially for coaches who are able to position themselves as a critical resource for small-business owners.

Here are some interesting facts about this growing market:

- Even though the traditional media largely ignore small businesses, they account for almost 75 percent of the total revenues generated by all U.S. companies.
- Three out of every four people in America are employed by a company with fewer than 100 employees.
- There are almost 6 million businesses in the United States with fewer than 100 employees and more than $100,000 in revenue.
- There are at least 2 million small-business owners who have a net worth between $500,000 and $5 million.
- Sixty percent of all millionaires are business owners.

- The average small-business owner has a net worth five times greater than that of people who are employed at a regular job.

Small-business owners are totally committed to building their business. They are passionate about what they do, and this passion pervades every area of their lives. To be effective in marketing to this audience, you must position yourself as a resource to them. You need to have a broad base of knowledge, with at least one specialty that you focus on: sales, marketing, finances, customer relationship management (CRM), operations, manufacturing, creating a workable vision, or turning your vision into reality. This specialty must be seen as something credible and meaningful to the small-business owner—so emphasizing your specialty in using spiritual meditation to find new business clients won't impress too many small-business owners!

Many large companies are starting to target small businesses aggressively. For example, American Express has a large contingent of financial advisors. In 2000, the company spent approximately $4 million on advertising targeted at small-business owners. Somewhere between 2000 and 2001 American Express recognized the potential for this untapped market. All the rest of its competitors were going after either large corporate accounts or individuals of high net worth, but largely ignoring the small business community. So in 2001, American Express increased its marketing budget for targeting small-business owners from $4 million to $114 million! Assuming its financial advisors know how to follow through on this marketing blitz effectively, the company may well be on its way to becoming a dominant player in the small-business financial market.

Positives
The small-business market is a critical one for anyone serious about succeeding as a business coach, and it is much more open to personal coaching than the larger-company markets.

- There are hundreds and even thousands of small businesses in most metropolitan areas, many of which need, want, and can afford your services.
- Even though these small businesses are in many different kinds of industries, the good thing is that they all face pretty much the same kinds of basic problems: developing leadership, managing growth

spurts, dealing with change and transitions, managing finances, handling sales and marketing, improving communication skills, developing the ability to delegate important tasks, dealing with a chaotic environment, coping with conflict, and finding and keeping solid talent.

- Small businesses can be great to work with because of the passion the owners have for their business, the speed at which success can happen, the great potential for growth, and the fact that most small-business owners can afford your services. It's up to you to demonstrate the value.
- When you approach a small business you can generally speak directly to the decision maker, the owner and operator. This usually makes the sales cycle much shorter and often leads to a quicker decision.
- Assuming you do a great job and build a solid relationship with the owner, there are many opportunities for more jobs as the company grows.

Negatives
- Getting direct referrals from small-business owners is often difficult because most of them don't know people outside their industry. In fact, most small-business owners are so busy, they don't even know people inside their industry.
- They typically don't do a good job of staying connected to their community or other professionals; as a result, they tend to feel rather isolated.
- They can seem overwhelming with the number of tasks they try to do simultaneously.
- It can be hard to work with clients who say they will accomplish a certain task, but always offer legitimate-sounding excuses as to why they were unable to finish the task.

Basic Marketing Strategies
- Build strategic partnerships with other service professionals who work exclusively with small-business owners (lawyers, accountants, financial planners, bankers, commercial loan officers).
- Become a regular speaker at small-business events, chambers of commerce, and Rotary Club meetings.

- Offer low-cost products or services (less than $300) that act as an introduction to your services.
- Emphasize the free coaching session.
- Look to see which small businesses are hiring. This usually indicates either a change in leadership or a growth spurt in business.
- Join traditional networking groups; chambers of commerce and industry associations are usually two good choices.
- Make sure all your marketing efforts talk about the hot buttons for small-business owners: lack of time, work-life balance, cash flow, lack of funding, way to find and retain top talent, means of motivating employees without using money, sales and marketing strategies, and steps to develop a business plan (40 percent of small businesses do not have a business plan).
- Educate them about the benefits of having a small-business coach and the kind of results you generally achieve.
- Offer a 100 percent money-back guarantee. This reverses the risk they take in purchasing your services.
- Be careful in selecting the title you use for your company and yourself. Many small-business owners are turned off by "touchy-feely spiritual energy" coaching. They don't want to feel like they are in therapy or consulting a psychic. They tend to be very focused on their business and respond best when you use business-related terms.

MIDSIZED COMPANIES

Midsized companies, those with 100 to 1000 employees and annual revenues of $50 million to $500 million, are characterized by a series of transitions. The transitions can be found in hiring larger numbers of employees, finding and retaining top talent, training new managers, changing technology requirements, restructuring the company pay scale, implementing customer relationship management (CRM) initiatives, moving to bigger facilities, going from being a regional to a national company, bringing on and training a national sales force, and making big changes on the executive level. A midsized company no longer has the luxuries of a small business—it has hundreds of people, employees and customers, depending on it, but now it is playing on a much bigger field, often going against competitors 10 to 100 times its size. A wrong step could send it quickly back into oblivion, but the right step could propel it into the top tier of American companies.

In many cases, the original founder of what has become a midsized business either has recently left the company, is in the process of leaving in the next few years, or is being moved out of a leadership position by the board or outside investors. It takes one type of person and skill set to start a company, a different one to build a successful company, and yet another one to build a small business into a much larger, midsized one. There are very few people who have mastered all of those different skill sets and are both knowledgeable and flexible enough to make it work.

Positives
- Coaches who have worked in a company that has undergone these types of growing pains or perhaps have even taken part in leading a company through such changes are best prepared to understand and take advantage of the challenges that a midsized company faces.
- Midsized companies usually have all the problems of a large company without having the processes and procedures in place to handle them. This provides many opportunities for coaches who know how to identify these problems and are able to clearly articulate how they can help. Coaching is the perfect medium for helping a person or company through a transition. It can be a very powerful tool useful for the following tasks:

  - Developing a strategic plan for training new managers
  - Helping the team train new managers or new salespeople
  - Helping individuals and the organization make the transition go more smoothly
  - Increasing critical communication skills between departments
  - Enhancing the management team's ability to work together
  - Creating a succession plan
  - Helping executives determine what types of people they need to bring in to increase their chances of success

- Midsized companies will often receive a sizable cash infusion from outside investors in order to take the steps needed to make the

Wendy Johnson, MA, CEC, CMC
President and Chief Executive Officer
Worldwide Association of Business Coaches
www.wabccoaches.com
presidentceo@wabccoaches.com

Wendy Johnson is president and CEO of the Worldwide Association of Business Coaches, the only international association dedicated to developing, advancing and promoting the business coaching industry. Johnson's vision is a business coach working with every business, organization and government.

How did you get into the business coaching field?

I have an extensive background in human dynamics, behavioral science and criminal justice. Prior to earning my Master of Arts (MA) degree in Counseling Psychology, I served in several highly selective positions within the British Columbia (BC) government, including several years as a "street cop" and a high profile investigator. In addition to my psychology background, I became certified in a number of advanced programs in mediation, negotiation, conflict analysis, management, interrogations and multiple areas of investigations.

A work related injury invited me to look at other ways in which I could apply my expertise in human dynamics. In 2001, I received my first Certified Executive Coach (CEC) designation through Royal Roads University (Victoria, Canada). Also in 2001, I was selected to study with internationally renowned Master Coach, Dr. Susan Skiffington, of Sydney, Australia, earning a Certified Master Coach (CMC) designation. In March of 2002, I received a second CEC designation through the former National Association of Business Coaches.

In the Spring of 2002, I became the President and CEO of the National Association of Business Coaches and led the organization through a year long transformation including changing the name to the Worldwide Association of Business Coaches (WABC) (www.wabccoaches.com).

What makes the Worldwide Association of Business Coaches (WABC) distinctive?

I believe there are three broad categories of coaching today; sports, personal, and business.

What makes us distinctive is our:

> *Focus* — Business Coaching, by our definition, is the umbrella term for all facets of coaching done in a business setting. Executive, corporate, entrepreneur, leadership, organizational development, and small business coaching are examples of niche specialties within the realm of business. In our Association, we have members who specialize in one or several niches, however, our unifying principle is business.

Exclusivity—WABC is the only international professional association dedicated exclusively to the business coaching industry.

Credibility—We require candidates to meet rigorous admission and renewal standards that differentiates professional from unqualified practitioners.

Client Services—Clients are attracted to WABC as the premiere business resource for coaching services.

What do you believe are the future trends in business coaching?

Both the personal coaching industry as well as the business coaching industry will continue to struggle over the next decade with issues specifically related to credibility and identity.

Our Association is focused on key initiatives aimed at refining, elevating and self-regulating our emerging business coaching profession. With broad stakeholder involvement, the next decade and beyond will be about:

Creating a Common Body of Knowledge
Embracing our Code of Business Coaching Ethics and Integrity
Standardizing Core Competencies, Training and Certification
Measuring Impact and Return on Investment (ROI)
Initiating Business Coaching Advocacy Programs

In terms of future trends in business coaching specifically, I think we will see:

Increased demand for ROI measurement
Merging of solo-practitioners to form networks, alliances, and formal business coaching firms
Increased competition, particularly from professionals migrating out of consulting, project management, organizational development, and counseling
Increased emphasis on advanced degrees
Influx of older practitioners as they retire and leave their former traditional positions
Amplified focus on corporate ethics and corporate governance
Multi-level projects too big for the solo-practitioner

What are some critical questions coaches should ask when evaluating training from all the different coaching schools?

As a self-regulating industry, there are currently no unified standards for comparison. However, there are a number of highly credible organizations that provide coach training. To find the right fit with your specific objectives, here are a few questions to consider:

(Continued)

1. *What type of coaching do you want to do?*
   If you are interested in business coaching, seek programs that offer curriculum in business. Most coaching programs today introduce both tracks (personal and business coaching), but you should be selective in choosing the program that provides the most emphasis in your area of interest.

2. *What is your past experience?*
   Coaching schools vary greatly between basic training and advanced or accelerated training. If you have had experience in human dynamics, seek a program that assumes basic knowledge so that you may benefit from a more advanced program. If this is a complete career change, consider taking a few free classes in coaching to see if it's a fit before you invest heavily in a field that may not be what you thought.

3. *What do past graduates say?*
   Many times we are shy about asking for references. This is not the time. Most active coaches have taken classes from more than one organization and can be helpful in clarifying the strengths and need areas of the organizations you are researching.

Peer Resources has a great comparison chart of various coaching schools at: http://www.peer.ca/coachingschools.html.

---

transition to the big leagues. This is often the time in a company's life cycle when the owners or investors decide to take the company public. Again, being able to identify companies in the appropriate stage and industry is imperative if you are going to take full advantage of targeting them in your marketing efforts.

- Growing a business to this size involves a lot of time, energy, and resources. The executives know they have a good thing going and are more likely to turn to outside help when they need it to keep a problem from damaging the company.

Negatives
- As a company grows larger it becomes increasingly difficult to talk directly to a decision maker. Gatekeepers become more prominent and more sophisticated.
- The owner or founder has often had to give up a substantial part of the company in order to get funding, so the owner or founder may still need to run your proposal past someone else for ultimate approval. Or, the owner or founder may have become discon-

nected from the day-to-day operations and may not be entirely aware of all the problems that are occurring.

- It can be difficult to find these companies at the exact time when they both need your services and have the available funding to pay for your services. Keeping in regular contact with your target market is critical here, because when the need arises, potential clients may act quickly to resolve it.

Basic Marketing Strategies

- Good referral sources include corporate law firms, large HR outsourcing companies, merger and acquisition firms, large accounting firms, business brokers, law firms that specialize in taking companies public, investment bankers, and venture capitalists.
- Focus your networking time on larger, more prestigious groups that target CEOs, presidents, board members, and movers and shakers in your business community.
- Hire a professional designer to rework your corporate image, and make sure all your marketing materials (business cards, brochures, and web site) are professionally designed. The people at this level will spot a do-it-yourself approach a mile away. Remember, tangibility enhances credibility, but if your tangible marketing materials are not top notch, they can degrade or destroy your credibility.
- Emphasize your company's experience with large, name-brand, and *Fortune* 500 companies. A midsized company often is looking to join the ranks of the major players and wants to work with companies that work with the majors and can possibly provide introductions to them.
- Ask industry insiders where you can find information about companies that are growing, what the current trends are, what kinds of questions to ask to determine how a company is doing financially, and where to look to find out which companies are looking for or receiving additional funding.
- This is the level at which you need to seriously invest time and money in your marketing efforts. It will take more time, more money, and more resources to make this target market a successful one. The sales cycle will lengthen noticeably, the level of sophistication will greatly increase, and the number of gatekeepers will be enlarged.

- Here is where the fun and games stop and, pardon the expression, the grown-ups are separated from the kiddies. If you're not dead serious about building your company and willing to dedicate everything it takes to make it happen, you will not be successful at this level or above. This is not the time to skimp by with the cheapest of anything. It really does take money to make money.

LARGE TO *FORTUNE* 500 COMPANIES

Research indicates that 30 to 45 percent of all *Fortune* 500 companies use either internal or external coaches for a variety of issues. Although this may seem like a lot, it is not enough to indicate a critical mass has been reached. This could mean there is still plenty of potential for coaching, or it could mean that the rest of the *Fortune* 500 is skeptical of coaching as being simply another fad developed by consultants trying to increase their business. In order to be successful in the long term, each coach in a *Fortune* 500 company must work extremely hard to show a direct correlation between their coaching and a positive impact on either the top or bottom line.

Positives
- Working for large, well-known companies can bring prestige to your company and open doors with other large prospects.
- Once you get in the door of a large company and are successful in a small project, you often find the door becomes wide open for other projects in other departments.
- Good news! Other departments you go to within the same company often have the same problems you just solved in the first department.
- Better news! In a large company there are many other departments with many other problems. Often these problems are systemic—on some level the organization allows them to begin and enables them to continue.

Negatives
Regardless of the prestige, honor, and multiple opportunities you can gain when coaching in a large company, some professional coaches do

not work for larger companies because of the problems and frustrations they have experienced.

- It's a very difficult culture in which to make a real difference. Corporate culture is so ingrained that it often seems impossible for real change to take place. This can be very frustrating for coaches who are results driven and change focused, especially when they see the same problems occurring time and time again (such as incompetent people being consistently promoted into positions of power — a phenomenon known as the *Dilbert principle*).
- It often seems as though there is no such thing as a decision maker in a large corporation. It takes real persistence to get past the multiple levels of red tape in order to get to someone who actually has hiring authority to get your project going.
- The sales cycle is often extremely long and frustrating! From the time of your first contact until you receive the first contract can be 9 to 12 months, and often much longer.
- Any project can be cut at any time with no warning or reason. My firm recently spent the better part of eight months cultivating a relationship with a senior vice president of a *Fortune* 500 company. Everything seemed to be going according to schedule for the launching of a $50,000 pilot program when we received an e-mail one day that simply said, "Sorry, budgets have been cut for this next year and we can't do the project." That was the end. All future phone calls and e-mails went unanswered.
- It often takes a very long time to receive payment (expect a three- to six-month delay), because everything is passed through "corporate," where you are seen as simply another vendor with an outstretched hand. Last year a West Coast coach told me she performed $40,000 worth of work for a *Fortune* 500 company and received a solid letter of recommendation from the division president, but did not receive any payment for nine months and ultimately had to threaten a lawsuit before they finally sent her the payment.
- It is virtually impossible to move beyond being viewed as simply another vendor and reach the position of critical strategic partner, where the best coaching occurs.

- Most big companies strongly prefer to work with other big companies or with a small company that has worked with several large companies in their industry. It can be very difficult and time consuming for a one-person coaching company to land its first big client. Today's Leadership Coaching has worked with more than 23 *Fortune* 500 companies, and we still have to jump through hoops when targeting other large companies.
- You have to be willing to invest a fair amount of money in creating top-notch marketing materials (brochures, web site, collateral material) if you want to be taken seriously.

Basic Marketing Strategies

- Do not expect to make quick money from these companies. The sales cycle can be extremely long. Be prepared to spend a lot of time following up and trying to secure appointments with decision makers. Be sure to have other businesses in the sales pipeline that you can depend on to come through while you are waiting for the big contract.
- Emphasize your previous experience working in and with other large, nationally recognized companies.
- Very few traditional sales strategies will help you reach the true decision maker. Clearly, the best way is to network your way to the top.
- You can easily be sidetracked or stymied by pseudo–decision makers, people who want you to believe they are the decision maker, but actually have no influence or authority.
- Attend only elite, prestigious networking groups where there is a relatively high entrance fee. (They often do this for three reasons: it allows them to pay for well-known speakers, to hold meetings in nice venues, and to keep pesky vendors away.)
- Unless you have expertise in marketing, hire a professional to help you design a creative and effective marketing strategy for reaching the real decision makers.
- Don't try to go straight to the top of the entire company—start with a department, division, or subsidiary. Many larger companies have several regional general managers who function as divisional presidents, complete with responsibilities for profit and loss. It can be somewhat easier to reach them, and they often have projects and people that could use your help.

- Try targeting a rising star in the company—someone who is on the fast track to management. If your coaching produces real results, they may be in a position to recommend you for other projects as they rise through the ranks.
- I encourage coaches and consultants to avoid targeting the human resources (HR) department. Unfortunately, in many large companies the HR department is viewed not as a necessity but as a necessary evil, and personnel are usually overworked, underpaid, and understaffed. It is often the last department created and the first one to be cut when layoffs hit. It is unfortunate, but realistic, to note that the typical HR department in today's large company has little or no influence on hiring, firing, promotion, or development decisions. The best you can hope for by using HR is to be introduced to someone with influence; the worst that can happen is to be permanently associated with the same negative stereotypes as the HR department. Although this is not true in every company, this kind of attitude is more the rule than the exception. If you are considering using HR as the entry point, I would encourage you to do two things: First, research a particular company to get a better understanding of how the HR department is viewed and treated, and second, use HR as a last resort. Try every other angle first, and then try the HR department.

SEGMENTATION BY INDUSTRY

This is not designed to be a comprehensive list of all the industries that use coaching. Instead, I have presented the top industries where coaches are currently reporting success. Which industry you target will largely depend on which industries you have an interest in, are geographically close to you, and you have experience with, unless you live in a major metropolitan area or want to have a nationwide coaching practice.

PROFESSIONAL SERVICE FIRMS

Professional service firms—such as law firms, accounting agencies, physician groups, executive and management recruiting companies, financial planners, architectural firms, psychological practices, consulting firms, large dental offices, and outsourcing agencies—can be a good source of clients for the coach who has the background and the necessary marketing skills. Unless you have previous experience in a field, I highly recommend that you invest time in researching the field you are interested in targeting: Talk to current professionals about their challenges, talk to owners of practices, interview former professionals about why they left the field, read a few of the field's major journals to find out the current trends, or target a specific area of interest. Some of the recurring hot topics among service firms are the following:

- Marketing their practice
- Helping every partner become a rainmaker
- Increasing their referral base
- Coping with conflict in the office and among the partners
- Refining their office management techniques
- Finding and keeping top talent

Positives
- Most professional firms need your coaching help. They often face very similar problems: they are great technicians, but know very little about sales, marketing, or people management skills.
- Many professionals like to practice their trade and dislike any area that infringes upon their billable hours, including sales and marketing activities.
- Most professionals understand if you bill by the hour because they likely do the same thing in their business.
- Most professionals stay connected in their field, and if you do an outstanding job, they will often refer you to their closest friends and colleagues.
- Professional firms can give you wonderful testimonial letters that are very clear, concise, and well written.

Negatives
- Many professional firms want the coach to meet many specific qualifications:

  - Be highly educated (at least a master's degree).
  - Have specific experience in their field (former or current practitioners strongly preferred).

- Provide a reference list of other professional firms the coach has coached (preferably in their field).
- Be able to virtually work miracles, such as turning a problem partner around in 30 days or less, or doubling their revenues with one simple technique.

- Firms are reluctant to pay more for coaching than they charge their clients for services, even though they view higher hourly rates as indicating a higher level of expertise and demand. If they charge $100 per hour, they believe you should, too.
- They don't like to use the word *coach;* they much prefer to work with a *consultant.*
- Professionals are so busy, overworked, and overstressed that they may not have time to see you for coaching, much less have time to implement all the strategies you talked about in your last session.
- Many professional services firms use democratic decision making, which usually involves all the partners or owners and can often hold things up inordinately.
- Some fields are very stingy when it comes to spending money on anything other than a tangible asset, and they may try to nickel and dime you for the lowest possible fee.
- It is often difficult to convince these firms to invest in the development of a manager or partner; instead, most times your work will revolve around a specific area of expertise you have or remedial coaching. In other words, there is a specific problem, such as anger outbursts or conflict management, that they want to have resolved.
- They also frequently wait way too long before calling for help. This kind of work is usually more difficult and has a much lower rate of success.
- It can be difficult to obtain references from professional firms because they may see coaching as an indication that they have a problem, and they don't want their public image tarnished.

Basic Marketing Strategies
- When talking to professional service firms, be sure to present yourself as experienced and knowledgeable in their field.
- Understand the challenges they face and how the field typically tries to resolve them.

- Know their language and be very comfortable with their buzz-words and acronyms.
- Speak to their local associations about relevant topics.
- Publishing articles or books will greatly increase your credibility among professional firms, because professionals were taught in their graduate programs that only the top people publish (most of whom were their professors).

TECHNOLOGY COMPANIES

In various parts of the country, technology firms have become a large part of the economy, hiring and firing thousands of employees at a time. With each new technology that comes out, there seems to be an entirely new surge of companies that are started, and a number of others that fail. When categorizing technology companies, there are primarily two different kinds: product-based companies and service-based companies, also commonly known as hardware companies and software companies. Most small to midsized companies focus on one line or the other. They sell products (computers, networks, parts, peripherals) or services (web site design, customized software creation, database administration), while larger companies typically sell both (e.g., they'll set up a network for you and create customized software to run on the network, then sell you a five-year service plan and $100,000 worth of consulting services to show you how to best utilize the solution they just gave you). Generally speaking, software companies have a better track record when it comes to developing their people. The explanation for this is simple: Intense competition in the hardware arena has collapsed the profit margins of most companies (which are often 0.5 to 5%), while profit margins in the software arena can be large (even a company as large as Microsoft can maintain about a 20 to 35 percent profit on each of its Windows applications), and margins of custom software companies can be enormous (often 20 to 60 percent). In addition, you are likely to find more highly educated and highly paid employees at a software company. The 2002 average starting salary for a new college graduate in computer science in the Chicago area was $47,000 to $52,000. So if you are going to target technology companies, it will be much easier to find software companies that can afford to hire you.

When I first started out, I coached numerous engineers, managers, and executives from several small and large technology companies, including Microsoft, IBM, Motorola, Lucent, Tellabs, and Wang Global, and regardless of the specific technology they use, whether hardware or software, or the ownership of the company (private or public), the fundamental issues remain the same. Here are some of the perennial hot buttons:

- Most tech companies provide little or no specific management training, and when they do, it is often not used by most employees.
- Many technical employees, including managers, have poor interpersonal and communication skills.
- Tech companies are renowned for regularly promoting great technicians who turn out to be mediocre managers who try to use their technical skills to manage people. (Hint: It doesn't work.)
- There is often a lack of time management skills which results in projects not getting done on time, which increases costs, decreases company profits, and damages customer relationships.
- There seems to be regular conflict between the marketing department, the sales team and the engineering division, which often stems from a lack of respect and communication between the three departments. The marketing department sees a need and launches a campaign for a solution that doesn't exist yet, the sales team promises prospects everything under the sun to get them to sign up, and the technical team is stuck with trying to build and deliver a product that doesn't even exist on an unrealistic time schedule.

Positives
- There are plenty of opportunities for coaching employees, project managers, and directors, all the way to the CEO. This environment is filled with people who are highly paid and highly intelligent, but who often don't feel appreciated and consistently underperform.
- Most of the people you coach are well paid. Most software engineers start out making $40,000 to $50,000. Within five years on the job, it is not that uncommon for a good engineer to make in excess of $100,000. High-tech companies will not be bothered by higher than standard rates ($250 to $400 per hour of coaching is not uncommon).

- If you can coach the right people, it is easier to prove how your coaching impacted the bottom line (e.g., the project was completed 15 days ahead of schedule; there is a significant decrease in the amount of team conflict).
- Most of the help these companies need consists of building basic skills that most coaches could assist them with: communication, interpersonal relationships, time management, stress management, conflict resolution, employee motivation, and team building.

Negatives

- It can be difficult to land your first project, because most high-tech companies want you to have direct experience coaching in their industry.
- It is definitely an industry that uses a lot of jargon, and either you know it or you don't. If you don't, you will not be as respected by the technical people. But if you do know the jargon, it will open a lot of doors for you.
- You have to like working with geeks. If you can't stand talking to the neighborhood technology expert, this isn't the field to coach in. The majority of people employed by high-tech companies, even the managers and executives, are either technology geeks or *former* geeks. (By the way, I'm using the term *geek* in the nicest way possible. After all, I'm married to one.)

Basic Marketing Strategies

- Read widely in the technology field, looking for trends and patterns in how the economy is impacting the field, which companies are going up and which are going down. There is often a big difference between which companies are successful and which are only squeaking by, even within a particular niche.
- Build your track record by first looking for work with engineers and managers at smaller high-tech companies before targeting the major tech companies.
- Go to technology conferences or networking events. Engineers like to hang out with other engineers.
- Learn the basic industry jargon, but be very careful about showing off your knowledge to engineers. They may take that as a challenge to find out just how much or how little you really know. Just drop

a few hints or abbreviations that let them know you are following them and understand what they are talking about.

- Design and develop a workshop or seminar that targets one of their major needs, such as "Successful Management Strategies for Engineers."
- Coaching at high-tech companies can be very cyclical and dependent upon the economy. Work hard to get into companies when the economy is good and high-tech companies are hiring; look to branch out into other industries when they are laying workers off.

SEGMENTATION BY POSITION AND DEPARTMENT

Targeting different departments or positions requires different strategies and different services. It may seem obvious, but many coaches make the mistake of using the same strategies and techniques when marketing to the accounting department as when they target the CEO of the company, and then wonder why it doesn't work. Here are a few common departments and positions that use coaching and training.

SALES PROFESSIONALS AND SALES TEAMS

More training and development dollars are spent on the sales department than any other part of a company, because anything the company can do to raise a salesperson's closing rate, even by a percentage point or two, can have an immediate positive effect on the company's top line. Targeting the sales department via presentations, seminars, or coaching programs can provide a great opening to other parts of the company.

Here are some common topics for presentations to sales professionals:

- Improving morale when sales are down
- Staying on top when the bottom falls out
- Discovering the top-10 tips for managing a sales team
- Building a referral network
- Developing power networking skills
- Increasing your communication level
- Understanding individual differences
- Adopting new closing techniques
- Developing strategies for following through with prospects

- Discovering your individual selling style
- Selling to top executives

Positives
- If you begin the coaching period with specific, measurable objectives, you should be able to see a direct correlation between your coaching and an impact on the company's top line, via increased sales.
- If you fit the profile (dynamic personality, excellent communication skills, history of success in sales), you can do rather well with this target market.
- Most of the skills sales people need to succeed are directly in line with what most coaches offer: communication skills, interpersonal relationships, building rapport, and self-motivation.
- Sales professionals are not afraid to ask for and receive coaching. They come from a long history of going to training sessions, workshops, and seminars. If your coaching produces results, they will gladly refer you to their friends.

Negatives
- The competition for this market is tough. There are entire companies dedicated to training sales professionals, many of which dominate a particular niche.
- Due to the number of companies vying for this market, it is very difficult not to be seen as just another vendor, rather than as a critical strategic partner.
- Even though companies spend a lot on training their salespeople, most of the training is done in group settings. They typically do not have a large budget for one-on-one work.
- A lot of the time, the people who hire you to "train" their salespeople really seem to want just fluff—motivational speaking that gets the salespeople all excited about nothing, instead of real content that could make a difference.
- You will experience a lot of apathy about your "new approach" among sales managers, because they have seen it all, and many have *tried* it all.

Basic Marketing Strategies
- Develop seminars and brief workshops around the hot buttons faced by salespeople and account executives.

- Most salespeople have one thing in common: They want to make a lot of money without working too hard. If you are going to have success in this field, you must be able to show them how to increase their sales. The only real way to do this is to be an expert in sales yourself, preferably by personal experience. You have to show them you have real content knowledge they need and that by hiring you, they can get this knowledge and become better salespeople.
- If you are targeting the sales department within a company, don't target an individual salesperson. Start higher up the chain, at least at the sales manager's level, if not the vice president's level.
- If you want to work with individual salespeople, try to price your services so they will be able to afford them on an individual basis. Top sales professionals are always looking for something that will give them an edge against their competitors.
- Focus on the benefits and results of the services you provide. Be sure to point these out for the individuals as well as for the department and organization.
- Work hard to include follow-up coaching after a training event in a proposal.
- Whenever you provide training or coaching to salespeople, try to track the results. If you can demonstrate how you impact the top line, obtaining new projects will become much easier.
- Become known as a specialist in a particular field, such as high-tech sales, service versus product sales, financial services sales, life insurance sales, or retail sales.
- Become a published author, either with a book or a newspaper or trade magazine column.
- Do a lot of speaking to groups of sales managers or executives of companies who use a sales force.
- Package your materials on tapes and CDs. Most salespeople do a fair amount of driving and often will listen to motivational or sales strategy CDs when traveling between appointments.

NEW MANAGERS

Most small to midsized companies have little or no formal training programs for new managers, and larger companies mostly ignore the ones they have. The companies that do have a well-laid-out program for training new managers by and large focus on sending them to one or two classes put on by large seminar companies and perhaps assigning them to a mentor within the company.

However, most adult educators can tell you that the best learning does not take place in a sterile classroom environment, and irregular meetings with a mentor who doesn't seem to have time for you does not constitute training. The best way to develop leadership skills is through regular one-on-one interaction with an objective, wise, and knowledgeable person who works with you on specific goals, action steps, and measurable outcomes. In other words, a personal coach!

Some common issues new managers need coaching around include the following:

- Communication skills
- Management skills for understanding and utilizing individual differences
- Team-building strategies
- Conflict resolution
- Time-management skills
- Stress management training
- Coaching skills for managers
- Strategies for a successful transition from technician to manager

Positives
- New managers are excited about their positions and want to do everything right the first time. This can be an ideal opportunity for them to receive development coaching.
- Coaches are generally not used to helping new managers who have a lot of problems. Generally, such managers are just outright fired or demoted back to their former position. Unless, of course, they work at a company that follows the Dilbert principle, in which case they are swiftly promoted.
- This can be a good entry point into a company by providing skill-building seminars and workshops for new managers.
- Most coaches can provide the skills new managers need most—the soft skills of business.

Negatives
- If a company's managers believe they already have a training program for developing new managers, you will not have much suc-

cess in changing their minds or getting them to spend more money by adding another service.

- Most companies do not truly believe in developing their new managers, and thus anything they do that is even remotely connected to training and development is construed to be a formal program.
- Many companies do not have any budget in place for training their new managers. Those that do often load so much work onto their new managers that the managers don't have the time or energy to leave the office to take advantage of the training budget.
- It will be difficult to target new managers directly and ask them to pay for coaching out of their own pockets, because most cannot afford your prices, unless you are relatively inexpensive.
- You typically cannot command top dollar for coaching and training new managers. They are not seen as particularly valuable to an organization, as they have not had time to make a major contribution. In addition, they were likely promoted because of their capabilities and competencies, not their interpersonal problems.
- New managers often don't feel the need for coaching because they have not been around long enough to experience real defeat or frustration.

Basic Marketing Strategies
- New managers tend to be in their midtwenties to midthirties. Remember this when you develop a marketing plan to target them.
- Focus on skill building, not remedial coaching or enhancement.
- Highlight the key points new managers need and want, focusing on the benefits for both the individual and the organization.
- New managers typically will not be the ones hiring you. You will be hired either as part of an overall company initiative to train the new managers or because the owner or top executive wants to bring you in to work with a new manager who is struggling with a specific problem. If it's the latter, be sure to study the following section, on Senior Managers, for some tips.
- Offer a community seminar for new managers or a series of inexpensive workshops (less than $200 each) focusing on skill building.
- Offer a group discount if a company hires you to work with a number of new managers.

- Put together a package of services designed to meet the needs of new managers.
- When pricing your services, try to keep the top amount to around $1,500 to $3,000 per person per year. Most midsized to large companies don't budget more than that for training new managers.
- Research companies in your target market to find out exactly what they are currently doing to train new managers, and try to develop services that complement their offerings without overlapping their existing ones.

REAL CASE STUDY

Bill is a senior software programmer who has been at his company for five to seven years and has reached the top of the company pay scale. The vice president has recently told him that in order to continue advancing, he will need to move into a management position. They offer him a project management position responsible for three technical teams with five to seven people per team. In order to ensure his success, they encourage him to sign up for a couple of new manager's classes through a national seminar company when he has a chance and to talk to Frank, the senior project manager, once a month if he has any questions.

Bill hits the ground running and his days are immediately filled with learning his new position, coordinating all the teams, and going to more meetings than he thought possible. The technical teams are constantly fighting with each other, trying to get more budget money to hire more help or get paid for the overtime they are putting in. Thirty days after he starts his new position, the company makes an announcement that 15 percent of employees will be laid off, and they ask Bill to choose which people on his teams should be let go.

Right about now, Bill sure could use some help—even those classes sound good—but there is no time, and he just learned that Frank, his senior manager and mentor, is one of the people being let go.

Two questions:

1. What are the biggest challenges Bill faces in the upcoming months?
2. What kinds of services could you develop that would target Bill's situation and his company?

SENIOR MANAGERS

It seems that the only time a coach is called in to work with senior managers is when there is a specific problem. Perhaps a manager has just been slated for a big promotion when an executive discloses some concern about the manager's outbursts of anger, or a senior manager (of the Builder or Boomer generations) has been placed in charge of younger employees (Generation X or Y) in a reorganization, and the difference in leadership styles is causing conflict.

When coaching a senior manager, the majority of the time you will have been called in either by the Human Resource department, which will have been told to find someone who can quickly solve this problem, or by a top executive with whom you have built a relationship or who has some level of responsibility for the senior manager. It will most likely be to help the manager with a specific interpersonal problem. If that problem is not resolved, it could lead to career derailment or even result in the manager's termination.

It cannot be stressed enough that in these situations, how coaching is presented to the senior manager is absolutely critical to its success. Too many times the opportunity has been ruined because HR or an executive has told the manager something like, "You have a big problem! You need serious help!" Then a coach shows up, and everyone wonders why the manager is resistant.

When called into situations like these, I immediately recommend that nothing more be said to the senior manager until I have met with the executive and the HR department together. During that meeting we discuss the issues involved, the history, what has been tried before, and what success would look like. I make it very clear in that initial meeting that if they are simply looking for a way to cover the company legally when they fire the senior manager, I am not interested in pursuing the matter any further. I personally do not believe coaching should be manipulated as another way for a company to cover its butt. Nor do I believe coaching will have a fair chance of success in these kinds of situations. I have learned from experience that trying to coach a person who has been threatened with termination unless they drastically change some attitude, behavior, or personality style is generally pointless. The decision has usually already been made to eventually terminate the manager, at least in the minds of the executive and the HR department. If I believe this is the case, I either try to bow out gracefully or recommend that they face the reality of the situation and agree to provide some transition coaching to help the individual move to another division or another company. I may or may not be willing to provide this, depending on the circumstances.

Unfortunately, these kinds of situations are not always cut and dried. They may initially state that they want to work with the manager and want to see the manager succeed, but halfway through the coaching they may realize that drastic changes will take more time than they are willing to grant (usually more than 30 to 60 days), or they may begin placing unreasonable demands on the manager as a way of testing to see if the changes will last. For whatever reasons, you must be careful to go into these situations with your eyes and ears wide open! When working under these circumstances, there are a number of risks you and your company take on:

- You may be pushed to break confidentiality to assure management that things are progressing at the speed they want.
- The company may try to change the rules or measurement of success in the middle of the coaching.
- If the situation turns bad, it could hurt your reputation in that industry.
- The employee may become disgruntled and sue the company, and throw your company into the lawsuit for good measure.

Unless you have a lot of experience in corporate coaching, feel you are very comfortable taking on these risks, and are able to help quickly turn the manager around, I recommend you refer this kind of situation to someone else. It can turn ugly very quickly when someone's livelihood or pension plan is at stake.

Assuming you have decided to take on this kind of situation and the company is really interested in working with this manager, the next step is to make sure everyone is on the same page. In a joint meeting with the coach, the senior manager, the executive, and a senior HR member should discuss and agree on the limits of confidentiality, specific problem issues, the measure of success, and precisely what the goals are and the timelines for meeting them. Each of these points is important. Everyone needs to agree on what success would look like—yes, everyone. For example: no more anger outbursts, a 15 percent increase in sales by the end of the quarter, or no more requests for six months by employees to be transferred to another division because they cannot get along with the senior manager. Use your coaching skills to set SMART goals: *specific, measurable, achievable, realistic,* and *timed.*

The concept of coaching as a form of development and as a way the company can show its concern for and commitment to the manager should be presented. It should also be talked about in a way that focuses on the benefits to the individual—it is a positive sign that the company believes in the manager's competence and desires to see the manager succeed in the company. Hiring a coach is a clear sign that the company wants to invest in the senior manager's success and help the manager to maximize his or her strengths and overcome any stumbling blocks in the way of advancement.

Positives

- If you succeed in quickly turning around a top-level manager at a company, you will have the door opened to multiple opportunities. The company will be very grateful, as will the senior manager. This is a difficult job and not for the meek of heart, but it can be very rewarding.
- Since this is a difficult situation in which you must make rapid changes and which involves a heightened level of risk, you should charge and receive top dollar. Top turnaround coaches are receiving $300 to $700 per hour for this kind of work.
- If you're looking for a serious challenge you should check this out!

Negatives

- Unfortunately, a company often doesn't bring you in until the last minute or just after everything else they have tried has failed. A personal coach is often seen as a last resort.
- You usually don't have the opportunity to talk with the company representatives about how to present coaching as something positive, because they have already told the senior manager they are getting a coach. The result is that you may be stepping into a situation where coaching has been presented as punitive—not the easiest barrier to overcome.

- You probably will experience the worst side of corporate America—dirty politics, people refusing to take personal responsibility, blame-shifting, the loss of friendships, and feelings of revenge.
- Many people would say you can't really target this audience; it more likely happens by default. You get called in to coach a senior manager, and it turns out to be a turnaround situation.
- More often than not, the outcome is not overwhelmingly positive or negative, but mixed. The senior manager doesn't explode in anger anymore, but his or her direct reports still don't like him or her and still ask to be transferred out of the department, or sales go up for one quarter, but are down the next.
- Regardless of how much the company states the opposite, the senior manager may still believe you were sent there to cover the company legally so he or she can be fired. This can become a major barrier to a successful outcome.
- You have to be clear on who your client is, the senior manager or the company. And everyone has to know it and agree on it.

Basic Marketing Strategies
- To be financially successful in targeting senior manager turnaround situations, you have to become known as a specialist. This usually takes a long time and comes as the result of leading several successful turnaround situations.
- You can help to establish yourself in the turnaround field by publishing articles, columns, and books.
- You have to establish a credible reputation to target this audience.

BUSINESS OWNERS

Owners of small to midsized businesses are a prime target for business coaching because of their position of influence and the common issues they face, including:

- Developing leadership
- Focusing company resources strategically
- Managing personnel issues
- Balancing work and life
- Finding and retaining top talent

- Managing conflict among staff members
- Managing in times of transition
- Keeping the staff satisfied
- Planning for succession
- Feeling isolated and alone
- Building teamwork
- Managing strategic planning issues
- Maintaining focus
- Motivating the sales team
- Making tough decisions about layoffs
- Making the next payroll
- Rolling out new products or services

Business owners look for a coach who has an outside objective point of view, acts as a solid sounding board, and is a wise mentor, an expert by experience, and a thick-skinned, results-driven, goal-focused person who tells it like they see it. Business owners don't want a yes-person— they want a person they can trust.

Positives
- Business owners usually have a high amount of energy, above-average intelligence, and a strong drive for success—the perfect candidates for coaching.
- If you help them be more successful, they will gladly provide you with a strong reference and a string of referrals.
- If you can help business owners, they will turn to you for advice on how to help their employees. This can easily turn into new, ongoing projects and training contracts.
- Coaching business owners allows you to charge above industry rates ($250 to $400 per hour). In fact, charging too little will be a turn off, because a business owner would interpret that as saying your services are not that valuable.

Negatives
- Business owners can be very demanding. They expect a lot from themselves and others.
- In most cases, business owners want coaching to produce real results, not fluff or good feelings. They are always asking the ROI

question, "What return on investment will this give me? Is this the absolute best way to spend my money?" You must be able to clearly and concisely answer all of their ROI questions, including the infamous ones, "How do you measure results?" and "How many other business owners have you worked with, and how have you helped them?"

- Business owners only want to work with experts, and they respond better to coaches who are comfortable being part coach and part consultant.
- Be prepared to comfortably respond in a nondefensive way to very tough questions and objections, because business owners will ask all of them, including the ones you fear the most. Your response, verbal and nonverbal, will determine whether you get their business.

Basic Marketing Strategies

- To work with business owners, you need to act like and think like a business owner. You must be willing to recognize that ultimately your client is the *business*, not just the owner—a difficult and sometimes precarious position to be in. At times business owners do not see their business clearly, and they need that outside perspective to help them guide the company through a difficult time.
- Find ways to relate your coaching directly to the top line (increases revenues) or the bottom lines (decreases costs).
- Most business owners see themselves as having their life together and being relatively successful. They may not want to work with a personal coach who emphasizes that aspect too much. Instead, focus on how you can help them and their employees become more productive and increase their performance levels.
- Present yourself as an expert in a specific area they need help in: sales, marketing, operations, customer relationship management, employee relations, or conflict management, to name a few. Owners want to work with an expert.
- Be careful what title you use. Owners do not want to talk to a sales coach, nor do they want to work with an employee of a coaching company. They want to deal with other owners, presidents, and CEOs. If you own your business, don't hide this. In fact, if you are

going to target business owners, you should have the title President, CEO, Principal, or Owner on your card, in addition to your specific coaching title, such as Business Coach or Executive Coach.

- Be careful how you approach business owners. If you come off too much as a salesperson, they will quickly dismiss you and your company.
- Package your services to respond to the specific needs of business owners. One size does not fit all. Find ways to attract business owners in terms of how you price the service, the length of time, what it focuses on, and who it includes.

GENERAL MANAGERS OF DIVISIONS IN LARGE TO *FORTUNE* 500 COMPANIES

General managers (GMs) in many large companies function similarly to a president in a small to midsized company. They usually have a certain amount of decision making capability, profit-and-loss (P&L) responsibility, and all the accountability that goes along with it. They have all the problems and possibilities of a smaller organization, but without the ultimate say in how to run their business.

Positives
- If you are successful in coaching a GM, it can open the door to multiple other opportunities within the division and in other corporate divisions.
- You don't have to be working as a turnaround coach to work with a GM. You could work with them to enhance their leadership skills, help them avoid burnout, increase their ability to delegate, or help them manage personal work-life balance issues.

Negatives
- GMs are typically very hard to reach because of the multiple gatekeepers you have to go through in order to talk to them, much less meet with them.
- GMs are very busy people with little free time. If you meet with them you must get straight to the point and clearly state what you

are looking for (how you can help and the results your clients typically achieve).

- There are situations where you may find it impossible to coach other people in the same division if you coach the GM of the division, due to confidentiality constraints, or concerns about conflict of interest.
- More often than not, GMs want you to have previous experience with midsized to large companies. If you have this experience, emphasize it in your marketing materials and when using illustrations. If you don't, talk about experience you have had coaching executives in other situations.

Basic Marketing Strategies
- Many GMs are natural networkers and tend to know a lot of other influential people in their company and in their community. They often ask for and give direct referrals for particular business issues.
- GMs may belong to prestigious clubs and elite networking groups. Research the groups in your area and find out which ones attract these kinds of people.
- GMs are apt to be involved in their community and are often found on the boards of nonprofit organizations.

YOUR OWN INDUSTRY OR PROFESSION

Often, one of the best places to target clients is in the industry you came out of. If you have worked in a specific field or industry for the past several years, you probably have insights that other coaches don't about the important people and right companies that need your services, the challenges they face, future trends, in their field, and their ability to afford your services.

WORK EXPERIENCE EVALUATION

Make a list of the industries you have worked in over the past 20 years (Figure 3.1). Of this list, which ones do you feel most comfortable with and knowledgeable about? Which ones can you envision yourself working with and coaching in?

Industry	Amount of experience you have	Do they need coaching?	Can they afford coaching?	What are their top 3 challenges?	How many contacts do you have in that field?

FIGURE 3.1   Work experience evaluation chart.

EIGHT KEY QUESTIONS TO DETERMINE IF AN INDUSTRY IS A GOOD TARGET FOR YOU

As you study each of these key areas and industries, you may wonder if a particular one is the right one for you. Clearly, there are some areas or industries that would not be right for you due to any number of factors, but no one can definitively tell you whether a particular area is the best or right one for you because it depends on your personality, your interests, your personal and professional experience, your level of familiarity, and many other intangibles. However, here are eight questions that can quickly help you narrow the field down to the top two or three, which is about the most any one individual can handle.

1. How much does the average company in this industry spend on the training and development of its managers, leaders, and executives? If the target is an individual, how much do they typically spend on personal and professional development activities? ("I don't know" is not acceptable; look on the Internet or ask your local librarian for help.)

2. If you are a working professional, how much does your company have in its annual budget for training and development?
3. How big an issue do you believe the performance and productivity of employees and managers is in your industry or company?
4. Do you know of people or companies in your industry who have hired coaches to work with their employees? How did it turn out? Would they do it again?
5. How comfortable would you be coaching a person around one of the biggest challenges this industry faces?
6. What kind of resources, internal or external, does this kind of person or industry typically use or turn to to deal with those challenges?
7. What kind of resources, internal and external, do individuals or companies in this industry typically use to maximize the performance of their employees?
8. Have you kept in contact with people you know in the field, and would any of them be in a position to assist you in locating good prospects?

SUMMARY

We have covered 12 of the largest markets for business and personal coaching. As I mentioned earlier, most individuals cannot effectively target more than two or three of these markets, so choose carefully when deciding which ones you will go after. Your choice will determine, to a great extent, how quickly you can build a successful practice, how much time it will take to land each new client, and how long the average client will stay with you, as well as how much money you can charge for your services. Make your selections, write them into your marketing plan, and stick with them. Do not make the mistake of chasing after every lead that comes your way, unless you can land it with little effort. Your time, energy, and resources are very limited—use them wisely and success will follow.

CHAPTER 4

It Takes Money to Make Money: Financing Your Business

What Does It Really Take to Start a Coaching Business?

You say you want to start a coaching practice, but wonder how much time, energy, and financial resources it will take. In the next couple of chapters we will fully explore this question, going into depth about the financial aspects of starting and sustaining a coaching business. In this chapter we will cover:

- Several specific recommendations for what you need before you officially launch your business
- The wisest purchases you can make in the first few months of your start-up
- The different marketing materials and tools necessary to build your business quickly
- A breakdown of the actual costs you can expect to spend for these products and services, based on industry averages

The next chapter is closely linked to this one because you can easily use the information and recommendations in this chapter to create your financial plan in the next chapter, but please note that neither this chapter nor this book was written to provide specific tax, financial, or legal consulting. Please talk to your trusted accountant, financial planner, and lawyer for specific help in any of these areas and to validate all tax, financial, and legal implications for your particular situation.

Perhaps before we go any further we should briefly examine the two big questions in the forefront of your mind right now, "Exactly how much money do I really need to start my business?" and "Where am I going to find the cash?" Unfortunately, there are no easy answers to either question, but regarding the first question I thought it might be interesting to look at a number of very successful small businesses, such as are to be found on *Inc.* magazine's annual *Inc.* 500 list of the nation's fastest-growing small businesses for 2002, to see how much capital they started their now financially successful companies with. See Table 4.1.

As you can see from Table 4.1, there is little correlation between the amount of money people have started successful companies with and their eventual success. Does this mean you don't need any money to make it big? No, but it does point out that the amount of start-up capi-

TABLE 4.1　Initial Cash Reserves of *Inc.* 500 CEOs Surveyed

Reserves	Percentage of CEOs
Less than $1,000	14
$1,000–$10,000	27
$10,001–$20,000	10
$20,001–$50,000	15
$50,001–$100,000	12
More than $100,000	22

Note: Reserves include CEOs' personal assets.
Source: Susan Greco, *A Little Goes a Long Way,* www.Inc.com.

tal you have is not nearly as good an indicator of your success as your ability to manage and operate your business (i.e., to keep operating costs within budget, develop and implement a strategic plan, and make wise decisions). Assuming you have enough income from somewhere else to cover your living expenses, through an employed significant other, previous investments, a company buyout plan, or even living with your relatives, you should have at least several thousand dollars set aside for your first year's budget in order to maximize your chances for success. You do not want to be in a position of begging for money every couple of months or wanting to target a specific market but not having enough marketing funds to do so.

Quickly following the first question is, "Where am I going to find this kind of money?" There are several common sources of money you may be able to tap into, depending on your particular circumstances:

- Personal savings (more than 85 percent of small-business owners use their personal finances)
- Second mortgage on your house
- Personal credit cards
- Money from a partner (about 30 percent of successful small businesses start this way)
- Bank loans (about 60 percent of owners turn to banks after they get started)

- Family and friends (also known as "F&F loans"—these can be dangerous to your relationships, but around 20 percent of people use them)
- Inheritance
- Microloans
- Small Business Administration guaranteed loans

TIME AND ENERGY

In launching any small business your largest expenditure will be your time. Make no mistake, starting any business takes a lot of time and energy, but building a successful business takes even more. Before you go too far in your business plans, you need to answer some very serious questions:

- Is this going to be a part-time or full-time endeavor?
- If you are planning to start out part-time until you build up your coaching practice enough to go full-time, how long are you anticipating this will take?
- What is the longest amount of time you are willing to wait before you go full-time?
- How much actual time are you willing to spend each day and every week toward building your coaching practice?
- If you're just starting out, how long do you think it will take to obtain your first paying client?
- How long are you planning it will take to find your first 10 paying clients?
- What are your personal and professional goals in starting your own company?
- If you have a significant other, how supportive are they of your new endeavor?
- Do you have an alternative revenue stream with enough financial support to allow you to go full-time right now?

Assuming the owner is working full time, it takes the average professional service business a full 12 to 18 months to generate enough revenue to become profitable. Even if you are extremely good at sales and marketing and can quickly build up a clientele at half the industry average, you should count on spending at least the next 6 to 12 months building your practice. If you are only working part time on your practice, it could take twice as long. This directly relates to how much time and energy you are able to put into building your practice.

Over 50 percent of small businesses fail in the first four years — not a very good success rate. While there are many variables that contribute to business failure, some of the top ones include:*

- Lack of financial funding at the start (undercapitalization)
- Inability to generate revenues (lack of clients, poor utilization of resources)
- Outside business problems (poor economic conditions, increased competition)
- Personal reasons (illness, divorce, not enough time or energy)
- Taxes and debt problems

> It will take you three times as long, require twice as much energy, and cost four times as much as you think it will to get your business off the ground.

To be successful in starting and maintaining a small business, you must be absolutely committed to making the time, energy, and resources available that you will need. NASA reports that on launching, the space shuttle uses approximately 80 percent of its rocket fuel in the first mile. Once it gets moving, momentum builds and carries it forward, significantly reducing fuel requirements. A good rule of thumb is that it will take three times as long, require twice as much energy, and cost four times as much as you think it will to get your business off the ground. Be sure to count the cost before you decide to launch your new business.

Most of your financial expenses will fall into one of three categories: start-up marketing materials, office equipment, and ongoing sales and marketing efforts. We will discuss each separately along with some typical prices you can expect to pay in 2003–2004, but overall your first-year financial plan should break down along the lines shown in Figure 4.1.

*Source: U.S. Small Business Administration, *The State of Small Business: A Report of the President*, 1997.

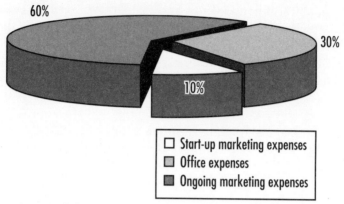

FIGURE 4.1   First-year financial plan for a start-up: percentage breakdown of total marketing budget.

OFFICE EQUIPMENT

COMPUTER

The consumer computer industry changes significantly every three to four months, so by the time you read this any specific recommendations I could make about buying a computer system would be out of date, perhaps even along with the company that made the computer. I come from a family of computer professionals. My brother is a network administrator, and my wife is a former senior software engineer. We currently have a network of five computers in our house (including two laptops), and I have built two computers from scratch. Based on my personal and professional experience, here is a condensed list of my recommendations for buying a computer:

- Educate yourself somewhat about the important specifications involved in buying a computer (CPU speed in MHz, RAM, CD-R/DVD, hard drive space, monitor size, etc.). Do not trust a salesperson to tell you what you need. Read an introductory article on the subject in *PC World* (www.pcworld.com) or *PC Magazine* (www.pcmag.com). Both are very informative and relatively unbiased. These magazines also have "Top 10 Budget PCs" features every few issues that list the specifications and names of their current favorites.

- Find out what the top computer currently is and buy one model down. You don't need the top of the line and you'll pay a fairly nice premium for it when the next step down will likely give you more than enough computing power.
- Don't let anyone push you into a sudden decision with the line "This is a one-time-only sale." There is one thing for certain about computer prices—for every two to four months you wait, you can *always* get a better computer for a lower price (especially right before or after the holiday season).
- Accept the fact that as soon as you buy the computer—regardless of how great the deal was—within 30 days you will find a better deal and experience buyer's remorse. It is simply a fact of buying a computer. Live with it!
- A computer is not—repeat, *not*—an investment. In fact, it will depreciate faster than almost any other piece of office equipment you buy. Recognize that computers are made to be disposable. Use one for a few years, then pass it on to your children or donate it to a charity and buy a new one. As you build your business you will probably rely more and more on your computer, and you cannot afford to have it die on you at the worst possible moment. All other things being equal, the older a computer is, the more likely it is to develop problems or die. Most companies make computer parts that should last three to five years. If your computer is more than five years old, count your blessings that it has lasted that long—then go treat yourself to a new one.
- Don't buy the cheapest, no-name brand you can get. Stick with the well-known name brands. Dell (my current favorite), Gateway, Toshiba (they make good notebooks), and Sony are a few. Yes, you will pay 5 to 20 percent more for a brand-name computer, but these companies also tend to use better-quality parts that last longer and are less likely to fail, and they provide better technical support.
- For the average consumer, I do not recommend buying a computer from a local computer shop that custom builds computers. Most of them claim to save you a lot of money, but they usually do so in three ways: They give you low-quality, no-name parts, which have

a tendency to wear out faster; they typically do not provide even basic technical support, unless you purchase it from them at additional cost; and you are never quite sure if they will be there to support your computer three months or three years from now when you really need them. The computer hardware business is extremely competitive, with very low profit margins and a high rate of business failure. The exceptions I would make to this recommendation are for consumers who are computer savvy and know exactly what they do and do not need, or for people who have a family member in the business of building computers who is willing to give them a really good deal, but if you fall into this category you probably aren't reading this section anyway.

- Only buy a computer from a company with a good reputation for customer service and technical support. Many companies have terrible technical support. If you ever need help, you will be very sorry if you ignore this warning. How do you find out? Use the Internet and check out *PC Magazine* and *PC World* for their evaluations.
- If you plan on using a particular computer for your business, buy an extended warranty of at least one year for a desktop and three years for a notebook. Why the difference? Because it is relatively easy and inexpensive to repair a desktop, and if yours is going to go bad, it will likely do so in the first year. With notebooks, it is almost impossible for anyone other than the manufacturer to repair them. The components used in notebooks are usually specifically designed for that specific computer and are tightly packed together. The cost of warranties can vary greatly, so take this into account before you purchase from a company. The usual variables involve how much the computer costs, what the warranty covers (e.g., a notebook's screen is easy to break, very expensive to replace, and often not covered) and how long the warranty period lasts. Expect to pay $200 to $600 for a two- to three-year warranty on a desktop or notebook, respectively.
- If you need to spend more than $400 to $500 to upgrade your current system to get the performance you need, you will be much happier simply buying a new computer in virtually every situation.
- Buy an uninterrupted power supply (UPS [*not* United Parcel Ser-

vice!]). It functions as a battery backup in case of a brief power outage. Here in Chicago the power doesn't go out very often, but when it does, it's always at the most inopportune time. A UPS typically costs $50 for a basic one to $200 for an advanced model, and they last three to five years.

- The two biggest enemies of computers are excessive heat and dust—avoid both and you and your computer will live happier lives.

- Generally speaking, you will get twice the computing power in a desktop as in a notebook for about the same price.

- As of this writing, with the current trend in the prices of computer hardware (they get cheaper every six months), most people will be able to buy a nice desktop system for $700 to $1,500 and a nice notebook for $1,000 to $2,000.

- Whatever you do, buy at least two options to back up your data and use them regularly. These can include a second hard drive and a CD-R burner, a tape drive, or a Zip drive. The reason to buy two is that hopefully you will use at least one of them on a regular basis. I cannot stress this enough—if you use this computer for your business, you must develop and follow a stringent plan for backing up your data. Everyone has heard horror stories of crashed hard drives and electrical surges that have fried computers. I have experienced the horror of having a new hard drive crash—*twice*—on the same computer within two months! This spring I backed up my data by burning the files onto several CDs and copying them to a second hard drive. As Murphy's law would have it, when my primary drive failed, I found out that most of the files I had burned onto CDs didn't format properly and couldn't be read, and I hadn't updated the files on the second hard drive for three months. At that point I had the choice of paying $1,000 to recover some of the files on my corrupted drive or chalking it up to a lesson learned the hard way. Back up your data!

- Find a way to store an extra copy of all your files and documents off site. Use a lock box or burn them onto a CD (double-check the files to make sure they open), and send them to a relative's house for safekeeping. In the event of a natural disaster, a total home loss due to flood or fire, or even an act of terrorism, you will feel much more comfortable knowing you have a copy of all your important documents and files.

- There are a number of new services designed for small businesses that automatically back up your files every day over the Internet. I personally recommend Connected (www.connected.com).

PRINTER, COPIER, SCANNER, AND FAX

It was not long ago that in order to have all these functions in your office, you needed three different pieces of equipment. Not any longer. There are now several manufacturers that offer three-in-one (printer, copier, and scanner) and four-in-one (printer, copier, scanner, and fax) machines, including Hewlett-Packard (HP), Panasonic, Brother, Lexmark, and Canon. Most of these are relatively low priced—in the $200 to $400 range. I recommend you test them out, read a few articles about the newest ones, and buy one of them. It will be a great investment for your new business. The results you can achieve with these printers is nothing less than phenomenal, especially if you use the right kind of paper (which does make a big difference). When starting out, I purchased an HP three-in-one machine (I already had a separate fax machine) and some HP high-gloss brochure paper and printed my own company brochures. I had several prospects ask me who my printer was because they were so impressed. Most of these printers will last a very long time and do a great job. In fact, after the first year, the biggest cost will not be your original purchase, but the price of the ink ($25 to $50 per cartridge)—so when you find your cartridges on sale, buy several!

Some people may also want to consider a laser printer. Companies are coming out with relatively low cost black-and-white ($300 to $500) and color laser printers ($600 to $1,500). If you plan on doing a lot of printing (more than a few hundred copies a month), consider a laser printer; otherwise, stick with an inkjet printer.

PHONE SYSTEM AND VOICEMAIL

The phone system, voicemail, and how you answer the phone directly affect the impression your prospect has of you. Don't miss this opportunity to make a positive impact. Don't use your old answering machine.

Don't use an answering service. (Ever been put on hold by one even before you could get "Hello" out of your mouth?) Either purchase voicemail service through your phone company or buy a small-business phone system (a good example is the BizFone at www.bizfone.com). The cost for these alternatives can vary from $300 to $3,000. The more sophisticated systems give callers a number of options, like these:

Press 1 for the general voice mailbox.

Press 2 for sales.

Press 3 to speak to our president.

Press 4 for more information about our company.

Keep your message short, professional, and somewhat energetic, with a little bit of information. For example:

Thank you for calling Today's Leadership Coaching. We use executive coaching and leadership development to help companies develop leaders who deliver results. For immediate information, please visit our web site at www.TodaysLeadership.com. To leave a message in the general mailbox, press 1. For sales, press 2. To speak to our president, Stephen Fairley, press 3. To leave a message for one of our other business coaches, press 4. For more information about our upcoming seminars for small business owners, press 5.

Another example:

Thank you for calling Today's Leadership Coaching. We cannot take your call right now; please leave your name, number, and a good time for us to get back to you, and we will return your call within two hours. If you would like more information about our company, please visit our web site at www.TodaysLeadership.com. Have a great day!

You can easily use your phone system to promote your web site, your latest book, or your speaking engagements (if you already have several speeches lined up).

Have a separate line for your business phone and another for your computer and fax (unless you have a separate broadband connection). One advantage of this is that it then qualifies as a tax deduction. There is nothing less professional than calling a "business" only to have the machine answer "This is the Frank's residence. If you're calling for the I'm-A-Cheapskate-Coaching Company, press 1. To leave a message for Bill, Suzy, or Thomas, press 2."

Be sure to get caller ID on your business line. I have been saved several times when someone has called on a cell phone, and just as they were leaving that all-important call-back number, their signal broke up. With caller ID, this is no longer a problem. That's another important thing to remember when you are signing up for that second line—make sure your prospects see your business name on their caller ID, not your personal name.

Basic Software Programs

The majority of your software needs will come from one of the office suites, such as Microsoft Office Professional—which includes Word, Outlook, Excel, and PowerPoint. However, one software program that every coach should invest in is Client Compass (www.ClientCompass.com). Client Compass Software, designed for coaches by coaches, is the ultimate business management software system for coaches. Whether you are just starting your coaching practice, or have a thriving business already, Client Compass will help you make your coaching business more successful! Keeping your programs up to date can help protect you against various viruses. One required piece of software is a separate antivirus program. All it takes is one good virus to kill your system—or worse, your reputation.

I know of a coach who was wrongly accused by an association of sending out spam (unsolicited e-mail) to a large group of association members. The coach had previously purchased a list of members from the organization. When confronted, the coach denied sending out the spam, and the association at least partially believed him. Later it was determined that another company had sent out the e-mail mentioning his name without his knowledge or approval. But in a very unfortunate confluence of events, within two weeks of that false accusation, the coach's secretary fell prey to a computer virus that replicated itself and sent out a virus to everyone in the coach's e-mail list—including the large group of association members.

The coach was innocent, but when this e-mail went out, the damage to his business reputation was done—all because the coach did not have an updated antivirus program on every computer. You can pay to get your computer restored after a virus attack, but no amount of money can restore your reputation. Heed the warning! Currently, the two best antivirus programs are from MacAfee (www.macafee.com) and Norton (www.norton.com). Contrary to the marketing efforts of these two companies, I do not know of any evidence that conclusively demonstrates that either one is better than the other. Some antivirus programs also integrate with the Microsoft Outlook e-mail program so that it automatically scans every e-mail attachment you receive.

OFFICE SPACE

Approximately 70 percent of coaching is done over the phone, so in most cases, you will not need to have an outside office. However, a certain percentage of your clients will want to meet face to face—or, conversely, you may feel more comfortable meeting face to face—and for those of us who have been trained to provide our services face to face, I suspect we will gravitate toward that model. In fact, I currently meet about 50 percent of my Chicago clients in person, most of the time at their office or a restaurant, but sometimes at my office. While some may perceive this to be a limitation of my practice, I don't experience it as such. I enjoy the variety. Also, on more than one occasion, I have used this as a selling point—most coaches don't offer the option of meeting face to face. I offer this benefit to my local clients for no extra charge.

If you are thinking about renting or buying outside office space, be sure to consider all the up-front start-up costs as well as the ongoing expenses, including security deposits, monthly rent or mortgage payments, utilities (if they are not included with rent), secretarial support, office furniture, Internet access, telephone lines, telephone usage, copier, another computer, insurance, cleaning services, security issues, and any additional setup fees.

There are a few national companies that can be ideal for someone looking for a small office space. In the typical situation, you pay a low monthly fee and in return they set you up with a professional-looking mailing address, use of office space for a limited number of hours per month, a phone number, a live answering service 9 A.M. to 5 P.M. Monday through Friday, and access to light secretarial support as needed. Some of these companies allow you access, for a fee, to office space in other cities all over the nation, which can be very convenient if you want to have a nationwide practice and still meet occasionally face to face. Two of the most well-known office-sharing companies are HQ (www .HQ.com) and Regus (www.regus.com). If you anticipate needing an office for client meetings a few hours a month, you may also find other professionals willing to share their office with you on a limited basis for an hourly fee.

Whether you work out of your home or an outside office, be sure to make it comfortable, secure, silent, and a place of solitude. It simply won't do to have your dog barking in the background of your coaching session, or to have the big prospect you have been working on for the past six months hear your small child crying in the other room. You need a place to call your own—make it a room in the back corner of your house, not in the middle of a living space. Enclose it with a solid-core, soundproof door. Have everything you need within easy reach. Stock up on office supplies when they are on sale. Keep it organized and somewhat clean.

If you decide to have a home office this can also be a great tax write-off (please consult your tax accountant for specifics), but in many cases you can deduct the following:

- Part of your mortgage interest, based on the percentage of your home used for business
- Part of your real estate taxes, based on a home business
- Depreciation on office space in your home
- Part of your utilities, based on the percentage of your home used for business purposes
- Office furniture
- Expense of cleaning your home office
- Rent paid for office space
- Telephone line costs (if you have a separate business phone line)

You will also want to explore adding a special rider or separate policy onto your homeowner's insurance because your personal insurance company may not pay for any loss if the adjusters determine you were running a business out of your house at the time of the claim. There are many different kinds of insurance, including liability, business property, business interruption, errors and omissions, malpractice, health, disability, and workers' compensation. Conduct some research to find out which ones you need and how much would be reasonable to protect you in case of a claim or loss.

BUSINESS FEES

Do you need to incorporate your coaching practice? Short answer: Yes. I believe there are a number of reasons why incorporating your practice is a good idea, including the following:

- It can help lower your overall personal tax exposure.
- It provides your personal assets with a level of protection against a lawsuit filed against your company.
- It helps in establishing your business with banks for setting up corporate checking accounts and obtaining business loans. (You will still have to personally sign for your loan in most cases.)
- It presents a much better image, especially to midsized to large companies. When a prospect asks you if your business is incorporated, the only acceptable answer is yes.

There are several kinds of incorporation, the most popular ones being sole proprietorship, S-corporation, C-corporation, and limited liability company (LLC). Each has its own positives and negatives. It seems more lawyers prefer the limited liability partnership (LLP) because it is relatively newer and has less established case law (and perhaps more loop holes to exploit), whereas more accountants favor the S-corporation because the rules are more straightforward when doing the company taxes. When you make the decision to incorporate, you have at least three choices: hire a lawyer or small-business accountant to do it, hire a company that specializes in incorporation services to do it, or find out how to do it yourself. The first option, hiring a lawyer or small-business accountant, will usually cost you $1,000 to $3,000. If you choose to go this route, try to find one who specializes in small business and has performed this service for a few dozen companies. You don't want to be the guinea pig for a newly graduated law or accounting student. There are many, many pieces of paperwork to file, each of which requires different information and must be sent to different addresses at different times. There are also now several dozen companies that specialize in incorporation services. Go to your favorite search engine and type in "incorporation services" for a current list. The prices range from a few hundred dollars to several thousand, depending on which services you want. Most are between $400 and $1,500. While you can learn how to do it yourself and save a few hundred dollars, plan on spending several weeks to learn which specific forms you need to fill out (local, state, and federal), gather all the appropriate information, and file all the documents. In my opinion, I would recommend option 2, hire a company that specializes in incorporation services, unless you have a previously existing relationship with a lawyer or accountant who does these services and will give you a decent deal. Incorporating your company is time consuming and paperwork heavy, and an improper filing can invalidate the process. There are usually local, state, and federal filing fees along with annual fees that vary from state to state.

CASH RESERVES

Money creates options. When you are cash poor, your options become very limited; having cash on hand allows you to take advantage of opportunities when they arise. I strongly recommend you take into consideration all the possible costs of starting up a business before you actually get going and create enough cash reserves to cover at least 9 to 12 months of operating expenses. If everything goes well, you can use the funds to further your sales and marketing efforts, but every business experiences tough times and unanticipated costs. Don't let poor cash flow ruin your chances for success by trying to ignore it or believing tough times won't happen to you. Undercapitalization is the biggest reason for new business failure. As a general rule of thumb, first determine all your costs for the first year in business, then multiply that by 1.2 to 1.6 to give yourself a general range for cash reserves.

START-UP MARKETING EXPENSES

We will discuss the details of developing a corporate identity package ($400 to $700), printing business cards ($100 to $300), and printing your company brochures ($500 to $2,000) when we discuss making a first impression in Chapter 7. In today's technologically sophisticated world, many coaches are finding the power of the Internet to be invaluable in giving them an online presence, enhancing their credibility and attracting new clients. There are five basic costs associated with having a web site:

- *Domain registration.* Purchasing a domain name you can use for your web site costs $10 to $35 per year.
- *Text and layout development.* This involves writing the text for the web site and planning the overall layout of the site. Most of this work you do yourself, so there is very little cost unless you hire it out.
- *Web site design.* This involves the actual process of building and coding your web site. This can range in cost from $500 to $2,000 or more.
- *Web site hosting.* You pay a hosting company to store your web site on its computers so people all over the world can access it. This can cost anywhere from $120 a year for a very basic web site to $1,200 per year for an e-commerce web site.
- *Upkeep and maintenance.* A web site has to be maintained as changes take place in the company, new services are offered, or great client testimonials come in. Expect to spend $300 to $500 a year on upgrades, modifications, and overhauls.

We will take a more in-depth look at each area in Chapter 12.

RECURRING MARKETING INVESTMENTS

Once you pass the start-up phase of establishing your business, the biggest recurring expense will come in the form of sales and marketing activities. To have a financially successful business, you must have a constant influx of new clients to replace the ones who leave.

MARKETING CAMPAIGNS

For each of your target markets you should design an ongoing marketing campaign that includes a mix of several different strategies, such as sending direct-mail letters, postcards, e-mails, and faxes; networking in groups your market frequents; asking strategic partners to provide you with an introduction; and making phone calls. In general, the greater the mix, the more likely you will receive a higher response percentage. Some of the ongoing marketing expenses can include:

- Developing and printing direct-mail materials (letters, postcards, and flyers)
- Purchasing mailing lists
- Paying postage costs
- Maintaining your web site
- Developing e-mail campaigns
- Maintaining memberships in networking groups
- Entertaining prospects and strategic partners
- Advertising at trade shows, on the radio, or in a trade magazine

Here is a common marketing campaign you might conduct as a business coach targeting small-business owners.

Month 1   Develop a list of 50 to 100 companies within your target market.

Determine the exact person(s) you will target within each company.

Prioritize the list and group them into tiers of 10 prospects.

Find out their contact information: phone, e-mail, fax, mailing address.

Write 3 to 5 compelling direct-mail letters.

Develop 3 to 5 concise presentations that you can deliver over the phone or to the prospect's voicemail.

Month 2   Send out first letter to 10 prospects (Group 1).

Wait 1 week, then begin follow-up calls to Group 1.

Meet with qualified prospects.

Month 3   Wait another week, then call Group 1 again.

Send out first letter to next 10 prospects (Group 2).

Wait 1 week then, begin follow up calls to Group 2.

Send out second letter to Group 1.

Send out article of interest to Group 1.
Call Group 1 again.

Month 4   Wait another week, then call Groups 1 and 2.
Send out first letter to Group 3.
Wait 1 week, then begin follow-up calls to Group 3.
Send out postcard reminder to Group 1.
Wait 1 week, then call Group 1.
Send out article of interest to Group 2.
Send out second letter to Group 2.
Wait 1 week, then call Group 2.

Month 5   Send out second letter to Group 3.
Wait 1 week, then call Group 3.
Send out fourth letter to Group 1.
Wait 1 week, then call Group 1.
Send out article of interest to Group 3.
Send out postcard reminder to Group 2.
Wait 1 week, then call Group 2.

The cycle can go on forever, and it becomes a lot of work, especially if you don't particularly like cold calling. There are coaches who emphatically say you'll never get any clients by cold calling. They even offer tele-classes on "No more cold calling!" However, I know several successful coaches who have used cold-calling techniques very effectively as one of their primary marketing strategies. (Notice I did not say their *only* strategy.) They have been able to get in the door of some very well respected companies. Remember, every person is unique, and what may be anathema to you may be a wonderful technique for another person. Also, like it or not, salespeople have used cold-calling techniques for decades. This is an individual choice (as is every marketing strategy). Some people are at their best in front of a large audience; others would rather be shot dead than give a public presentation. You must be comfortable with whatever strategy you use, but the more strategies you use, the more people you'll reach, and the faster you will build your practice.

If you decide to go with a more traditional approach involving purchasing direct-mail lists and following up via phone, here are a few points to consider:

Susan Ennis
Founder
Leadership Communications
Canton, Massachusetts
www.toLead.com
Susan@toLead.com

Susan is the founder of Leadership Communications and is an executive development consultant with over 22 years of direct leadership experience in corporate America.

How did you first get started in coaching?

There were three phases that really launched my coaching career. About 10 years ago I was working at Digital Equipment Company running an internal consulting group doing competency evaluations for succession planning and turnaround work. We created a highly quantitative 360 instrument, which was perfect for an engineering company, but the difficult question was how to use the data effectively as an individual to best position yourself for succession and promotion. From there I went to Bank of Boston to do competency modeling for executive teams, and I realized the work I was doing was more than just assessing individuals, it was executive coaching.

By 1996, the profession of coaching was very accepted in Massachusetts, and my job became to set the standard of leadership development and coaching in my company. I was trying to answer the same question that people are asking today, "How do I manage executive coaching for my company so that it's best both for the individual and the company and obtain the best ROI?" From that position, I transitioned into becoming an internal coach with the bank.

About four years ago I officially launched my company, Leadership Communications, in Boston, and one of the things I immediately missed was all the support I had back in my corporate job—assistants to send out letters, tech support for my computer, and a secretary to manage my schedule. I guess that's one thing a lot of people don't think about before they launch their company.

What is one piece of advice you would give to a new coach just starting out?

To be successful in this field, you have to really understand the business side. Especially people coming out of the clinical background are not trained in how business works. Sometimes people spend so much time developing themselves personally, they don't know how to coach business people. It is difficult to find coaches who can be really effective in a business setting.

For example, a coach who wants to be effective in corporate America needs to understand the feeling when an executive client says they are not making their numbers. When an executive doesn't make their numbers, that means people are going to get laid off. A coach needs to know what that feels like, how to help that client, and how to best support the organization.

What web site would you recommend the readers visit?

The Executive Coaching Forum is a great place to learn more about professional guidelines and standard practices in the field. The address is www.executivecoachingforum.com.

What tips would you give a new coach?

Be very clear about the kind of coaching you want to do and can do. You need to clearly understand your limitations and only coach people you are qualified to help. Answer the question, "Who am I really good at coaching?" And "everybody" is not an acceptable answer.

From your perspective, what do you believe coaching will look like in five years?

I believe coaching will become either more of a commodity or programmatic. Meaning, companies will try to take a programmatic approach to their coaching like insurance companies do to health care: "You have four hours to turn this team around" or "six hours to work with this high-potential manager to help him modify his interpersonal communication style." They will struggle to cap their costs, but one of the reasons why coaching works is because it is so customized, so coaches will have to push back.

- *The list you buy will make you or break you.* Do not waste your money buying a mailing list of a million names for $29.99 or any other such promotion. Only use a reputable list company. A good list costs money, and oftentimes the best list is the one you don't buy, but have developed from your extensive networking activities.
- *Less is better.* Don't waste your efforts trying to target a few thousand people or companies at the same time. Your results will be much better if you spend more time targeting fewer people. Thirty to forty companies or 75 to 100 people are more than enough for the average coach to actively target using a comprehensive marketing campaign.
- *If you are not experienced at writing direct-mail letters, either educate yourself about how to do it or hire someone to help.* The Direct Mail Association is a good place to start for books, seminars, tapes, and professionals.
- *You will never get a decent response by simply sending out a bunch of letters or postcards.* The only way to get a response is to be committed to actively following up on the letters by phone on a regular and consistent basis. If you are not willing to spend the time or effort it takes to follow up, then don't bother sending out the letters.
- *Each target market must have its own specially designed campaign.* This is because every market is different and has different needs, wants, and purposes for hiring a coach.
- *Set realistic goals and deadlines for yourself.* For example, mail out 10 letters a week, make 10 follow-up calls per week, set one face-to-face appointment for every 20 letters sent, and land one paying client for every five free coaching sessions.
- *The goal is the face-to-face appointment.* The goal here is to get an appointment with the prospect, because you will almost never go directly from sending a letter to landing a coaching client. The letter only gets your foot in the door. What you do in the appointment will determine whether there is a next step. It's kind of like a resume. Any good career coach will tell you that having a fantastic resume will never get you the job. The only thing a resume is designed to do is to get you the interview. It's during the interview that the person will determine whether you are the one to do the job.
- *If you are targeting a business, make absolutely certain that you are directing your efforts at the right audience within the company.* The only per-

son you want to spend time on is the decision maker. Many coaches make the mistake of spending time with people who have no authority.

- *From the outset determine how much time, energy, and resources you will put into this effort.* How long are you willing to go before you either call it quits, change your target, modify your efforts, or call for help?
- *Direct mail and cold calling is one of many strategies you can use to get in the door, not the only or necessarily the best one for you.* Diversify your efforts by attending networking events that your targets frequent, publishing articles, and tapping into your strategic network for personal introductions. Use multiple marketing strategies for every target market.

Assuming you have two or three target markets and you conduct ongoing marketing campaigns for each one, you can easily see how the costs add up. When starting out include several hundred dollars in your annual marketing plan designated for ongoing campaign expenses. Most coaches making more than $75,000 a year spend at least $200 to $500 per month on marketing-related activities.

Networking Events

Networking is consistently in the top four ways coaches find new clients. I have talked about networking in depth in two other chapters, so I will not reiterate all that information here, except to say that you should find two or three great networking groups to attend on a regular basis. There are usually four types of costs associated with attending an event: membership, a per-meeting fee, your transportation costs, and the cost of any food or beverage you consume at the event. These costs can quickly add up, so be sure to account for these on an annual basis.

Traditional Advertising

Even though some coaches use traditional advertising, such as television, radio, newspapers, yellow pages, and trade publications, I do not recommend it. The overwhelming majority of advertising today is totally ineffective for three groups of buyers:

- Small-business owners
- Companies with small marketing budgets
- Businesses that offer services rather than products

A quick look at this list confirms that all coaching companies meet all three criteria. You may think I'm cynical, but the only time I can really recommend using traditional advertising is after you have tried everything else, it hasn't worked, and you still have a lot of money left over that you can't think of anything better to do with. If you find yourself in that last situation, give me a call and I'll give you a few ideas.

Summary

We have covered a lot of territory in this chapter, much of which will be used in the next chapter to create your financial plan. We learned that you don't have to have $100,000 to start a successful small business, but that you do need some money, as it opens up doors of opportunity that you may want to take advantage of to grow and develop your coaching practice. I hope you also realized that the largest percentage of your financial plan will go toward recurring marketing activities, after your initial start-up costs. There are two primary reasons why I wrote this chapter: First, to counteract the simplistic and overly naïve belief propagated by certain members of the coaching community who teach that you can become wealthy by following some universal principles or philosophies (usually as part of a program, seminar, or book they are trying to sell you). Building a successful business is not easy or immediate. It takes time, lots of energy, and the wise use of finances. The other reason is to help beginning coaches overcome their fear of spending money. This is not to say you should be reckless or apathetic about where your money is going. I firmly believe in fiscal responsibility. However, I personally know seasoned coaches who could have had significantly larger practices than they do now, simply because they let their fear of investing any money back into their practice keep them from growing.

Some people live their lives out of poverty—always worrying about where the next dollar will come from. Other people live their lives out of abundance—leveraging their money in a responsible manner so as to produce the greatest return on investment. As you create your financial plan in the next chapter, remember: The first attitude will kill your business.

CHAPTER 5

What to Buy on a Budget: Creating Your Financial Plan

Every person has their own specific reasons for making the leap from being an employee to starting their own company, but the decision usually revolves around the themes of freedom, the ability to make their own decisions, a yearning for a more balanced life, the desire to control their own destiny, the desire to create something of lasting value, or the aspiration to wealth. Regardless of your reasons, the chances of realizing your dreams significantly increase if you have a plan to guide you. Part of this preparation includes creating a financial plan, which we will start to do in this chapter.

Everyone has a different budget, different experiences, and ultimately different needs, but over the next few pages I would like to do the following:

- Suggest some guidelines for those who are trying to start up a coaching practice on a budget (that probably includes everybody).
- Make specific recommendations about what to buy, based on three financial plans: $2,000 to $4,000, $5,000 to $10,000, and $10,000 to $20,000.
- Help you make wise financial and business decisions such as asking the question, "Assuming I am starting out with a rather fixed amount of money, what should I spend it on that would provide the absolute best value given my situation and help my company get off the ground faster?"

Following here are my suggestions, based on various budgets, of the most important products and services you should consider buying when starting up your company. Obviously, every person and situation is different, but I have tried to list the major categories, with rough guidelines as to how much you should expect to spend for both the basic and deluxe models as of 2003. Every year prices in every category typically increase by 5 to 10 percent. Within these three broad budget ranges, I have categorized items into what I would consider to be the highest, middle, and lower priorities.

RECOMMENDATIONS FOR A
$2,000 TO $4,000 START-UP BUDGET

I would purchase the following products and services:

Highest Priority

$150 to $200 — Purchase a decent answering machine, cordless phone, and high-quality headset to use during your coaching calls.

$150 to $250 per year — Have 1,000 to 1,500 business cards professionally printed using your company colors and design. Your goal is to hand them *all* out *every year* you are in business.

$360 to $600 per year — Add another phone line to your home just for your business. Put the phone number on all your marketing materials.

$360 to $1,200 per year — Spend time with every single person in your existing network, educating them about your new business, who your ideal client is, how you help them, and the results they can expect to achieve. Meet with them on a regular basis (every four to six weeks), especially with those in a position to refer business to you. Offer to buy them lunch or a coffee. When they do refer you business, be sure to thank them and send them a small token of your appreciation. Amount is based on meeting with three or four people per month for 12 months and spending an average of $10 to $20 per meeting.

Middle Priority

$200 to $360 — Attend two or three networking events each month, pass out your business cards, and work hard to land at least one or two free coaching sessions at each networking event. Do not purchase membership unless

131

	you have to. Amount is based on spending $10 to $15 per meeting.
$500 to $2,800 per year	Meet with your prospects face to face whenever possible, especially for the initial free coaching session. If you don't have an office where they can come, go to a local restaurant or coffee shop. Meeting face to face can significantly increase your ability to make the sale. The amount is based on meeting one to three people every week, four weeks per month for 12 months and spending an average of $10 to $20 per meeting.
$180 to $600 per year	Sign up for Internet access (dial-up or broadband) and add your e-mail address to all your marketing materials.

Lower Priority

$250 to $350	Basic corporate identity package: Hire someone to design your logo, business cards, letterhead, and envelopes. While this price is a little on the low side, I would scour the Internet and local colleges until I found someone qualified who would do it for this price. Keep the designs handy, but don't print up any letterhead or envelopes yet unless you can afford to. As a last resort, do this yourself.

RECOMMENDATIONS FOR A $5,000 TO $10,000 START-UP BUDGET

In addition to the preceding recommendations, for those with a larger budget, I would purchase the following products and services in the following order:

Highest Priority

$200 to $300 per year	Set up a do-it-yourself web site using either a software program you learned or a tem-

Ed Shea, MSW, LCSW
Relationship Coach
Elmhurst, Illinois
www.ImagoByPhone.com
CoachImago@AOL.com
(630) 530-1060

As a Relationship Coach, Ed Shea focuses on empowering couples who desire a stronger, healthier, and more satisfying bond to achieve the relationship of their dreams and experience a new way to love. While his practice is physically located in Elmhurst, Illinois, Ed works with couples all over the United States via telephone. He is a clinical member of the American Association of Marriage and Family Therapy.

You started out as a marriage counselor, but now practice as a relationship coach. How did you make the transition?

I started out practicing social work back in 1972 and found I really enjoyed working with couples on their relationship. So I started my own practice specializing in marriage counseling, but was always looking for more effective ways to help relationships work.

I was first introduced to coaching at a conference in early 1996 where I met someone who said he wanted to coach me. We sat down and I had my first experience being coached. I was hooked! I immediately saw the power that coaching could have on helping relationships work and knew I had to explore this new field.

So that fall I went to a conference sponsored by Thomas Leonard and told him of my desire to coach couples about their relationship over the phone. He agreed to support me in advertising my practice to the growing coaching community. Thomas also encouraged me to practice the art of giving—which is giving for the simple joy of giving, rather than for what you can get. This principle is something I've taken to heart in every area of my practice.

Tell us about your current coaching practice.

I currently work only with couples, not just individuals. I work with couples all over the continuum—from those people who have a great

(Continued)

133

relationship and want to create an even better one all the way to couples on the brink of divorce, but truly want to renew their love and passion for each other. That's actually one of my specialties—I'm a "near-divorce specialist." I coach couples where both people want to make the relationship work. I typically work with about 25 to 30 couples per week, with about 75 percent of them over the phone.

You were taught by Harville Hendrix, the author of Getting the Love You Want: A Guide for Couples *(Owl Books, 2001), in the Imago model of relationships. Tell us what that means.*

Imago is Latin for "image" and refers to the positive and negative images I have of my caregivers. It's a new way of relating that allows you to experience your partner in a completely different light. Probably the best way to illustrate this is by the following metaphor.

As we journey along in our relationship we come across impasses and obstacles. In order to move beyond them, we must first build a bridge to cross the great divide that separates us and our points of view. Crossing over the bridge from my world into yours requires a great deal of trust on both our parts, because it requires me to temporarily leave my world behind. When I do cross the bridge, a powerful transformation occurs within me. I can suddenly learn about your world in a new and exciting way—from your perspective instead of mine. Before I came across your bridge, I didn't want to understand your world. I wanted you to understand, and agree with, my world view. But now I can truly understand who you are and where you're coming from in a way that I've never been able to fully understand before. That creates a powerful change in our relationship because now I'm not just seeing reality through my own eyes, but I can begin to also see it through your eyes. I'm no longer just concerned with getting my own way, but I start being concerned with meeting your needs as well. And when the time is right, we can switch places, where you can learn about my world from my point of view. This is how I help couples with my relationship coaching.

How is what you do different from traditional marriage counseling?

That's a great question, because in my coaching practice I make every effort to not be a traditional therapist. I see myself as the coach on the sidelines. I teach people a process of healthy relating in which I view the couple as the experts on their relationship, not me. Their relationship is a vehicle for personal growth and development. I am simply there to guide them along in their journey. As a relationship coach I don't focus or talk about pathology and illness; rather, I help couples to build on their strengths, focusing on personal growth and empowerment.

As a relationship coach, I help couples to create a safe space where they can feel free to focus on their needs, removing all danger from the relationship, and ending all criticism.

In the early days of our country in the wild, wild West, there were times when you needed to pass through someone's land to get to your destination. As a matter of courtesy, you would ask them for permission to cross their land, and in return they would guarantee your safety as you traveled across their land. They would create a safe passageway for you to walk on in your journey. That's exactly what I do for couples in my coaching.

How are you finding clients these days?

I firmly believe in the model of servant marketing—the best way to build a business or fill a practice is to be a servant to other people by supporting them in their work and connecting them with great resources. Let me give you an example. I enjoy supporting coaches and being a part of their support network. Part of my joy is connecting them with resources so they can do their work better.

One of the ways I do this is by volunteering my time to help coaches set up AudioPodiums. An AudioPodium records teleclasses, promotions, panel discussions or interviews for your business, product, or practice. Up to 240 people at a time can dial in and listen to your recording. This is a powerful resource I help coaches set up so they can use it, and I often get three to five coaches calling me a day asking me about AudioPodiums. Even though I do this for the simple joy of giving, I have the joy returned to me when grateful coaches refer couples who need help to me. That's part of being a servant marketer. You can find more information about them at www.ImagoByPhone.com/AudioPodium.

(Continued)

What would you say to a new coach trying to build a coaching business?

First, I can't emphasize enough the importance of knowing who your target market is. You need to invest your time in focusing on that market rather than spreading yourself out too thin and trying to be all things to all people. There are people out there who need exactly what you know the most about and you must focus on finding and helping those people.

Early on in my practice I learned the Disney model of marketing: first, you develop the product, then you tell everyone about the product, then you keep on telling everyone about the product. Don't ever stop telling people how you can help them as a coach. Find effective ways to keep in touch with them and never lose touch. One of the best examples I know of that practices this principle is the summer camp I went to when I was age 12. I still get a postcard from them every year on my birthday.

plate-based web site from a recognized Internet company. Cost includes domain name registration, setup, and hosting fees.

$100 to $300 per year Use your existing network and contacts you make at events you attend to slowly build your database. Keep in touch with targets on a regular basis (every four to six weeks)—send them a letter, an e-mail, a fax, or an interesting article, or phone them. Cost is for reproduction costs and mailings.

$400 to $1,200 per year Visit two or three high-quality networking events a month. Hold off on paying for membership unless the cost of attending monthly meetings is equal to the annual fee. Amount is based on attending two or three meetings a month and spending $20 to $35 per meeting on transportation, entry fee, and beverages.

Middle Priority

$150 to $400	Purchase a new printer/scanner/copier/fax machine
$200 to $2,000	Incorporate your business. Amount varies based on doing it yourself or hiring a professional to do it for you.
$600 to $1,500	Obtain a merchant account to accept credit cards. This involves getting approved, purchasing or leasing a credit card terminal, and paying monthly fees plus a percentage of every transaction you make.

Lower Priority

$150 to $600 per year	Write and design your own brochures, then purchase high-quality paper and print out the brochures 20 at a time from your new printer. Cost is primarily for paper and ink.
$200 to $400 per year	Buy and immerse yourself in a dozen of the best sales and marketing books to help bring you quickly up to speed. If you don't know of any, visit my web site (www.TodaysLeadership.com), and look under Free Resources.
$200 to $300	Use your existing computer, but upgrade one or two of the components (e.g., add more memory or another hard drive). Buy a used or new computer only if you absolutely have to, and don't spend more than $500 to $700.
$400 to $800 per year	Stock up on a wide variety of high-quality office supplies (ink cartridges, various high-quality paper, notebooks, various presentation binders, generic portfolios for proposals).
$300 to $2,000	Purchase a phone system that includes multiple voicemail boxes, auto attendant,

call forwarding, and multiple phone line capability.

RECOMMENDATIONS FOR A $10,000 TO $20,000 START-UP BUDGET

Highest Priority

$300 to $700	Invest in a better corporate identity package with a more experienced and sophisticated graphic designer. In addition to developing your logo, business cards, letterhead, and envelopes, have them carry the design over to your future web site.
$500 to $2,000	Hire a professional web designer to build you a solid web site.
$240 to $1,200 per year	Budget hosting fees for your new web site. Cost varies according to company and complexity (brochure site versus e-commerce site).
$60 to $100 per year	Buy an 800 number for your company and put it on all your future marketing materials. This promotes an image of an established, credible business or organization.
$100 to $400	Hire a graphic designer to design professional-looking brochures.
$100 to $500 per year	Develop and send out a professional-looking electronic newsletter (e-zine) every three to four weeks to your entire database. Be absolutely sure to give recipients the opportunity to opt out of receiving the e-zine; otherwise you will be accused of sending spam (unsolicited e-mail that people do not want). Amount includes purchasing a software product to help design it, mail it, and track subscriptions or hiring a company to take care of it for you.
$200 to $400	Professionally print your envelopes and company letterhead.

$3,000 to $6,000 per year   Invest in working one on one with an experienced, successful sales and marketing coach to help you market your coaching business and dramatically increase your sales. Alternatively, there are a number of sales and marketing programs designed for coaches who need professional help. They may be less expensive, but typically are not completely customized to meet your specific needs, are usually held only over the phone and with large groups of people, and may not provide the level of personal assistance you need.

$300 to $1,500   Put together a professionally designed marketing kit, including presentation portfolios, coaching packages, client list, testimonials, company overview, a list of your background and accomplishments, articles you have written and published, and a copy of the company brochure. The kit should be printed on high-quality paper and designed to catch a prospect's eye, draw their attention to the appropriate areas, and make the sale easier by increasing your company's credibility and trust level. You can either print them on your new printer as needed or have them professionally printed if you are planning to launch a major marketing campaign.

Middle Priority

$200 to $700 per year   Invest in two or three local sales or marketing training events to help you increase your closing ratio, use new sales techniques and direct-mail strategies, learn how to market a professional service, and so forth. Be careful, because many of these events are simply one long sales pitch for a

	company's products or services. Typically, if it's free, expect a little bit of interesting content, along with seven reasons why you can't do it yourself, and a sales pitch at the end. If you have to pay for the seminar, expect real content.
$700 to $2,000	Purchase a new computer.
$200 to $500	Purchase an extended warranty for your new computer.
$500 to $2,500 per year	Go to one or two coaching conferences a year. If possible, select local ones to decrease travel-related costs. Conferences are a great way to find out new trends in the field, learn more about coaching and cutting-edge ideas, build relationships within the coaching community, find a mentor, discover the newest books and available research, and soak in the excitement and enthusiasm of being around a large group of people who are of like mind and attitude about coaching. Amount ranges from local to national conferences which require travel, food, and housing expenses, in addition to conference fees.
$500 to $2,000	Have the brochures professionally printed instead of running them off on your new printer. (If you don't have a new printer, do this much earlier.)
$1,000 to $3,000 per year	Invest in some initial coach training from a recognized coach-training program to sharp your skills. Work toward or obtain a coaching certification.

Lower Priority

$360 to $500 per year	Get high-speed Internet access. Amount varies by location and upload/download speeds.
$200 to $700	Buy a top-notch list of 50 to 100 people or companies in your target audience. Alter-

natively, use your local research librarian to help you identify ways to find people or companies in your target audience.

$600 to $1,200 per year Mail to the targets on that list every four to six weeks, following up each letter, e-mail, or fax with a personal phone call until you have met face to face with at least 10 to 15 percent of them. Amount includes printing and mailing a simple letter (versus a full-color, four-page booklet, which would involve printing costs).

ADDITIONAL RECOMMENDATIONS

You may want to consider the following recommendations based on your specific situation.

$500 to $3,000 Hire a professional copywriter to help you design or revise your brochures, web site, or three to five direct sales pieces you can use in your direct-marketing efforts, such as multiple sales letters, postcards, marketing e-mails, banners, posters, flyers, and the like. The difference between an average sales letter and an expert one is the difference between spending your money and investing it.

$2,000 to $5,000 Work with a professional web development firm to create a great web site that will be the foundation of your current and future marketing campaigns.

$6,000 to $10,000 per year If your strength is not in sales, consider hiring a part-time professional salesperson on a contingency basis (they receive a percentage of any sales they generate). Some salespeople will want an hourly fee in addition to the percentage. Amount is based on paying an hourly fee of $10 to $20 per hour for 10 to 15 hours per week, 12 months a

	year, not including any commission you might offer them.
$200 to $2,000 per year	Invest in learning how to get publicity for your company via publishing newspaper articles and being interviewed in print, on the radio, or on television. This can be done by reading books, hiring a media coach, going to a seminar, or hiring a one-person public relations agency, depending on the level of assistance and sophistication you want.
$2,000 to $6,000	Hire a professional marketer to help you develop and market several products (books, tapes, videos, CDs, etc.) to enhance your credibility and develop additional revenue streams for your company.

ACTION STEPS

1. Go back through this chapter and circle the general amount of capital you are anticipating having available to spend over this next year.
2. Place a mark next to each item or service you want to consider purchasing, regardless of what general range it falls into. This will be helpful for the next section, where you begin actually setting up a financial plan.
3. The next section includes charts with all the preceding categories and their respective price ranges. Photocopy the charts and begin researching the actual costs in your area or over the Internet.
4. As you find out each cost, place it in the appropriate category for your records, and create your financial plan over the next two weeks.

CREATING YOUR FINANCIAL PLAN

MARKETING MATERIALS

Marketing Materials	One-Time Start-up Costs	Recurring Annual Fees	Actual Costs Based on Your Research
Corporate identity package (Includes a logo and design costs for business cards, letterhead, and envelopes)	$400–$700	None, unless you update or change your image	
Brochures professionally designed	$100–$500	None, unless you create additional brochures	
Professional printing			
• Business cards	$100–$250 for 1,000 cards	$100–$250 for another 1,000 cards	
• Letterhead	$100–$200 for 1,000 sheets	None, unless you do a lot of writing	
• Envelopes	$100–$200 for 100 envelopes	$100–$200 for 100 envelopes	
• Brochures	Price varies greatly, $500–$2,000 for 1,000	None, unless you run out	
Web site			
• Register a domain name	$10–$35 per year	$10–$35 per year	
• Build the web site	$300–$2,000	None	
• Host the web site	$10–$30 per month for a basic one, $20–$100 per month for an e-commerce website	$240 per year for a basic web site up to $1,200 per year for a secure e-commerce site (at $20–$100 per month)	
• Updates and modifications	$300–$500 per year (at $15–$20 per hour)	$300–$500 per year (at $15–$20 per hour)	

(Continued)

Marketing Materials	One-Time Start-up Costs	Recurring Annual Fees	Actual Costs Based on Your Research
Other:			
Other:			
Other:			
Subtotals (Range is based on lowest and highest figures in each category, but does not include costs for categories only marked "Varies." It also assumes you purchase every category with an associated dollar amount.)	$1,950–$6,485	$750–$2,185	
Totals for your first year			

OFFICE COSTS

Office Costs	One-Time Start-up Costs	Recurring Annual Costs	Actual Fees Based on Your Research
Technology costs			
• Computer	$700–$1,500 for a new desktop and $1,000–$2,000 for a new notebook	$100–$200 for upgrades (more RAM, another hard drive, a new mouse, a bigger monitor, etc.)	
• Computer warranty	$200–$500 for a 2 to 3 year warranty, respectively	None	
• UPS/battery backup	$50–$200	None	
• Printer, copier, scanner, fax	$200–$400	None	

Office Costs	One-Time Start-up Costs	Recurring Annual Fees	Actual Costs Based on Your Research
• Ink cartridges	$25–$40 per cartridge (usually 2–3 separate ink colors), replaced 3–5 times per year)	$150–$600 per year depending on how much printing you do	
• Phone system and voicemail	$300 to $2,000	None, unless you choose voicemail service through your phone company	
• Business phone line	$30 to $50 per month depending on features.	$360–$600 per year	
• Internet access	$15 to $50 per month (dialup versus DSL)	$180–$600 per year	
• Basic software programs	$250 to $500	None, except when you upgrade to the newest version every few years.	
Merchant account to accept credit card payment	$600–$1,500	$100–$400 per year in monthly fees and per transaction fees	
Other:			
Other:			
Other:			
Home office space			
• New desk	$200–$1,500	None	
• New ergonomic chair	$300–$600	None	
• Miscellaneous office supplies	$200–$400	$400–$800 annually	
• Separate fax or modem line	Varies	Varies	

(Continued)

Office Costs	One-Time Start-up Costs	Recurring Annual Costs	Actual Fees Based on Your Research
• Separate insurance policy to cover home office and equipment	Varies	Varies	
Other:			
Other:			
Other:			
Rental office space	Varies greatly	Varies greatly	
• Monthly rent			
• Security deposits			
• Utilities			
• Secretarial support			
• Office furniture (desk, chairs, filing cabinets, etc.)			
• Internet access			
• Telephone lines			
• Copying service			
• Another computer			
• Insurance coverage			
• Cleaning services			
• Additional setup fees			
Business fees and insurance			
• Incorporating your business	$200–$2,000	None	
• State and federal fees	$100–$300	Usually $50–$300 annually depending on your location	

Office Costs	One-Time Start-up Costs	Recurring Annual Costs	Actual Fees Based on Your Research
• Various insurance policies: liability, business property, business interruption, errors and omissions, malpractice, health, disability, and workers' compensation	Varies greatly	Varies greatly	
Other:			
Other:			
Subtotals (Range is based on lowest and highest figures in each category, but does not include costs for categories only marked "Varies." It also assumes you purchase every category with an associated dollar amount.)	$3,570–$12,600	$1,240–$3,500	
Totals for your first year			

SALES AND MARKETING

Sales and Marketing, Professional Development, and Services	One-Time Start-up Costs	Recurring Annual Costs	Actual Fees Based on Your Research
Recurring sales and marketing costs			
• Attendance at monthly networking events	$100–$200 per month	$400–$1,200 per year, based on 2–3 networking events per month spending $20–$35 per meeting for transportation, attendance fee, food and drink	

(Continued)

Sales and Marketing, Professional Development, and Services	One-Time Start-up Costs	Recurring Annual Costs	Actual Fees Based on Your Research
• Full membership in 2 or 3 profitable networking groups	Varies greatly	Budget for $300–$1,000 for joining 2 or 3 profitable networking groups.	
• Direct-mail campaigns (including development cost, postage, and follow-up costs)	Varies greatly	Varies greatly; typically $600–$2,000 for a 6-month campaign	
• Regular mailouts to existing database of contacts	None	$100–$300 per year	
• Monthly professional-looking electronic newsletter (e-zine)	None	$100–$500 per year; includes a software program to design it, mail it, and track your results	
• Business lunches with strategic partners and prospects	$100–$200 per month	$950–$1,750 per year, based on meeting with 2–3 people per week, 4 weeks per month for 12 months, spending an average of $10–$20 each meeting	
• Business lunches with prospects you meet at networking events and people who are referred to you	$100–$250 per month	$500–$2,800, based on meeting 1–3 people per week, 4 weeks per month for 12 months, spending an average of $10–$20 per meeting	
• Seminars, training events, or presentations you want to hold to promote your business	Varies greatly	Varies greatly	
Professional development			
• Coaching seminars, training events, and conferences	Varies greatly	$500–$2,500 per year for 1 or 2 events	

Sales and Marketing, Professional Development, and Services	One-Time Start-up Costs	Recurring Annual Costs	Actual Fees Based on Your Research
• Sales and marketing books for business development	$15–$40 per book	$200–$400 per year	
• Attendance at local sales and marketing training events	$50–$300 per event	$200–$700 per year	
• Effort toward a coaching certification in your field	None	$1,000–$3,000 per year	
• Membership in a coaching organization to help you develop professionally	$300–$600 per year	$300–$600 per year	
Other professional services			
• Hiring a marketing and sales coach	$500–$1,200 per month	$3,000–$6,000 per year	
• Hiring someone to professionally design a marketing kit you can give to prospects	$300–$1,500	None, unless you decide to update it or modify it	
• Hiring a professional copywriter to assist you with direct-mail campaigns	$500–$1,000 per campaign	None, unless there are multiple campaigns	
• Hiring a part-time professional salesperson		$6,000–$10,000 per year, based on paying $10–$20 per hour for 10–15 hours per week, plus commission, for 12 months a year	
• Hiring a professional marketer to help you develop and market several info products	$2,000–$6,000 per product	None, unless you develop and market additional products	
Other:			
Other:			

(Continued)

Sales and Marketing, Professional Development, and Services	One-Time Start-up Costs	Recurring Annual Costs	Actual Fees Based on Your Research
Subtotals (Range is based on lowest and highest figures in each category, but does not include costs for categories only marked "Varies." It also assumes you purchase every category with an associated dollar amount.)	$3,965–$11,300	$14,150–$32,750	
Totals for your first year			
Subtotals			
• Marketing materials			
• Office costs			
• Sales and marketing			
Total costs			

SUMMARY

In this chapter we have introduced the hardest part of planning a new business start-up—money. It seems there is never quite enough to do all you want to do and never enough left over after you have purchased everything you need; thus, you have to plan ahead, based on your priorities, what you believe will be the best for your particular business at your specific stage. Creating a financial plan is a necessary part of business, yet year after year companies fail because they have failed to plan ahead. When creating a financial plan take into consideration which products or services will give you the greatest return on investment in terms of increasing your personal productivity, expanding your ability to attract new prospects, or enhancing your effectiveness in landing new clients.

CHAPTER 6

Building a Successful Business Requires a Solid Plan

Most books talk about writing a business plan as an academic exercise—the creation of an all-important document that sits proudly on your shelf to show to interested parties or give to potential investors. However, I believe creating a traditional business plan the way most people write about it is a complete waste of your time—and let's face it, the majority of coaches are not interested in seeking out venture capital. Instead, I want to encourage you in this chapter to think about this process in a very different way. So in this chapter we will cover the following points:

- Why you don't need a traditional business plan
- The top 10 reasons why you must have a marketing plan
- Ten easy steps to writing and using your marketing plan

THE RIGHT REASONS

Do you really, truly need a plan to build a successful coaching business? No. My answer may surprise you, but research shows that people have built successful companies without a business or marketing plan. Anything is possible, but the real question is: Is it probable? What does having a plan really do for you and your business? Here are the reasons why you need a plan:

It increases your chances of long-term success. It is possible to succeed without a marketing plan, but historically speaking, having a solid marketing plan that you can follow will significantly increase your chances for success in your business endeavor. A solid, well-thought-out plan keeps you from making serious mistakes later that can sink your business.

It gives you structure in an otherwise unstructured business. Part of the appeal of starting your own business may be the freedom—no one to tell you what to do. This is great, especially when you know exactly what to do every day, month in and month out, year after year. However, most entrepreneurs are new entrepreneurs. If this is your first try at building a business, having a plan can help give you structure and a context for your everyday activities.

It keeps you on the right track. One of my favorite quotes is from Lewis Carroll's *Alice in Wonderland,* when the Cheshire cat meets Alice for the first time and responds to her question with the classic reply, "If you don't know where you're going, any path will do." One of the best reasons to develop a plan before you get started is to help you stay on the right track. It is so easy to become distracted by problems that arise or opportunities that sound great, but don't exactly fit with your long-term goals. A plan is not designed to be unduly constrictive, but to provide you with freedom within defined boundaries, the boundaries being your short- and long-term goals.

It helps you count the cost before you start building. Critical to any marketing plan is an outline of your anticipated expenses, your marketing budget, your sales goals, and your path to profitability. Knowing your costs ahead of time can be invaluable in planning out your growth strategy.

It makes you think outside of the box. It's very easy to copy someone else, which is what most people end up doing when they don't have a personal plan. There are several potential dangers to copying someone else when it comes to marketing your small business:

- You miss opportunities that are perfect for you but not for other people.
- You take advantage of "opportunities" that are not right for you.
- You make the same mistakes as the person you copy.
- You stop thinking strategically about your business, instead focusing on duplicating others' efforts.

It exposes holes in your plan. Regardless of how advanced your thinking skills are, you probably can't think of every major challenge you will encounter while building your business. Writing down your plan will help you expose the traps that could derail your efforts. It's easy to overlook areas that you are unclear about or that are outside of your expertise.

It forces you to become clear. A great reason for having a written plan is that it forces you to become clear about your personal and business goals, your target market, your financial goals, and how and when you are going to implement parts of your plan. There is something about the disciplined exercise of writing these down that solidifies them and drives them into reality.

It helps you create a vision for what you want in the future. Where do you want to be in 12 months? How about three to five years? Ultimately, your business will be driven by your vision, and the process of developing that vision is critical to your long-term success. The real value of a marketing plan is not in just having it done; it's in all the time, energy, and research you put into thinking about your business in a strategic way.

It sets up measurable objectives for you to use to evaluate your success. How will you know if you've had a successful year? Will it depend on how you feel, or can you set up measurable objectives to compare your results against? If you fail to do so, how will you know whether your specific efforts were rewarded? How will you determine where to put your future efforts if something didn't work? A marketing plan with objective goals can help you ask and answer the right questions when it comes to evaluating your marketing and sales efforts. The answers give you indications as to your next steps.

It sets you apart as being committed to your business. Let's face it, if you're not willing to spend a few days writing up a solid marketing plan to grow and develop your business, why should anyone take you seriously? Do you really have anything better to do than to take some time and write down your plan for how you are going to succeed in your business? Writing up a working marketing plan sets you apart from other would-be entrepreneurs.

THE RIGHT ATTITUDE

Many people just don't take the time to write a solid, actionable plan before they start their business. If they do it at all, it is usually after their first year didn't go really well or just after they come back from a conference where a presenter has talked about all the positive aspects of creating a business plan. However, I would argue that not developing a plan is totally contrary to the very foundation of coaching. A core principle of coaching is to identify where you are, decide where you want to be, and create a plan to get there. That's exactly what a business plan does for your coaching company. A business plan is simply a written plan that details these points:

- What your business does
- Who your business helps

- What your goals and objectives are
- What financial, marketing, and sales strategies you will use to get there

Don't think of it as a business plan—think of it as a marketing plan.   About 80 percent of your plan should be focused on sales and marketing strategies, because these are the two areas where most small businesses have the most problems and these problems are the largest reasons why they fail. It makes sense to spend most of your time on the part that makes the biggest difference to your success.

Don't look at it as an academic exercise—look at it as a living document.   It is something you should refer to on a daily and monthly basis, not a long essay you write only to put on your shelf.

Don't see it as a just one more thing to do—see it as a plan for all the things you must do to succeed.   Your marketing plan becomes the driving force for all your actions and financial expenditures. It is your personal success plan.

THE RIGHT PLAN

If you're still reading this chapter, there is a good chance you will take the next crucial step and set aside some time to start working on your marketing plan. The whole process will probably take you anywhere from a few days to a few weeks, from start to finish, depending on the time you have available and how much time you have already put into thinking about all the pertinent issues. Much of your time will be spent researching and rethinking your original plans and ideas.

There are many ways to write a marketing or business plan, some of which are more helpful than others. Here are the 10 critical components I believe you need to create a solid marketing plan:

- Executive summary and company overview
- Services and products
- Target market
- Competition
- SWOT analysis
- Positioning, competitive advantage, and unique selling proposition

- Marketing strategies
- Financial plan
- Contingency planning
- Your biography

Over the next few pages we will talk about the specific sections you should include in your marketing plan. I strongly encourage you to work along in your notebook or on your computer as you read through each section, rather than waiting until a later date to start writing your plan.

EXECUTIVE SUMMARY AND COMPANY OVERVIEW

An *executive summary* is a one-page overview of your entire company, designed so that a person totally unfamiliar with your business can easily and quickly know exactly what you offer, who you service, and how you help. It should be the last part you write in your marketing plan, because most of the information you need to put in it comes from the other sections. The common parts of a summary are the company mission statement, goals and objectives, and a brief description of services and products offered, target market, and marketing strategies.

Company Mission Statement
Include a short mission statement of 30 words or so that succinctly states why your company exists, what it will provide, and to whom it will provide it. Let's use a fictional small-business coaching practice for example purposes.

> The Chicago Coaching Network (CCN) is a premier executive coaching and leadership development firm specializing in work with top-level executives, entrepreneurs, and small-business owners to help them experience significant increases in performance, productivity, and profitability.

Write down your company mission statement in your notebook.

Company Goals and Objectives
Describe the top three to five goals and objectives you have for your company. For example:

- To experience at least a 50 percent increase in annual revenues every year.
- To make more than $75,000 annually just from your coaching services.
- To focus at least 60 percent of your time, energy, and resources targeting small business owners and entrepreneurs. The other 40 percent will be spent targeting midsized companies.
- To build solid, lasting relationships with clients so that you work with them an average of 9 to 12 months instead of the current 4 to 6 months.
- To invest at least 50 percent of your time in marketing-related activities until you have a steady stream of new clients and are able to build up at least a three-month waiting list or give these new clients to another coach and take a percentage of the fee.

Write down your top three to five goals and objectives for your company in your notebook.

Services and Products Offered

List the full range of services and products you will provide. For example: one-on-one business coaching, career coaching, executive coaching, leadership development, team coaching, corporate training, workshops, seminars, coach-training events, and a how-to book on strategies for leadership development. You will explain each of them in the next section.

Write down a list of the services and products you will offer in your notebook.

Target Market

Provide some details about your top target markets. For example:

CCN will target owners of small businesses within 20 miles of downtown Chicago. A *small business* shall be defined as a company with less than 100 employees, privately or family owned, with $5 million to $50 million in annual revenues.

Write down a description of your target markets in your notebook.

SERVICES AND PRODUCTS

Describe which services you will offer and to whom you will offer them. Explain why you are offering that particular service to that specific market. For example, perhaps you offer career coaching to midlevel executives, creative workshops to aspiring authors, or team-building experiences to professional service firms. Why does that specific market need your particular services?

List as many features and benefits of your services and products as possible. You will use these over and over again in your marketing efforts, so spend a good amount of time on this section. Some benefits for personal coaching might include the following:

- Achieving your life goals faster
- Moving from a life of success to one of significance
- Ceasing to tolerate the things in life that keep you down
- Identifying and overcoming the obstacles to your personal success
- Experiencing more satisfying relationships

Possible benefits for small business coaching might include the following:

- Enhancing leadership performance in times of change and transition
- Experiencing significant increases in employee motivation and productivity
- Understanding the difference between building a company and having a job
- Decreasing conflict between owners and partners
- Discovering how to use your competitive edge for maximum impact
- Creating a business environment that produces better results faster with fewer resources

Write down the services you want to offer, which target market you will offer that service to, and why that specific market needs your particular services, using Chart 6.1 as a model.

Write down the specific benefits, results, and value each service brings to each target market, using Chart 6.2 as a model.

Service	Target Market	Why Market Needs Service

CHART 6.1   Services offered to target market.

Service	Benefit, Result, or Value to Target Market

CHART 6.2   Benefit to target market of services.

TARGET MARKET

Provide detailed information of who the members of your primary and secondary markets are, including age, gender, location, income level, socioeconomic status, education, industry, profession, title, position in company, life stage, personal interests, motivational methods, major personal and professional challenges, all their points of pain, buying habits, and any other distinguishing characteristics about them. The point is to create a comprehensive profile of everything you know about the members of your target markets, because the more you know about who belongs to your markets, the easier it is to identify them and market to them. If you need more help, please see Chapter 2.

Write down a description of your target markets in your notebook, using the information you have gathered.

COMPETITION

Every company has competition, and regardless of how unique you believe your services are, there are many other people and companies doing exactly what you do—or, at least, your prospects *believe* they do exactly what you do. Take for example, a business coach practicing in Chicago who does executive coaching and leadership development for small to midsized companies. The most obvious competition is from other business coaches, but our coach has many other competitors, including:

- Business consultants
- Small management consulting firms
- Large national management consulting firms
- Other consultants who focus on the exact same market as our coach
- Executive recruiting firms
- Some law and accounting firms
- Personal coaches who work with businesses and professionals
- Industrial and organizational psychologists
- Organizational development consultants
- Workshops and seminars put on by major companies (e.g., Linkage, Skill Path, Dale Carnegie, Stephen Covey, Anthony Robbins, and the American Management Association)
- Local graduate business programs with courses in leadership
- A stagnant economy, because companies cut back on their budgets during these times
- Best-selling books and tapes on leadership
- National conferences on leadership development

A competitor is anyone or anything a prospect can and will spend money on that they perceive will achieve the same or similar results and benefits as you state that your services will provide. Reread that carefully, because who your competition is depends on *your client's perspective*, not yours.

You do not need to know every one of your competitors, nor do you need to know everything about them. You do need to know who the key players are in your area, which ones target your exact market, which ones are the most aggressive in their sales and marketing efforts, and which ones are the best of the best. What do you need to know about them?

- Name of company and key executives
- Who some of their clients are
- What kind of fees they charge and any hidden costs
- How they price their services (by the hour, six-month packages, a percentage of revenues)
- How their business has been going in the past 6 to 12 months
- What they do for marketing (networking, direct-sales force, the Internet, advertising)
- How to differentiate yourself from competitors when talking to prospects
- Their strengths and weaknesses
- The 10 best reasons why prospects should buy from you instead of them

How do you find out all this information? Here are two simple ways to do a competitive analysis:

- *Use the power of the Internet.* Many companies have web sites; read through every page and take notes. Use your favorite search engine to track down articles they have published, stories about their key executives, or their company history (www.hoovers.com can be very helpful, especially for larger or well-established companies).
- *Send for some information.* Call them up as a prospect, ask their sales department several key questions, and request that they mail you some information. (If you don't feel comfortable doing this, ask a friend, a trusted client, or business associate).

Chart 6.3 is a great chart you can use to segregate your competition. In the "My Company" column, briefly state how you compare with other companies you have researched. In the "My Strength" and "My Weakness" columns, mark each factor according to whether you believe, as objectively as possible, that this area is a strength or a weakness for you. Briefly describe your top three competitors in the next

Factor	My Company	My Strength	My Weakness	Competitor	Competitor	Competitor	Importance to clients
Types of services							
Variety of services							
Quality of services							
Price							
Experience with the industry or situation							
Level of expertise							
Company reputation							
Location							
Company image							
Sales methods used to attract and acquire clients							
Differentiation from competitors							
Level of marketing sophistication							
Financial resources							

CHART 6.3   Segregating your competition.

columns, and in the final column mark down how important you believe each factor is to your clients, on a scale of 1 to 5.

SWOT ANALYSIS

SWOT stands for *strengths, weaknesses, opportunities,* and *threats.* Look at your new venture as objectively as possible to determine what strengths you have, the weaknesses you need to be aware of, the opportunities you need to explore, and the potential threats to your plan. To give you a better idea, here is a SWOT analysis based on our fictional example of a Chicago-based small-business coaching company called the Chicago Coaching Network:

Strengths. CCN has two coaches who have strong skill sets in business, sales, and psychology. Because coaching includes dealing with clients' behavioral and interpersonal issues, this professional training in psychology ensures that clients will not be adversely affected by a lack of training on our part. Our extensive business and sales experience ensures that clients will be provided with access to some of the best business techniques and sales strategies available today. We are highly skilled in helping small-business owners in critical areas such as teamwork, motivation, conflict resolution, and achieving goals.

Weaknesses. CCN has three primary weaknesses:

- *Undercapitalization.* There is only $5,000 in the budget for all sales and marketing activities, so each activity will have to be closely monitored, and low-cost strategies will be preferred. This will hamper our ability to aggressively target our market.
- *Long sales cycle.* Given the state of the economy and the cautious buying habits of small companies, the sales cycle can vary from a low of 30 days to a more typical 4 to 6 months. This impedes cash flow and drains much needed people resources for targeting new prospects.
- *Finding ideal clients.* Even though there are a great number of small businesses in the Chicago area, they are often isolated and unconnected, making them difficult to find. After identifying people in our target market, we must know how to quickly dis-

tinguish suspects from prospects who need, want, and can afford our services.

Opportunities. While there are several hundred coaches already in the Chicago market, there are significantly fewer who specialize in business and executive coaching. Furthermore, there are even fewer who aggressively market their services, which CCN is willing and wanting to do. Most small companies in this area are not aware of the power of business coaching, which can be both a positive and a negative—a positive in the sense that they have not been tainted by a bad experience, and a negative in the sense that it always takes a longer time to sell the service if you have to educate your prospects about what you do and how it can help.

Threats. It is estimated that the number of coaches entering the field is doubling about every year. The barriers to entry are currently minimal. Also, because of poor economic conditions, many other types of consultants are moving into coaching, including human resource consulting firms, traditional management consultants, psychologists, executive recruiting firms, organizational development companies, law firms, and accounting agencies, as well as a growing number of personal coaches. We must clearly and concisely distinguish our company from all of these competitors, and we must be very intentional in educating our clients about those differences.

Start working on the SWOT analysis of your company in your notebook. Be sure to list:

- Strengths
- Weaknesses
- Opportunities
- Threats

POSITIONING, COMPETITIVE ADVANTAGE, AND UNIQUE SELLING PROPOSITION

Using the information, research, and analysis you did for the competition and SWOT analysis sections, outline how you will position yourself and your services. Here are some good questions to get you started:

- How will you take advantage of your competitors' weaknesses?
- In light of what you know about your competitors, what are the top 5 to 10 reasons why someone should buy from you rather than any other company?
- Why are you the best and only person for the job?
- What skills, abilities, and experiences do you offer clients that they can't receive elsewhere?
- How can you emphasize the value you bring to the table?

Start developing your positioning, competitive advantage, and unique selling proposition statement in your notebook.

MARKETING STRATEGIES

Here is where you list all the different marketing techniques and strategies you will use to identify prospects and land new clients. This is the heart of this book, so if you don't have a lot of ideas right now, that's okay, because you will have more ideas than you can possibly handle by the time you finish this book. Here are a few common strategies coaches use:

- Referrals from former and current clients
- Referrals from strategic referral partners (SRPs)
- Contacts from speaking engagements
- Publicity from writing books and articles
- Internet strategies (web site, e-zine)
- Direct sales efforts (sales letters, cold calling, postcards, direct-mail letters)

Let's briefly outline a sample marketing plan for increasing your referrals from SRPs:

1. Identify the industries, fields, professions, and positions that are in a position to refer prospects to you.
2. Create an initial list of people who meet the first criterion.
3. Call each person, briefly introduce yourself, and request an hour of their time to talk about possible mutual referral situations.
4. Go to the meeting and convince them you can help their clients and want to develop a mutually beneficial business relationship.

5. Follow up with them on a regular basis (every four to six weeks) with an e-mail, newspaper clipping, newsletter, or phone call.

Obviously, this is an oversimplification, but you get the picture. I go into much more detail in Chapter 8. The next step is to create a 12-month chart (we will use a 6-month chart for purposes of illustration) and place each of these steps within the chart (see Chart 6.4).

FINANCIAL PLAN

This is often the scariest part of writing a marketing plan. One of the biggest reasons for small-business failure is lack of available funding to keep the business going. This is certainly the case for many coaching practices. This section should include the following points:

- Your currently available funds (cash in hand for expenses).
- A list of your current monthly sales for every category (individual coaching clients, small-business owners, speaking engagements, training programs, product sales, etc.).
- A 12-month timetable in which you estimate how much revenue you will bring in per client per month (assuming you will not keep every client forever).
- A forecast of new sales—how many new sales you anticipate per month and at what rate.
- A comprehensive list of all marketing activities and the anticipated expense of each one.
- A simple profit-and-loss (P&L) statement in which you subtract your anticipated expenses from your anticipated revenues. This should give you a good idea of how much money you need to have on hand in order to properly fund your business.

Often, the easiest way to write up and keep track of these financial charts is by using Excel or another spreadsheet program, but the most important part is the actual process of running the numbers, rather than the program you use to calculate the numbers.

The following paragraphs give some examples of each category, using a well-established small-business coaching practice making about $125,000 a year.

Marketing Activity: Develop Referrals from SRPs

Activity	January	February	March	April	May	June
Identify industries, positions, and professions of SRPs.	Complete research by 3rd week.					
Create a list of 50 potential SRPs.	Start compiling list by 2nd week.	Finish compiling list by 2nd week.				
Start calling each contact and set up 1-on-1 meetings.		Start calling list by 3rd week. Make 10 calls per week.	Continue calling 10 contacts per week.	Continue calling 10 contacts per week.	Continue calling 10 contacts per week.	Continue calling 10 contacts per week.
Attend meetings to develop relationship and discuss referrals.			Set up at least 2 meetings by 3rd week.	Set up at least 2 meetings per week.	Set up at least 2 meetings per week.	Set up at least 2 meetings per week.
Follow up after every meeting.			Follow up every meeting within 24 hours with a thank-you note and next steps.	Follow up every meeting within 24 hours with a thank-you note and next steps.	Follow up every meeting within 24 hours with a thank-you note and next steps.	Follow up every meeting within 24 hours with a thank-you note and next steps.
Follow up every 4–6 weeks.			Follow up with each person.	Follow up with each person.	Follow up with each person.	Follow up with each person.

CHART 6.4 Developing referrals from strategic referral partners (SRPs).

Saralyn Collins
Certified Professional Consultant, Trainer, and Coach
The Training Bridge
Winter Park, Florida
www.thetrainingbridge.com
saralyn@thetrainingbridge.com
(407) 657-5788

Saralyn Collins is the owner of the Training Bridge and is a seasoned Certified Professional Consultant, a Certified Professional Marketing Consultant, a Certified Executive Trainer, and a Franklin Covey Certified Personal Coach.

You have been doing consulting for many years, but moved into coaching within the past few years. What helped you make that change?

Like many people, I now realize I've been doing coaching intuitively for many years, but I first realized I was doing coaching in the purest sense of the word when I was still a marketing consultant. I started researching coaching through books and the Internet, and I realized that my personal style was much more in line with coaching than a typical consultant. 2002 was the big year of change for me. I went to my first coaching conference, a CoachVille Coaching Intensive. While I was there I found it to be a very comfortable base, and at that point, I had no more questions. I knew I was a coach.

How has that changed your current practice?

I have a great mix of coaching, consulting, and training. With my consulting, I work with businesses, groups in a business, or an individual person in a business. With my training skills, I come in and help them with their soft skills, like team building, customer service, management growth and development, and communication skills. One of the keys to my success has been my ability to offer my clients a continuation of services, from consulting, to training, through coaching. I help them in designing the change, then implementing it.

What do you see as the primary difference between coaching and consulting?

In consulting, my job is to provide a specific solution to a specific problem. In coaching, I try to help my client to come up with as much of the solution as possible. I act as a checkpoint for the validity of the solution, and then I actually work with them through the implementation of the solution. I don't do a one-shot training as a trainer because I know the key to success, to truly change behavior, takes time and a lot of effort. I use coaching to build on the training to help them implement the behavior change necessary for their success.

Other than referrals, what is one of the top ways you are currently finding clients?

Eighty to ninety percent of my clients come from my speaking engagements to organizations and clubs all across my city. I speak four or five times per month to every type of organization you can imagine. Virtually all of my speaking I do for free. I speak for recognition, not pay. As a coach there are multiple topics you can present, like individual differences, determining behavior for enhanced performance, assessment tools, communication skills, how to identify yourself to attract your prospects, team building—basically, almost anything that is a people skill is greatly needed.

A lot of new coaches who want to do speaking struggle to get started. Do you have some suggestions for them?

Yes, here are the seven steps you need to take in order to start speaking to groups:

1. Develop a brief introduction that presents who you are and how you help in a clear and compelling way. Use your audio logo.
2. Review all the clubs meeting in your area and select four or five to go to. Use your audio logo at the meetings.
3. While you're at the meeting, seek out the program chair and acknowledge they have a difficult job in the association, then tell them you are a speaker and would like to speak to their group.
4. Here is where many coaches get stuck: After the meeting you have to be aggressive and follow through with the program chair. This is the key.
5. Have three to five topics of interest to their group that you can send. Try to get a specific date for a future presentation.
6. Every time you speak, create a handout with blanks on it so the group will follow along, and on the back give them an overview of your services, benefits, bio, and contact information.

(Continued)

7. Don't forget to volunteer to be an emergency fill-in speaker to the group. You wouldn't believe it, but it's not that uncommon for a speaker to get sick and leave the group in a pinch. To be a backup emergency speaker can get you into some great groups. Just be sure to have one or two key presentations that you can give in a moments notice.

What's one piece of advice you would have to a new coach just starting out?

Move from prospecting to positioning. At the core of your marketing message you have one key that holds you together—your reputation. You must work hard to build your reputation in the community for what you do and who you are. Have great passion for what you do and let it show! People are attracted to excitement, passion, and enthusiasm before they are attracted to knowledge.

What do you believe coaching will look like in three to five years?

While there will always be a need for people who do just life-strategy coaching, I believe the bulk of people will eventually look for a more inclusive coach who can give them business advice, professional advice, and personal life coaching. The more expansive your services are, the more value you can provide to your clients. I don't think we will see coaches who just do one thing, but people who can do multiple things and have multiple areas of expertise. Realize there is no hard and fast line between life and home and work; they each affect the other.

Chart 6.5: Monthly Revenues from New and Existing Clients
This chart gives an example of monthly revenues generated from new and existing clients on a month-by-month basis along with an estimation of long-term revenues. For example, for the first individual coaching client (line 1), it assumes you are charging $900 per month and that the client will remain with you for six months, bringing the total revenue from that client to $5,400 for the year. The example also assumes you will land your first new small-business owner for the year by March (line 9) and keep that client for six months. It further estimates that your second new small-business client will come by April (line 10) and last for 9 months, bringing in $10,800 for this year.

Chart 6.6: Marketing Expense Budget

This is a listing of all the new and existing marketing activities and projects you plan for the year and the anticipated costs, along with an estimated timeline for implementation. For example, you want to launch a new web site sometime between January and March, and you anticipate you will spend around $900 to do so. You also want to join three networking groups at an initial investment of $300 each, and spend about $50 per month on travel, entrance fees, and food at the meetings for the rest of the year.

Chart 6.7: Profit and Loss Statement

This is a simple Excel chart that shows the monthly profits and losses based on anticipated expenses and revenues.

CONTINGENCY PLANNING

This is another difficult section for many people to write, because you don't want to think about all the things that could go wrong. Most people are overly positive when starting up a business—and that's great, because you will encounter enough tough times without being cynical and pessimistic when starting out. However, the time you spend thinking through the major potential stumbling blocks and what you will do if you encounter any of them will be well spent. The following paragraphs discuss some of the common obstacles to small-business success.

Lack of Funding

Not having enough cash on hand to sustain your business while trying to grow it results in not being able to actively market your services, pay yourself a salary, or even pay your bills. Do you have a solid idea of how much money it will take to launch and sustain your business over the first year or two? If not, read Chapters 4 and 5. What are you really willing to do to make this business go? Are you really serious about it, or are you just playing around?

Economic Downturn

At the time of this writing, coaching is not considered by most people to be an absolute necessity on par with eating, housing, taking a long overdue vacation, or keeping the sales department happy. Ultimately, most

Sales Forecast Plan

Sales	Jan	Feb	Mar	Apr	May	Jun	Jul	Aug	Sep	Oct	Nov	Dec	Year
1. Current individual coaching client	$ 900	$ 900	$ 900	$ 900	$ 900	$ 900	$ 0	$ 0	$ 0	$ 0	$ 0	$ 0	$ 5,400
2. Current individual coaching client	675	675	675	675	675	675	675	675	675	675	675	675	8,100
3. Current small-business owner	2,100	0	0	0	0	0	0	0	0	0	0	0	2,100
4. Current small-business owner	920	2,120	1,200	1,200	1,200	1,200	1,200	0	0	0	0	0	9,040
5. Current small-business owner	2,000	2,000	1,000	1,000	1,000	1,000	1,000	500	1,000	1,000	1,000	1,000	13,500
6. Current individual coaching client	500	500	500	675	675	675	675	675	675	675	675	0	6,900
7. Current individual coaching client	675	675	675	675	675	675	675	675	675	675	675	675	8,100
8. Current training events	0	1,450	0	0	0	0	0	0	1,200	0	0	0	2,650
9. New small-business owner	0	0	900	900	900	900	900	900	0	0	0	0	5,400

10. New small-business owner	0	0	0	900	900	900	900	900	900	900	900	900	10,800
11. New small-business owner	0	0	0	0	1,200	1,200	1,200	1,200	1,200	1,200	1,200	1,200	9,600
12. New small-business owner	0	0	0	0	0	1,200	1,200	1,200	1,200	1,200	1,200	0	7,200
13. New midsized coaching client	0	0	1,000	1,000	1,000	1,000	1,000	1,000	1,000	1,000	1,000	1,000	10,000
14. New midsized coaching client	0	0	0	0	1,500	1,500	1,500	1,500	1,500	1,500	1,500	1,500	12,000
15. Product sales	0	0	300	600	900	1,200	1,500	1,800	2,100	2,400	2,700	3,000	16,500
16. Other	0	0	0	0	0	0	0	0	0	0	0	0	0
Total sales	$7,770	$8,320	$7,150	$8,525	$11,525	$13,025	$12,425	$11,025	$12,125	$11,225	$11,525	$9,950	$124,590

CHART 6.5 Monthly revenues from new and existing clients.

Marketing Expense Budget

Expense	Jan	Feb	Mar	Apr	May	June	July	Aug	Sept	Oct	Nov	Dec	Total
New web site	$ 500	$ 200	$ 200	$ 0	$ 0	$ 0	$ 0	$ 0	$ 0	$ 0	$ 0	$ 0	$ 900
Hosting for new web site	30	30	30	30	30	30	30	30	30	30	30	30	360
Market new web site	0	300	100	100	100	100	25	25	25	25	25	25	850
Join 3 networking groups and go to meetings	300	300	300	50	50	50	50	50	50	50	50	50	1,350
Postage for direct-mail campaigns	200	0	200	0	200	0	0	200	0	200	0	0	1,000
Mail out postcards and direct-mail letters	0	100	0	100	0	100	0	100	0	100	0	0	500
New business cards and letterhead	0	0	600	0	0	0	0	0	0	0	0	0	600
Market and hold 3 public seminars	0	600	600	0	600	600	0	0	600	600	0	0	3,600
Business lunches	75	75	75	75	75	75	75	75	75	75	75	75	900
Miscellaneous expenses	100	100	100	100	100	0	0	0	100	100	100	100	900
Total marketing expenses	$1,205	$1,705	$2,205	$455	$1,155	$955	$180	$580	$880	$1,180	$280	$280	$10,960

CHART 6.6   Marketing expense budget.

174

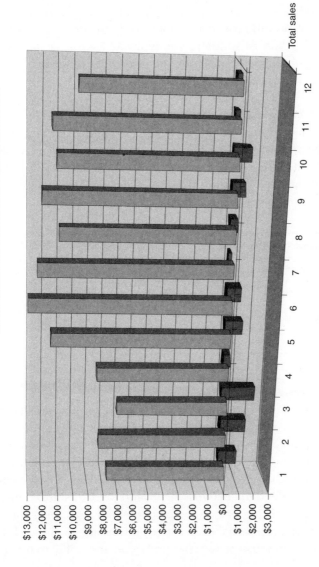

	1	2	3	4	5	6	7	8	9	10	11	12
Total sales	$7,770	$8,320	$7,150	$8,525	$11,525	$13,025	$12,425	$11,025	$12,125	$11,225	$11,525	$9,950
Total sales and marketing expenses	($1,205)	($1,705)	($2,205)	($455)	($1,155)	($955)	($180)	($480)	($880)	($1,180)	($280)	($280)

CHART 6.7   Profit-and-loss statement.

175

people and businesses see coaching as discretionary, and in an economic downturn people and companies tend to cut back on discretionary items. Coaching then becomes more difficult to sell, and finding people to pay for coaching takes more time.

Inability to Secure Many SRPs

Strategic referral partners (SRPs) can be the lifeblood of your new company, but it may be difficult to convince them to refer to you when you're just starting out. In addition, you typically have to spend a lot of time meeting with various SRPs before you find one who actually delivers on their promised referrals.

Missed Sales Goals and Lack of Revenue Growth

In order to cover your marketing and cost-of-living expenses, you need to be able to set and meet sales goals. Let's use the previous example of an established small-business coaching practice anticipating $124,590 this year in revenues — which, by the way, would place it in the top 9 percent of all coaching practices.

Total annual income	$124,590
Sales and marketing expenses	− 10,960
Subtotal	$113,630
Average of 35% taxes	− 39,770
Total	$73,860

A typical 40-hour work week for 48 weeks gives you about 1,920 possible billable hours. For the sake of argument, let's say you do work 2,000 hours in a given year, even though most small-business owners work significantly more, but you are a well-balanced owner. However, you are not able to bill all 40 hours per week — much of your time is spent marketing, attending networking events and business lunches, writing up and submitting proposals for new work, following up with leads, and so on. In an established practice you should be able to bill 20 to 30 percent of your actual time. That gives you about 400 to 600 total billable hours annually (40 percent gives you 800 billable hours). If you were able to bill 20 percent of your time (or 400 hours annually), you would need to average $311 per hour to make $124,590 a year. Billing 30 percent of your time allows you to average only $207 per hour. The average business coach charges about $197 per hour, so this latter price is not entirely out of market, but it is significantly higher than the rates charged by most personal coaches. The next question to consider is how many clients you would need to maintain in order to bill 20 to 30 percent of your time.

The average business coach spends four to six months per client, so in a given year let's assume there is about 100 percent client turnover. If a coach bills clients $207 per hour and spends 4 hours a month with them for 6 months, that would average $4,968 per client for 24 hours of actual coaching time. To make $124,590 annually, you would need to average 24 to 27 new clients per year, or about 2 to 3 new clients per month, and spend billable time with an average of 12 to 13 clients every month (48 to 52 hours of actual coaching). That doesn't sound hard, but 65 percent of all coaches report having fewer than 10 clients a month on average, which is why less than 9 percent of all coaches make more than $100,000 a year.

In your contingency plan, you need to account for what you will do if any of these cases arise. What measures will you take? How closely will you watch your new client sales, how many people you have in the pipeline at any given time, or your prospect-to-client conversion ratio? All of these questions are important to plan for in case they occur.

Write down the major problems that could keep your business from being successful.

For each major problem, briefly outline how you will recognize it and the specific steps you will take to overcome it if it should occur.

Your Biography

Talk about your background, focusing on the issues and experiences you believe will be important to your prospective clients. Remember, coaching is very personal. Ultimately, people are hiring you because of your interpersonal style, your experience, your background, and what you stand for, so be wise and honest about what you say and don't say in your biography.

Write down the four to six major points you want to emphasize in your biography.

SUMMARY

In this chapter we have focused on how to significantly increase your chances of building a successful coaching business by developing a solid marketing plan. There are two hard questions you need to consider:

- Will you follow through and write your marketing plan?
- If you do, will you use it to guide and direct your company?

Ultimately, your long-term business success depends on your ability to think strategically about services, uniquely position your company to your prospects, and consistently implement your plan.

CHAPTER 7

You Only Get One Chance: Seven Tools for Making a Great First Impression

As the old saying goes, you only get one chance to make a first impression, and every future impression will be based on the first. As a small-business owner, you must ask yourself three important questions:

- What kind of impression are you currently making?
- What kind of impression do you want to make on prospects?
- How can you best make that kind of impression?

Take a minute and write down your answers to those questions.

Everything about you and your business combines to create an image: your personal presence, your business cards or lack of them, the company name, the title you use for yourself, your brochure and web site. All of them must be:

Credible. Everything about you and your company must project competence and credibility. Not only can you do the job, you are the best person to do it.

Congruent. You can't afford to send mixed messages to your prospects. All of your marketing messages must be congruent. For example, it would not be wise to spend $5,000 creating a web site, but photocopy your brochures.

Clear. Prospects must be able to grasp quickly exactly what you do. They shouldn't have to translate your "coaching language" into their own; you must do it for them.

Compelling. When people in your target market hear and understand how you can help them and the results you achieve, they should feel compelled to contact you because of the power of your persuasion.

In this chapter I'm going to show you exactly what tools you need to create a credible, congruent, clear, and compelling first impression. Some of the more important topics we'll cover include:

- The top seven tools for increasing your company's tangibility
- Effective ways to identify, screen, and work with other qualified service professionals who can assist you in creating these tools
- The critical areas to focus on when creating your tools
- Helpful advice on how to effectively design and use the cheapest marketing tool ever created

> Tangibility builds credibility. Tangibility cannot create credibility, it can only build on it. The best source of credibility your company will ever have is *you*, because when people hire a coach it is a very personal decision—they are hiring you. However, everything you can do to make your coaching company, your services, your value, and your quality more tangible to prospects will make it all the easier to sell your services.

- Pointed questions to help you clarify your thinking and writing
- Specific recommendations on how to get the best return on investment for your time, energy, and money

HOW YOUR MARKETING MATERIALS AFFECT YOUR BUSINESS IMAGE

When planning, designing, and writing your marketing tools, my first general recommendation is to make sure all of your marketing materials focus on these points:

- Who your target market is
- How you help them
- What results and benefits your clients achieve

They should *not* focus on these points:

- A complete description of your biography or resume
- Long lists of all the different services you can provide
- A comprehensive listing of all your target markets (you should pick a specific target market for each marketing piece)
- Arguments to convince prospects to hire you (you should focus on getting them to contact you by phone, fax, or e-mail)

Try to read each of these descriptions from the perspective of a small-business owner who wants to work with someone who can help strategically build a small company:

Example 1.   Today's Leadership Coaching, Inc., is owned by Stephen Fairley, MA, RCC, and was founded to become the premier executive coaching firm in Chicago. At Today's Leadership Coaching they help businesses of all sizes, including more than 20 *Fortune* 500 companies, by focusing on leadership development, executive coaching, team building, management and corporate coaching, training, and seminars.

Example 2.   Today's Leadership Coaching, Inc., is a Chicago-based firm dedicated to helping small-business owners increase employee performance, managerial productivity, and bottom-line profitability. They use one-on-one executive coaching and business development strategies to help owners build a strong and profitable business.

Example 3.   Are you a small-business owner searching for ways to build your business? Today's Leadership Coaching has proven experience working one-on-one with owners to help them grow their company, increase their performance, and implement powerful strategies that result in significant growth and long-term success—guaranteed. Call today to set up your free coaching session.

Did you notice the differences? The first example has several problems, including these:

- It focuses on the company and its owner rather than the prospect.
- It is too generic and unfocused ("businesses of all sizes").
- It lists every kind of service the company provides with no apparent concern for what kind of service the prospect needs or wants.
- It does not mention any kind of results.

The second example is better:

- It focuses on small-business owners (who you help).
- It states that the company uses executive coaching and business development strategies (how you help).
- It emphasizes performance, productivity, and profitability (the results clients achieve).

The third example is even more focused:

- It is clear who they help.
- It is confident in the results they achieve.
- It offers a compelling reason to contact them.

Remember these three criteria whenever you are writing and designing your marketing tools and you will be three steps ahead of your competition.

Now, here are the top seven tools for giving your company the tangibility it needs and how to use them to enhance its credibility.

TOOL 1: A POWERFUL COMPANY NAME

One of the first exciting things you get to do in planning your coaching business is to come up with a name for your coaching practice. This can be a lot of fun if you enjoy creativity, but frustrating if it takes too long.

Give careful thought to the name you will give your company. It will often be the first thing your prospects hear and will give them the first impression they have about:

- If you are someone that can help them
- The size of your company
- The level of professionalism you have
- What your company does

Work hard and long brainstorming about possible options, but resist the urge to include your personal name in the company name (e.g., Fairley & Associates or SGF Consulting). It may be good for your ego to have a company named after you, but how many successful companies do you know that were named after their founder? A couple come to mind—Merrill Lynch and Arthur Anderson—but it's still Microsoft, not the Bill Gates Company. I usually go to three or four business networking events a month and meet between 20 and 30 people at each event, and every time I meet someone who has named their company after themselves three thoughts pass through my mind: Either they are not marketing savvy, or they are a small, fly-by-night organization, or they have a *very* healthy ego.

Here is a simple six-step process I use when coaching start-ups and entrepreneurs to help them create a business name.

Step 1: Write down what images you want your business to project. Consider your target audience, your various services (coaching, training, speaking, consulting, etc), and what kind of results you want your clients to experience. Do you want a strong image, one that is conservative, highly professional, or that sounds like a large or national company?

Some of these statements may stimulate your thinking:

Achieving your personal best	Reaching your professional best
A sense of forward movement	Built to last
Building trust	Being wise
Providing insight and clarity	Someone you can turn to and trust
Honesty and integrity	Reaching your goals
Achieving peak performance	Living your dreams
Focusing your energy	Current for today's needs

Here's an example:

I want my company to project an image that is attractive to small-business owners and leaders at midsized companies. It should sound like an established company that can provide various services, but focuses on coaching. I want it to be clear that I target leaders in companies. I want it to focus on being fresh and current—for the challenges companies are currently facing.

Step 2: Based on the preceding images, think about what words remind you of those images. Add to those words all the different words you are attracted to.

Here are a few starting points:

Advantage	Build	Clarity	Coaching	Compass
Confident	Consulting	Create	Deliberate	Develop
Development	Direction	Discover	Energetic	Enhance
Evolving	Excel	Focus	Global	Growth
Integrity	International	Landscape	Leadership	Maximum
National	Pathfinder	Peak	Performance	Persistence
Personal	Pinnacle	Potential	Power	Precision
Principle	Proactive	Productive	Professional	Progressive
Results	Strategic	Summit	Synchrony	Today
Training	Transcendent	Transform	Transformational	Vantage point
Vision	Wisdom			

Write down some other words you like that remind you of the images you talked about in Step 1.

Step 3: Start putting the words you came up with in Step 2 together using various combinations. Write down other attractive words as they come to mind. For example:

Creative Coaching	The Leadership Edge
Peak Performance Incorporated	Today's Leadership Coaching
Chicago Coaching Company	Maximum Coaching Advantage
Leadership Coaching and Training	Coaching and Consulting Company
Building for Today	Creating Powerful Leaders for Today
Leadership Performance and Power	Global Coaching and Consulting

Step 4: Come up with at least five different names you really like. Include what you think is best and worst about each name. For example:

- *Peak Performance Incorporated.* Sounds great, easily rolls off the tongue, sounds professional, sounds just like every other consulting company, not sure if it accurately reflects what I do.
- *Chicago Coaching Company.* Sounds prestigious, like a big name firm, can be too geographically limited if I ever wanted to build a national company, says we do coaching.
- *Leadership Coaching and Training.* Focuses on leaders, talks about coaching and training.
- *Maximum Coaching Advantage.* Tells what we do, describes it as an advantage, and plays up the power aspect—*maximum.*
- *Today's Leadership Coaching.* Wow! Now there's a great name! It talks about coaching and leaders, it is current and always fresh, and it has a well-recognized abbreviation (TLC). Sorry, but it's already taken.

Step 5: Obtain feedback. Approach several business associates and friends who are in your target audience. Ask them for their honest feedback: If

185

they heard about a company by this name, what image would they think of first, and what does the name say about that company, in their opinion?

Be careful about the final name you choose and its possible limitations. Before coming up with Today's Leadership Coaching, Inc., I strongly considered the name Chicago Coaching Company. It has a catchy sound, immediately defines what we do (coaching), and is connected with a well-recognized area (Chicago). However, my colleagues warned me that it could be geographically limiting if and when I expanded the company to reach outside Chicago. I tried to incorporate under that name anyway, but was refused because another company's name, the Chicago Coach Company, a limousine service, was too close. Looking back, I'm glad that happened, because I think Today's Leadership Coaching (TLC) is a much better name.

Step 6: Test it out. If you still can't decide, try going to a networking event and using the name to see how it sounds when you say it to your target audience. Don't worry, they will not remember if you change your name in a week. You'll be lucky if they remember you, much less your name.

It can take a few weeks and several brainstorming sessions to come up with a name you really like and that sounds great. If you reach a block in your thinking, pull out a thesaurus or ask a creative friend to help you with a brainstorming session over a cup of coffee. I don't recommend naming your company after yourself. At its worst, this comes across as a little too egotistical, smacks of a lack of creativity ("I couldn't think of anything better than my own name"), and portrays a small, unprofessional company (like Bob's Auto & Towing). There are some professions where this is commonplace and acceptable, such as accounting and law, but we all know lawyers never struggle with their ego, right?

Tool 2: A Corporate Identity Package

The foundation of your marketing materials is a basic business image, also known by graphic designers as a *corporate identity package* (CIP). A basic CIP usually includes the design of your company logo and the look of your business cards, letterhead and envelopes. The image your business projects will determine who is attracted to you. It should be an image that is professional, one you are proud of, one that grabs your target market's interest and draws attention to who you are and what you do. A full CIP can also include your company web site and multiple marketing campaigns designed to graphically tie into your company image.

Hiring a professional to develop a basic corporate identity package used to cost thousands of dollars, but not any more, thanks to the power of the Internet. A basic CIP can cost less than $200 from a student just starting out to several hundred dollars from a seasoned professional. It has become commonplace to find excellent designers with a lot of experience who will do a basic package for $500 to $1,000. If this is way out of your budget, spend extra time looking on the Internet and you may find a new designer with great ideas who will do it for much less. Unless you come from a design background, I don't recommend doing this yourself. This is one of those fun and exciting things you get to do when starting a business, but which can cause you a lot of turmoil and frustration if you do it yourself. I believe that in most cases you are much better off outsourcing this job.

Here are a few pointers to keep in mind when working with your designer:

- Do not be afraid to go with a small or single-person firm if their recommendations are strong. Often a small firm will give you more personal attention, and their overhead costs are much lower.

SMALL BUSINESS RESOURCE ELANCE WWW.ELANCE.COM

Elance.com is like an auction site for graphic design services. After you register and describe the type of work you are looking for, designers from literally all over the world bid for your contract. It allows you to view the contractor's portfolio and previous clients' testimonials and e-mail the contractors to ask any questions. Many of my clients have had great success with this service.

- Look over the individual designers' portfolios carefully to see what kind of companies they have worked for, the blend of colors and designs, and how unique each logo is.
- Determine all the costs up front by asking prospective designers the right questions:

  - How many original concepts will you provide me with? (Three to six is typical.)
  - How many revisions will you give me of those concepts? (One to three is typical.)
  - What if I don't like any of the ones you come up with?
  - Do you have a written 100 percent satisfaction guarantee?
  - How fast can you turn the ideas around?
  - What formats will you give the final product to me in?
  - Do you have any local printers that you have a relationship with that could give me a good price?
  - Can you provide at least three to five recent references? (Call them.)

- I recommend that when possible you work with a local graphic designer or someone who lives in a nearby state. I know of one coach who selected a graphic designer from a Middle Eastern country off the Internet because of the extremely low cost, but ended up totally dissatisfied with the finished product because she couldn't verify what the colors would actually look like in print before the job went to the printer, and she couldn't get in touch with the designer except by e-mail.
- When choosing logos, be sure you really like the logo in black and white. It's easy to dress up a poorly designed logo with a fancy color scheme, but more difficult in black and white.
- Be sure your logo is legible after it has been faxed (another reason to like your logo in black and white).
- Try to limit the number of colors you use in your designs and logos. Two colors are fine, but there is quite a jump in printing costs from two colors to three and an even bigger one when you move to full four-color processing.
- Have your designer or a printer carefully explain the differences between RGB (red, green, and blue) colors and CMYK (cyan, magenta, yellow, and black) colors. The colors you see on your

computer monitor screen are RGB based, and if you design or approve a color logo based on what your designer sent you via e-mail, you may be *very* surprised when you see it in finished, printed form, because it will likely look very different. Don't ask me why—I'm not a graphic designer, and I don't build computer monitors—but that's the way it is.

- There are 16 standard colors commonly used in the printing process. You will go a long way toward reducing your printing costs if your logo colors are from this palette. For example, when I first met with my graphic designer I told him that I wanted navy blue, but he encouraged me to go with a similar blue called *process* or *metallic blue*, one of the 16 standard printing colors. From what I understand, colors outside of that palette must be individually created by the printer, which increases the cost. After I saw the similarity, I decided to change to the process blue. That simple choice saved me over 30 percent in my printing costs. I'm still grateful for that little change.

- If you are at all particular about colors, stipulate that you will make all final approvals for colors only after seeing them in printed form, preferably from the same (or equivalent) printer that will be used for the final product.

- Be clear with your designer about what kind of business you are in and who your target audience is. Not only do you have to like your CIP, so does your target market.

- Try to get a package deal that includes designing your logo, business cards, letterhead, and envelopes all at once, even if you don't plan on using all of them right away. It may be difficult for another designer to duplicate your designer's work in the future if you can't get in contact with your former designer.

- Require the designer to waive all future rights to your logo and sign them over to you in writing.

- Before sending in your final payment, make sure your designer provides you with all the design work saved in multiple formats—jpg, gif, tiff, eps, and bmp. You never know which one you might need later on down the road for printing, your web site, or an e-zine.

- Talk to a printer about how the overall design of a business card, letterhead, envelope, or brochure impacts printing costs. For example, printing color to the edge of your business card or letterhead (called *bleeding*) can increase your costs by 5 to 20 percent, because they have to use a larger paper size and have more wasted material between cards. On a side note, many printers have designers working for them, and you may want to consider asking them to bid on the CIP, especially if they have a package deal that includes design and printing costs.

- Show the designs to as many people in your target audience as possible. Listen to their ideas and opinions, but remember that you will be the one who has to live with the design, and ultimately, company colors and a business logo are very personal choices. Be sure you love them.

Tool 3: Dynamic Tag Lines

The tag line for your company is a brief phrase or statement describing the theme, mission, goal, results, or benefits of your company. These can be powerful reminders to prospects about your company. See if you can correctly match these tag lines with the correct companies (the answers are at the end of the chapter):

Avis	When you absolutely, positively need it there on time.
Hertz	America's News channel.
Nike	Developing leaders who deliver results.
Allstate	Strong enough for a man, but made for a woman.
Memorex	The document company.
Xerox	We try harder.
FedEx	We're #1.
Fox News	Never let them see you sweat.
MSNBC	You're in good hands with ____.
Sure antiperspirant	Real journalism. Fair and balanced.
Secret antiperspirant	Just do it.
Today's Leadership Coaching	Is it live or is it ____?

Well, how did you do? More than 50 percent? How well you did is not a function of your memory or intelligence, but rather of how good a job these companies have done in branding themselves with their customers. You see, these companies have each spent millions of dollars over the years trying to create a name for themselves (except that last one), develop a brand image, and attract new customers and retain loyal ones. One of the ways they do this is by creating tag lines, often used over and over again in their commercials and advertisements in hopes that you will automatically think of the company every time you hear or see or read its tag line or anything like it. As a consumer, you are the real judge of whether these companies have done a good job of this, just as your clients will be the ultimate judge of whether you do a good job of using your tag line. This is precisely why you should take care to develop a strong and dynamic tag line for your coaching company.

Before developing your tag line you must be clear about four things:

- What your company really does (not just coaching or "helping people")
- Who you help (your primary target market)
- How you help them
- The results your clients achieve (does this list sound familiar?)

Clarity about what your company really does will help you think about what idea or concept you want to focus on in your tag line. Knowing precisely who your primary target market audience is will help you identify their specific pains and greatest challenges, which directly relates to how your company helps them, and ultimately to the results they achieve. These four concepts will help you craft a tag line that is meaningful to your target market.

ACTION STEP

Answer the following questions in one sentence or less than 10 words each:

- *What does your company really do?*
- *Who exactly is your primary target audience?* Use as few words as possible to meaningfully identify them, for example: top leaders in midsized companies, executive professionals in a midlife career transition, or former Catholics who are seeking spiritual enlightenment. But stay away from generic terms,

Sylva Leduc, MEd, MPEC
Executive Coach
President, TurningPoint Northwest
Chief Executive Officer, Client Compass
Phoenix, Arizona
www.TurningPointNW.com
skleduc@turningpointnw.com
www.ClientCompass.com
(425) 985-9244

Sylva Leduc is the president of TurningPoint Northwest, an executive coaching firm, and the CEO of Client Compass, a technology development company specializing in client relationship management software for coaches.

How did you first get started in coaching?

I've been coaching for over a dozen years. In 1990, I was contracted by a *Fortune* 500 company to develop and launch a career development program called "The Manager's Role as Coach, Information Broker and Referral Agent." It was very successful in helping managers develop their coaching and leadership skills. Shortly after completing the contract, I joined a firm specializing in executive outplacement and coaching. Over the years I was brought into many organizations to work with senior mangers and executives to help them with interpersonal communication skills and leadership development.

An intriguing aspect of your business is its diversity—not only do you have a successful executive coaching company, but you also have developed a widely adopted client relationship management system. Tell us more about this.

Currently my time is focused on developing two companies: Turning Point Northwest—a leadership development and executive coaching company—and Client Compass—a custom-designed client relationship management system developed specifically to help professional coaches to easily manage client relationships and track their marketing efforts. It's a customized software program that helps coaches who really want to take their practice to the next level by implementing client relation-ship management techniques and marketing strategies. I began using the software to streamline the processes at Turning Point Northwest and was so pleased with the results that I bought the software company in 2002.

What's one piece of advice you would give to a new coach just starting out?

First, learn ways to increase your efficiency by making sure you have your systems in place so you're not spending time on busy work, but on productive work. Second, you must develop a well-thought-out plan based on annual revenues you want to achieve. It needs to include measurements for success, a financial budget, and specific strategies to achieve it. Last, unless you have a lot of sales and marketing experience, a lot of contacts you can quickly tap into for referrals, and a well-thought-out plan, don't quit your day job. Starting up a coaching busi-ness is not something you decide in a weekend. It takes a lot of time, energy, and money. Most new coaches spend one to two years develop-ing their business before they reach consistent financial revenues.

What were some mistakes you made early on in your practice that you would advise new coaches to avoid?

In the beginning I didn't charge enough for my services. I didn't fully recognize the value my services provided to companies. Many new coaches shortchange themselves and downplay the power of their coaching by not charging enough. Also, because I was just starting out I wasn't as selective about my clients and ended up working with clients who were not a good fit for my personal style. Now that I'm established, I can afford to be more selective, but just to be on the safe side I often have prospects take an assessment to help me determine if they would be a good fit. The DiSC profile system by Target Training International is a good tool for that.

What do you believe are the future trends in coaching?

I believe coaching will be regarded as a fundamental component of per-sonal and professional development. Personal coaching will complement

(Continued)

and, perhaps, in many ways even replace some forms of therapy. It will become a norm within organizations, and in the corporate arena there will be a blended approach of coaching and consulting and facilitation.

A lot of new coaches are becoming certified. What are some critical questions they should ask when evaluating a coaching school?

- What is the primary approach the school uses—strictly telephone, some face to face, or a combination?
- What is the history of the school and its founders?
- Does the school primarily take an academic approach or an experiential one?
- Does it require a student screening process or can anyone get in? How selective is it?
- Will the training you receive help you build a successful coaching business or just to "be" a coach? Many coaching schools focus solely on coaching models, strategies, and techniques, with very little time on practice building.
- Does the school teach you how to develop a marketing and business plan?
- Does it have name recognition in the marketplace?

like *people* or *adults*, because they don't help you distinguish your target.
- *Precisely how do your company or services help your primary target audience?*   A good tag line must be clear, concise, compelling, and contagious to you and your target market.

Write down your initial ideas.

Tool 4: Business Cards (Cheapest Marketing Tool Ever Created)

Here is the major point to remember when deciding how much you are willing to spend on business cards—they are the cheapest form of marketing you will ever have! Almost every other kind of marketing material will cost you significantly more in the long run than business cards. They often make the second impression a person will have of your company (the first being made by you). As someone who handles 500 to 700 different business cards a year from various networking events, I have some relatively strong opinions about business cards. I can tell simply by touching a business card which people care about the image they present, and as a small-business owner, I am immediately unimpressed by anyone who gives me a flimsy, plain white business card—or worse, one that has perforations around the edges. It just does not leave me with a good feeling about doing work with that person or company. You say, "Stephen, that's ridiculous. After all, business cards are so trivial." That's *exactly* my point! If they are not willing to spend a little more time, attention, and money on a good business card, how would they handle my business account? I see myself as a professional and only want to work with others who see themselves as professionals. When I come across homemade business cards, two thoughts immediately cross my mind: They do not see themselves as professionals, and they need marketing help.

Here are a few other dos and don'ts:

Don't:

- Print your business cards on your home computer printer. No matter how tempting it is to try out your new inkjet or how good the picture on the box of the nonperforated business cards looks, they all have problems. Even the microperforated cards leave little bumps on the edges that you can feel, and the new laser nonperforated cards are too thin. Another problem is that ink from an inkjet smears if it gets wet.
- Get the cheapest business cards from a printer. Go for the upgraded, thicker paper.
- Use just black-and-white cards. Spend the extra money for a color card that looks sharp.
- Put your photo on them. I have met numerous powerful top executives from *Fortune* 500 companies and hundreds of small-business owners, and not a single one of them has their picture on the front of their business cards. I don't mean to offend here, but I believe this is a common mistake—it cheapens the effect of your card and makes you look like a real estate agent or a used-car dealer. Both are honorable professions, but do they really reflect the image you want to project as a professional coach? I

believe one of the reasons why people in these professions insist on having portrait photos on their business card is because they have not been able to clearly differentiate themselves from the thousands of others in each field—they have become a commodity, so they hope and pray people will at least remember what they look like. I don't believe this is the position you are trying to create for yourself.

Do:

- Have them printed on quality paper.
- Have them professionally designed and printed.
- Keep them updated if you change location, information, or web site domain name. (Sending out your updated cards also gives you a good opportunity to send them to everyone on your contact list as a way of staying in touch.)
- Put your logo and all your contact information on them.
- Be careful about using certain types of linen paper because it can obscure the print at times or even cause it to flake off.
- Hand them out everywhere you go.
- Keep a handful of your business cards everywhere: your car, suitcase, briefcase, laptop carrying case, wallet, and all your suit coat pockets.

Basic black-and-white business cards (which I do not recommend) can cost as little as $30 online (www.vistaprint.com) or as much as $300 or more for top-notch, custom-designed ones, but most will cost you $100 to $200 for 1,000 to 1,500 cards. Some printers may have a package deal if you order both business cards and letterhead at the same time, and unless you expect to change your contact information or revise your total business image in the near future, it is typically better to order more materials rather than less (within reason). It does not cost much more to get 1,500 business cards made than to get 500. The same goes for letterhead and envelopes. The biggest printing charge is the setup fee.

When designing your business cards, look at them as prime real estate—make maximum use of every part. Don't make them too busy or too drab; make them look sharp, attractive, and easy to read; and don't forget to use the back of the card. What can you put on the back of the card? You have several choices: a brief biography of yourself or your company, a description of your ideal clients, a list of services you provide, an offer for a free coaching session, a discount for services purchased, an advertisement for your new book, or my preference—a list of a couple of benefit statements, similar to your unique selling proposition (USP). Based on the pain my primary target market experiences, I have designed four specific statements that quickly describe how I help my target market:

EXPERIENCE OUR COACHING RESULTS . . .

Develop your leadership skills and performance

•

Experience remarkable growth in your business

•

Significantly increase employee motivation
and productivity

•

Achieve better results faster with fewer resources

Each one is targeted directly at the pain of my target audiences: executives, business owners, top-level managers, and professionals in leadership positions, respectively.

ACTION STEP

Based on your target markets, what are a couple of ideas you could use to maximize your business cards? Write them down for later use.

TOOL 5: COMMANDING COMPANY BROCHURES

After a good business card, a well-designed brochure is the next most important piece of marketing material you should invest in to command your prospect's attention, especially if you do not have a web site or your primary target is a business professional, a corporate executive, or a company. When you meet hot prospects at a networking event who want you to give them more information about your company and your services, you need to have something you can hand them or somewhere online you can direct them to. The most common item used is a company brochure.

Let me warn you, designing a brochure can take literally days and days of work. It can be very time and energy consuming and furiously frustrating. Unless you have a good amount of experience designing brochures, I recommend that you spend your time writing the copy and hire a professional to design it for you. Use the Internet to find a good designer who doesn't cost a lot. I have found quite a number on elance.com who will design a company brochure for less than $200.

A word of caution: Most companies waste way too much space in their brochures either listing their services or giving you a complete biography of the owner or the company. Do not make the same mistake. Do not make the brochure about you and your company. Instead, focus on talking to your target market audience and concisely answering their possible questions about who you help, how you help them, the results your clients achieve, and the problems you solve.

Your brochure should be targeted toward your primary audience and perhaps also your secondary audience, if they are similar enough. Otherwise, develop a second brochure. Here are a few guidelines to remember when writing and designing your brochure:

- Remember, people don't read brochures, they skim. Including too much text and too little white space in a brochure will quickly turn off your audience.
- Don't use paragraphs longer than four to six lines.
- Make liberal use of bullet points.
- Include a powerful testimony or two from former clients who are also a part of your target market.
- When possible, include a partial list of companies or organizations you have done work for.
- Make it absolutely clear who this brochure is for (your primary target market) and exactly how you can help them, and list as many benefits and results as you can. Don't confuse people by talking about all the different services you provide or all the different targets you market. When you meet prospects who are in your target audience, they should believe you wrote this brochure just for them. They must be able to quickly connect with what you are saying, and the brochure must convey that you know exactly what issues they are facing, and it must clearly state how you can help them.

- Minimize the amount of space you devote to listing your services. People do not care what services you offer, they care about one thing: Can you help them?
- Use a fair amount of white space. This is a marketing piece, not a technical white paper or an opportunity for you to tell people everything about you or your company.
- Remember, the primary purpose of your brochure is to give prospects just enough information to make them want to pick up the phone and call you for more.
- Think of your company brochure as a resume. The only purpose of a resume is to get an employer to pick up the phone and call you in for an interview. A resume will never get you a job. You have to ace the interview to be offered a position. The same principle applies to brochures—the best result you can ask for is to have a prospect skim your brochure and pick up the phone to ask you for more information—so make that your goal.
- The information you put in the brochure is just as important as the overall layout in helping prospects decide whether they want to know more about you.
- If you have your brochure professionally designed (which I recommend, unless you have direct experience creating multiple brochures or have a background in graphic design) be sure your designer uses a software program that you can access on your own computer and printer. Many graphic designers use very expensive software programs and Macintosh computers, but have the ability to design in simple programs like Microsoft Publisher. Here is one piece of marketing material I think you should try to print with your home computer, assuming you have a good printer. The reason is that you probably don't need to print 500 or 1,000 of these brochures at a time. All you need is 20 or so to take to a networking event, and it's much easier to print them as needed rather than have hundreds of them gathering dust and becoming outdated with every passing month.
- Before you finalize it, show the brochure to several business associates who are in your target market. A person who doesn't know anything about your business should be able to quickly figure out what you do, who you help, and what results you achieve just from scanning your brochure for less than 30 seconds. It must pass this test because 30 seconds is about as long as any prospect is going to

look at your brochure before they decide to either keep it or throw it away.

- Remember, your two goals are to build your credibility and to create a compelling reason why prospects should contact you.

ACTION STEP

Here are some questions to stimulate your thinking when writing your brochure:

- *What is the exact target you want to attract using this brochure?* For example: Small-business owners who run professional service firms.
- *What are the top four challenges this target is currently facing?* For example,

  1. They can't find enough clients.
  2. They are running low on cash flow.
  3. They are not enjoying their jobs because they are working way too many hours.
  4. They cannot seem to find and keep top talent.

- *Exactly how do you help them with each of these four challenges?* For example:

  1. I help them market their services more effectively to attract new clients.
  2. I help them increase the productivity of their employees so they can do more with less.
  3. I work with them to develop and implement strategies that allow them to work smarter and automate their business while spending fewer hours at work.
  4. I show business owners techniques that significantly improve employee morale and productivity without spending any more money.

- *What are four specific benefits of working with you and your company?* For example:

  1. Managers greatly increase their productivity.
  2. Professionals achieve work-life balance.

3. Adults can accomplish their personal and career goals five times faster.
4. Executives enhance their leadership skills.

Tool 6: Audio Logos to Attract Your Target Market

An audio logo is a simple statement that answers the question, "What do you do?" When asked this question most people state their job title ("I'm a salesperson," or "I'm the vice president of human resources"), their company name ("I work for AT&T"), or their industry ("I'm in the high-tech field"). Unfortunately, these are the least effective ways to answer that opening question. The best way to answer that question is to use an audio logo. An audio logo follows a simple formula:

"I help (*name your target audience*) to (*tell them one of the results or benefits you offer*)."

For example:

"I help small business owners to market their services more effectively."

"I coach entrepreneurs to focus their efforts and build their companies faster."

"I assist executives in reaching new levels of performance and productivity."

The reason why you work so hard in identifying your target audiences and their biggest challenges is so you can use this information to develop your marketing materials, including your audio logo. When properly designed, an audio logo will provoke your target audience to ask, "How do you do that?" This is precisely the response you desire. Develop three to four audio logos for each of your target markets, memorize them, and then test each of them out. When you visit your next networking event, ask each person you meet what they do first. Find out their industry, their position in the company, and how things are going for them. If they are in your target audience and ask you what you do, try out an appropriate audio logo and listen for their response. Try each one out three or four times until you find one that consistently gives you your desired response of "How do you do that?" or "That sounds interesting. Tell me more." If they simply respond with a casual nod or "That's nice" before going back to their drink, then either you are not talking to a person in your target market, you have focused on a pain that doesn't concern them, or your audio logo needs more refinement.

A few thoughts to remember when designing audio logos:

- They work only if you identify a specific target market. Using the words *people, adults, professionals* or another generic title will have significantly less results than using descriptive titles such as *CEOs, small-business owners, entrepreneurs,* and *managers in transition.*
- You must focus on a primary pain or pleasure you provide for that specific market. There are two theories about motivational marketing. One theory says people are more motivated by pain, so the best way to market is to focus on their pain and make them keenly aware of it. The other theory says people are more motivated by pleasure, so create a pleasurable vision for them of how you can help them. I have personally used both and have not found one to be decisively more effective than the other.
- Make the result or benefit as specific and tangible as possible. For example: "I help small-business owners increase their sales by 35 percent in six months or less" (pleasure). "I help small-business owners who are struggling to find new clients" (pain). "I coach busy professionals who are overstressed but still want to accomplish big goals" (pain mixed with pleasure).
- Have two or three separate audio logos for each of your target markets.
- Be sure to listen for your target's response. Remember when they ask, "How do you do that?" because that indicates you have developed a good audio logo.

Action Step

Write down your target market, identify one of the benefits or results you offer, then create the audio logo. Each target should have at least one or two distinct audio logos. Use the worksheet in Figure 7.1 as a model.

Target Market	Result or Benefit You Offer	Audio Logo
Entrepreneurs who are either starting up a company or currently run a small company	Focus their time and energy, find more clients, build their company faster	I coach entrepreneurs to focus their efforts and build their companies faster.

FIGURE 7.1   Audio logo development worksheet.

TOOL 7: DESCRIPTION OF SERVICES AND PROGRAMS

Prospects need to have a clear idea of what specific services you are offering along with the price for each service before they agree to purchase them. Most coaches provide a written list of three or four different coaching packages at varying prices. There are a couple of good

Charlotte Purvis
Communications Consultant and Coach
Purvis Communications, Inc.
Durham, North Carolina
charlottepurvis@mindspring.com
(919) 309-7878

Your coaching practice is a little different from the norm. Tell us about it.

I have been in business for myself for 17 years and I do communications consulting and coaching. I primarily coach people who are speaking to people they cannot see. It may be an executive doing a television interview, a business owner on the radio, or a salesperson on the telephone.

What are the top ways you are currently finding clients?

First let me say I am proud that I have not done any advertising in 17 years. My clients come from three *R*s:

- *Recruitment.* With my reputation for results, I have many people recruit me to coach them. Plus I get out into the community and let people know what I do and how I help.
- *Repeat business.* Much of my business comes from the same clients year after year. Typically, as the company grows they need the same services for more of their employees.
- *Referrals.* I get many referrals from former and current clients.

What is one piece of advice you would give to a new coach just starting out?

Pay attention to the business side of the business. Coaching is the service you provide, but the more important part is your overall business, like your taxes, finances, accounting, marketing costs, profit margins, client tracking, and record keeping. Don't be afraid to hire experts to help you out in managing your business. A great accountant, small-business lawyer, financial planner, and business coach can go a long way in helping you grow your business.

Also, track all of your business activities. Find out which ones produce results, where your revenue has come from, who has given you the most repeat business, and what kinds of clients you do your best work with.

> The person who is most likely to buy from you is one who has already bought something from you or the person who is currently buying from you.

reasons for this: First, it gives you an opportunity to upsell your prospect. The person who is most likely to buy from you is one who has already bought something from you or the person who is currently buying from you. When a prospect has made the mental decision that you are the right coach to help them and they want your services, you can often offer them a package of services for around the same price as your hourly rate, but as part of the package they agree to sign up with you for three, six, or more months instead of going on a month-to-month basis. Next, you may be able to offer them a lot of different services for a little bit more than your hourly fee, because when you sign up long-term clients you can spend more of your time servicing those clients rather than seeking more clients. Third, it should be noted that over 80 percent of coaches who make more than $75,000 per year offer prospects monthly coaching packages or project-based prices, rather than simply pricing their services per hour. One of the ways to significantly increase your annual income is to work with each client longer. Beginning coaches typically work with clients 1 to 3 months, but more experienced coaches have increased that to an average of 6 to 8 months, and one of the ways they do this is to offer 6-, 9-, and 12-month coaching packages.

For example, here is a typical list of services a personal coach would provide:

Level 1:	Four 1-hour sessions of personal coaching per month	Monthly price
Level 2:	Three 1-hour sessions of personal coaching per month	Monthly price
Level 3:	Four 30-minute sessions of personal coaching per month	Monthly price

You can find many more examples by looking at various personal coaching web sites. The idea behind this is that some people want, need, and can afford more coaching per month than others, and you want to attract the widest audience possible by offering different price points. This is an important and necessary step, but most coaches stop here, to their own detriment.

There are several other ways you can quickly enhance your coaching packages. Let me ask you a couple of questions:

- If a client called you between sessions, would you talk to them about a specific issue, assuming it didn't take more than 5 or 10 minutes?
- Do you offer clients a satisfaction guarantee?
- Do you answer e-mails that clients send you?
- Do you ever meet your clients face to face, or do you just coach them over the phone?
- If a client wanted to sign up for 3, 6, 9, or 12 months of coaching, would you give them a discount, throw in a couple of extra coaching sessions, or give them access to an assessment tool for low or no cost?
- Are your sessions customized to meet your client's needs (versus being standardized regardless of the client or their situation)?
- If a client wanted two 1-hour sessions instead of four 30-minute sessions, would you accommodate them?
- Do you have any kind of self-assessment tool you can offer to clients for no charge? This could be a life balance wheel, a coaching readiness questionnaire, or a career transition checklist.
- If you service more than one primary target market, do you give each of them unique coaching based on their needs, challenges, and primary issues (versus giving all of your targets the exact same coaching services)?

If you answered "Yes" to any of these questions, and you are not actively advertising these facts to your prospects, then you are missing opportunities. Assuming you responded "Yes" to all of these questions, here are a few specific ways you could spice up a list of your services:

EXAMPLE OF MONTHLY COACHING PACKAGES

Level 1: Four 1-hour sessions of personal coaching per month
Monthly price

- **Four 1-hour personal coaching sessions**
- Designed for serious professionals who want to achieve significant goals in a short period of time
- Coach-on-call between sessions
- Unlimited e-mail and fax support between sessions
- Unlimited brief phone calls between sessions

Level 2: Three 1-hour sessions of personal coaching per month
Monthly price

- **Three 1-hour personal coaching sessions**
- Designed for professionals who want to achieve success in multiple areas
- Unlimited e-mail and fax support
- Periodic brief phone calls between sessions

Level 3: Four 30-minute sessions of personal coaching per month
Monthly price

- **Four 30-minute personal coaching sessions**
- For professionals who value continuous development, are in a career transition, or have specific areas in their personal or professional life they desire coaching on
- E-mail and fax support as needed

All of our coaching services come with these additional benefits:

- All of our services include a **100% satisfaction guarantee.** If you are not completely satisfied after the first month of coaching, we will refund all of your money. No questions asked.
- Our sessions are **completely customized** to meet your current needs and goals.

Package Feature	Level 3	Level 2	Level 1
Amount of monthly coaching sessions	Two 1-hour sessions	Three 1-hour sessions	Four 1-hour sessions
For professionals in a career transition	X	X	X
100% satisfaction guarantee	X	X	X
All sessions completely customized to meet your needs and goals	X	X	X
Led by an experienced professional coach	X	X	X
Sessions can be combined	X	X	X
E-mail and fax support as needed	X	X	X
Periodic brief phone calls between sessions		X	X
Unlimited e-mail support between sessions		X	X
Designed to achieve significant goals in a short period of time		X	X
Includes a comprehensive personal assessment			X
Includes an additional 2-hour planning session			X
Unlimited brief phone calls between sessions			X
Unlimited fax support between sessions			X
Available in a 6-month program for a discount			X
Investment per month			

FIGURE 7.2   Graphic presentation of monthly coaching packages.

- Your coach has years of experience helping professionals **achieve maximum results.**
- Our sessions will help you rapidly take your professional and personal life to the next level.
- For local clients, your sessions can be held either in person or over the phone.
- Your sessions can be combined as needed (e.g., two 1-hour sessions instead of four 30-minute sessions).
- Ask about our 6- and 9-month programs for a discount.

You can also demonstrate your different packages visually, as shown in Figure 7.2.

Here is an example of a three month coaching program for professionals in a career transition.

THE PROFESSIONAL TRANSITION PROGRAM

What is the Professional Transition Program?

The Professional Transition Program is a highly-focused, all-inclusive, three-month program specifically intended to help motivated professionals quickly take their career to the next level using personal coaching, a comprehensive assessment, and self-directed learning.

Who is this program for?

As a highly trained professional, you have attained a good deal of professional success, but you realize you want something more. Your career choices are more critical now. You don't have time to make a major career mistake. You want to invest yourself in a career that you enjoy—one that brings a high degree of satisfaction and enjoyment. Your life is too important.

It is for people just like you that we have created the Professional Transition Program. It is specifically designed for professionals who:

- Make at least $80,000 a year
- Are currently in a career transition

- Want to focus exclusively on taking their career to the next level or desire to move out of a particular job or career path

How does the Professional Transition Program work?

Over the next three months, your personal coach will help you move through the following three stages:

Stage 1: Assessment and Goal Setting.   You will focus on active goal setting and developing a comprehensive career plan to efficiently reach your professional goals.

Stage 2: Career Development and Professional Planning.   You will discover your strength and growth areas, identify career characteristics that best fit your personality, and identify what you truly want out of your life.

Stage 3: Success, Significance, and Life Direction.   This advanced stage will help you determine how you can move from a career of success to one of significance.

What is so unique about the Professional Transition Program?

- It is offered only by our coaching company.
- Everything is completely customized, highly personal, and developed specifically to meet your needs.
- Our program focuses only on successful professionals like you.
- We offer a one-of-a-kind comprehensive personal, professional, and managerial assessment package.
- Everything is included in one low cost: executive coaching, comprehensive assessment, strategic career planning, skill development, goal implementation, between-session phone calls, e-mail contact, and business contacts.
- You work one-on-one with a highly trained Personal Coach several hours every month who has specialized training and is completely committed to helping you achieve your goals.
- We offer a 100% satisfaction guarantee on all of our services.

What does the Professional Transition Program cost?

The cost for the entire Professional Transition Program is ____.

How do I sign up?

Call us at (630) 588-0500 or e-mail us and ask about the Professional Transition Program.

The keys to developing compelling services are:

- Be crystal clear about the distinctions between your services
- Try to package your services into bundles (include more than one kind of service, such as assessment and coaching or training with follow-up coaching).
- Give prospects several reasons to upgrade to the next level of service.
- Give prospects a discount for signing up with you longer. You can afford to do this because it costs you eight times more to acquire a new client than to service an existing one.

There are many, many other ways to package your coaching services. Try to be creative and innovative when designing programs that fit your target markets. You can use these programs and packages to increase the amount of time you work with each client, to attract clients who are looking for an all-in-one package, or to find clients who want to focus on one specialty area that you coach around.

ACTION STEP

Based on this section, what are three specific ways you are going to improve or change your current offerings to prospects? When will you accomplish each one?

SUMMARY

In this chapter we have spotlighted the top six ways to give tangibility to your company and the coaching services you offer: your company name, a corporate identity package, a dynamic company tag line, business cards, a company brochure, audio logos, and a description of your services and programs. Here are some other common marketing materials coaches use to attract prospects and land clients:

- Printed or electronic newsletters (commonly known as *e-zines*)
- Postcards introducing your company, your services, your web site, or your new book
- Information sheets providing an overview of your company, the coaching industry, or other topics important to your target markets
- Brief biographical information on your company and leadership team
- Case studies based on your work with previous clients, identifying common challenges you work with (e.g., developing a leadership program in a midsized manufacturing company or helping a professional regain a balanced life and launch a new career)
- White papers that give helpful information on topics of interest to your target market
- CDs providing a number of your marketing materials or a PowerPoint presentation
- Published articles, media interviews, or reviews of a book you have written
- A sheet with a list of clients or testimonials about your services

You don't need to include all of these in your marketing materials—a mix of two to four, in addition to the top six tools, is a very good start. Carefully select an assortment of marketing materials that gives you a range of things you can send interested prospects, materials that show different sides of your company. Try to select items that follow a natural progression, so that as you make more contacts with a prospect, your marketing materials provide an increasing level of detail about how you can help them and the results they can achieve.

Always remember: The marketing materials you use will, to a great extent, directly affect the types of prospects you attract—so make sure your prospects are attracted to your materials before you finalize them. There is no need to spend several thousand dollars on any of these tools—you can do many of them yourself, if you have the time and patience, or you can find someone to help through the Internet. It is important to make them look professional and attractive, because they are the next closest thing to your personal presence for showing your prospects who you help, how you help them, and what results they can achieve.

ANSWERS TO THE COMPANY TAG LINES

Avis	We try harder.
Hertz	We're #1.
Nike	Just do it.
Allstate	You're in good hands with ____.
Memorex	Is it live or is it ____?
Xerox	The document company.
FedEx	When you absolutely, positively need it there on time.
Fox News	Real journalism. Fair and balanced.
MSNBC	America's News channel.
Sure antiperspirant	Never let them see you sweat.
Secret antiperspirant	Strong enough for a man, but made for a woman.
Today's Leadership Coaching	Developing leaders who deliver results. (We're still working on our branding program.)

Relationships and Referrals: Networking, Strategic Referral Partners, and Centers of Influence

This is a very important chapter, and I firmly believe that your application of this information has the potential to make or break your coaching business. Now that I have your attention, here is what we are going to talk about over the next few pages:

- The top two ways to find new clients
- How to identify strategic referral partners
- Eight great questions to guide your conversations with referral partners
- The top three ways to categorize potential partners
- More than 30 places to find your next partner
- A simple test to help you discover the best partners and
- How to leverage your most valuable asset

Let's get going.

THE POTENTIAL OF STRATEGIC REFERRAL PARTNERS

The number-one way every professional service business finds new clients is from previous or existing clients. The second best way is through a network of strategic referral partners (SRPs). In my survey, more than 60 percent of all top coaches rated these methods as the best two ways to find new clients. When just starting out, it is virtually impossible to build a sustainable business just from current and former clients because you may have neither, so the next best way is to rapidly develop strong, consistent relationships with numerous strategic partners. An SRP is a person who meets the following criteria:

- Is in a position of influence or power as part of their profession, education, or standing in your community
- Is in regular contact with your target audience
- Is open to the idea of coaching and understands how it works
- Is comfortable with you, your interpersonal style, and the quality of your work
- Is someone with whom you either already have a great and trusting relationship or can quickly develop one (it's usually too late to develop a trusting relationship when you're desperate)

- Is willing to openly agree to refer people to you when appropriate
- Is someone you feel comfortable with and are willing to openly agree to refer people to when appropriate

When looking for SRPs, you want to follow the same three criteria as prospects do when they look for a coach. They must know who you are, like you personally, and be able to develop a relationship of trust with you — know, like, and trust.

EIGHT POWERFUL QUESTIONS TO GUIDE YOUR CONVERSATION

During your meetings with SRPs, be mentally clear about your goals:

- You are not there to sell them anything, nor are you there to land them as a client.
- Aim to spend about 80 to 90 percent of the time learning more about them, their business, and how you can help them succeed.
- Inform them a little about your coaching business.
- Give them a picture of who your ideal target market is.
- Mention a brief illustration of how you help people, focusing on the results your clients achieve.
- Offer to coach them or their staff members two hours a month for free.
- If the situation arises naturally, ask them if they would have any reservations about referring people in your target market to you when appropriate.
- Carefully question them to see what their concerns or reservations are.
- Ensure them of your professionalism and the quality of your services (including your guarantee, if you offer one).

Let's expand a little on these points. When meeting with someone who may become an SRP, never make the mistake of trying to sell them anything. If you do, that relationship is probably lost forever. They will believe you misled them, and that's no way to develop trust. You also don't want to make the mistake of spending most of your time talking about yourself. You are there to learn about them, their business, and how you can be a part of their success. Here are eight great questions to ask them:

1. How did you first get started in your business?
2. What are some of your greatest challenges?
3. What do you believe sets you apart from your competitors?
4. What do you like best about what you do?
5. How has your industry changed over the past several years?
6. How do you find new clients or customers?
7. Has your business grown a lot in the past year?
8. How can I know if someone I'm talking to is a good prospect for you? (This is the question, Bob Burg asserts in *Endless Referrals* (McGraw-Hill, 1998), that separates the professional networkers from the amateurs.)

The appropriate time to start talking about your business is when the potential SRP starts asking questions about your business, not before. Often the last question will lead naturally in that direction, because most people will want to reciprocate your attitude of giving. Briefly tell them about what you do, using your audio logo, and give them a short illustration of how you helped a recent client (preferably a client with some similarities to the SRP's clients). You should specifically ask them for referrals only if and when you feel you have won them over (they both understand what you do and believe you can do it) and they ask you question 6 or something similar to it that lets you know they are open to referring people to you. Trying to tell potential SRPs how to refer a person to you before they are ready is unprofessional and a waste of your time. When describing your ideal referral try to give them a picture of that person. A response to a financial planner might be:

A good person to refer to me is someone who is financially secure and well on their way to achieving their financial goals, but unsatisfied with how fast they are reaching their personal or career goals. They might mention an obstacle that is keeping them from creating the life or business they really desire.

The key is that you want the potential SRP to walk away from your conversation with the feeling that you are a giving person and want to be of service to them, not that you are only interested in promoting yourself. You want them to see you as their strategic referral partner.

When an influential person refers one of their clients to you, recognize that they are putting their reputation on the line. If you mess up and fail to treat that referral in the best possible way—or worse, act in an unprofessional or unethical manner—you will never get another referral from that person. Plus, they may tell their other influential friends about the poor service their referral received from you and discourage them from sending additional referrals your way. As a professional coach, your reputation in the community is the most precious thing you have, so guard it with your life.

> *A good reputation is more desirable than great riches.*
>
> —Proverbs 22:1

SOURCES OF STRATEGIC REFERRAL PARTNERS

There are several practical ways you can categorize strategic partners: by industry, by "hunger quotient," and by membership in the elite ranks of those people known as centers of influence (COIs). The key is to think broadly and cast a wide net at first because you never really know where a great strategic partner can come from. After you explore as many different areas as is feasible, your experience will help you determine where to keep looking. Let's take a quick look at each category.

IDENTIFYING STRATEGIC REFERRAL PARTNERS BY INDUSTRY

When trying to build relationships with potential partners in different industries, look for industries that are built on trust. In other words, ask yourself: Which industries must build trust with prospects and clients in order to work? Think about your money; would you do business with a banker you did not trust? What about drawing up legal documents; would you use a lawyer who seemed a bit shady? How about your taxes; would you go back to an accountant who botched last year's taxes? What about investments; would you let an inexperienced financial planner handle your retirement stock portfolio? All of these situations have

Steve Lishansky
President
Success Dynamics
West Concord, Massachusetts
www.successdynamics.com
SteveL@SuccessDynamics.com
(978) 369-4525

Steve Lishansky is the president of Success Dynamics, an executive coaching and leadership development firm.

Tell us how you first started in coaching.

For years I thought about going into coaching, so in 1992, I set up Success Dynamics as an executive coaching firm. At that time, "executive coaching" was just a good title, but no one really knew what it meant. For the next few years, I did a lot of speaking, training, and consulting. Today, Success Dynamics is a leadership transformation company and coaching is just the process we use.

You find a lot of your clients from speaking and writing, but some coaches have tried speaking and not found it to be effective. Any tips?

Both speaking and writing are great ways to gain new clients, but if you're not getting results from speaking there are only two reasons:

- *You're not a good speaker.* The solution is to get some presentation training.
- *Your message isn't clear.* The biggest mistake I see coaches making is trying to sell people on coaching. Don't talk about coaching, talk about results your clients achieve, the value you provide, and the benefits of working with you.

Your coaching practice is very successful. What do you consider your secrets to success?

I teach three rules to success in coaching:

- You never sell coaching; you sell results, benefits, and value.
- You want to be absolutely crystal clear about the client's objectives and the measurements for success.
- You never discuss pricing until you have clearly established what the value is to that client and their organization.

Any tips for marketing a coaching business?

I believe there is a big difference between having a job and running a business. Coaching is a good thing, but if you're not coaching, you're not making money. That's why I added affiliates—to handle the overflow and build a business. When I landed my first big corporate coaching gig I instantly had 60 clients. That was more than I wanted to do or could do.

There are two critical factors in marketing a coaching business:

- *You must be confident in yourself in order to sell your value proposition.* This is the biggest issue new coaches face. Alan Weiss says, "Your first sale is to yourself." You must believe in what you offer and in your ability to help other people.
- *You must make your marketing message simple enough that others can easily carry it for you.* Your value proposition must be so clear that other people can easily say what you do and why someone should hire you. This is how you get referrals.

Remember to never sell your process, coaching, sell your results. If you're selling coaching you're selling a tool, and tools don't sell. Say, for example, you're looking to put an addition onto your house and you call up a carpenter to give you a bid. He comes in and says, "Let me show you all the tools I'm going to use to do this job." Then he starts pulling them out of his bag and explaining what each one does. What would you do with that person? You would probably throw them out. You want a carpenter that comes in and asks the right questions and helps you develop a vision for what your new addition will look like, how it will feel, and the value it will give you. You could care less about the tools he's going to use to do the job. When you're in front of a prospect, talk about the results you deliver. The tool you use is coaching.

(Continued)

You've been coaching a long time, but what were two mistakes you made early on in your practice that beginning coaches should avoid?

My first mistake was not getting referrals and collecting testimonials from clients. The second mistake was forgetting about marketing when the times were good. Consider marketing to be part of your day-to-day, month-to-month activities. If you aren't marketing, you aren't running a business. If you're not running a business, you're doing volunteer work. Even today I try to spend a minimum of 15 percent of my time in marketing activities like speaking, writing, networking, direct-mail efforts, and having conversations for new business.

What do you believe are the future trends in coaching?

In the future, I don't believe it will be called coaching at the top levels. Coaching will never disappear because it has been around forever, whether you call it mentoring or consulting. Coaching is hot right now because people are being told that it is *the* solution to their problems. Coaching is not a silver bullet. It is simply one of the best ways to help people.

two things in common: They are services performed by professionals, and every single relationship is built on a foundation of trust. In addition to your banker, lawyer, accountant, and financial planner, who do you know in other professions where the foundation of the relationship with clients is trust?

Here are just a few common fields and industries that I believe are primarily built on trust:

Primarily for Business Coaches

Community leaders

Meeting planners

Community career center managers

Executive, management, and technical recruiters

Psychologists who do consulting work

Organizational development consultants who don't do one-on-one coaching

HR consultants

Other coaches who have full practices

Bankers, lawyers, and doctors

Accountants and CPAs

Financial advisors

Investment bankers and stock brokers

Business brokers

Association presidents

Training firm managers

The Executive Committee (TEC) chairs

Church leaders and elders

Board members of nonprofit organizations

Professors at graduate schools of business, psychology, or counseling

Mortgage brokers

Insurance agents

Commercial real estate agents

Venture capitalists and angel investors

Primarily for Personal Coaches

Community leaders

Personal trainers

Chiropractors

Nutritionists and health food center managers

Therapists of all types

Members of the healing professions

Fitness center managers

Recruiting and job placement agency managers

Mental health therapists

Counseling center managers

Doctors and psychologists with large practices

Dieticians

Community career center managers

Other coaches who have full practices

Association presidents

Training firm managers

Church leaders and elders

Spiritual counselors

Financial advisors

Real estate agents

For each category where you do not personally know at least two or three people, your action step is to do some research until you gather some names. Then set up a meeting with each of them for the purpose of starting a business relationship (do not try to sell them your coaching services or they will see you as a salesperson instead of a potential strategic partner). You can start by making a list of all the influential people in your city and community. Perhaps you have met them at a party or a networking event, read about them in a local newspaper, or heard about them through a personal contact. Write their names down in your notebook.

ACTION STEP

Copy the appropriate list of professionals and place a mark next to each example where you personally know at least two or three people in that particular group. List each of their names, contact information, industry, and priority rank, using the worksheet in Figure 8.1 as a model.

After you have listed all their contact information, your next step is to gather the information you want to share with them. Some basic marketing materials would be helpful, such as a few business cards, a brochure, a brief biography, a list of your services, a short description of your target market, and a partial client list with testimonials. You should create a packet of information that you can give to each contact when you meet, which is the next step.

Start by calling the potential strategic partners you already have a relationship with. Try to set up at least two to four meetings per month (double that if you have time) with people in various categories until you have met with all of them. Write your target date for contacting each one in the Contact date column.

Priority Rank	Group or Industry	Name (2–3 per group or industry)	Phone, E-mail Contact Info	Contact Date

FIGURE 8.1 Worksheet for identifying potential SRPs.

IDENTIFYING STRATEGIC REFERRAL PARTNERS
BY HUNGER QUOTIENT

A few years ago I learned the hard way that the best referral partners can be measured by their "hunger quotient"—how hungry they are for new business. I held an all-day seminar for small-business owners, titled "How to Market Your Small Business Like a Pro," which was cospon-

sored by two financial advisors from American Express, an older partner with an established practice and a younger apprentice. The plan was
to have the advisors spend about 90 minutes explaining a few key ways
that small-business owners could save on their taxes by using various
financial strategies (such as a company savings plan, etc.). They weren't
two minutes into their time when I knew they hadn't prepared at all for
the presentation and were flying by the seat of their pants, so to speak.
Even though we had clearly set out the expectation ahead of time that
each of us would provide solid content, rather than just give a sales
speech, they were using this as simply another opportunity to pass out
their glossy brochures and fancy folders. Near the beginning of their
presentation, a small-business owner asked the older financial advisor
how he found new clients. His verbatim response was, "I don't accept
new clients. In fact, I don't even accept referrals from my existing clients
because most of them are just a waste of my time." By the time I picked
up my jaw from the floor, I knew it was going to be a long 90 minutes. I
had made the mistake of choosing to partner and cosponsor my seminar
with someone who didn't need, or even want, any new clients. From
then on I made it a point to partner only with people who needed and
wanted new clients. Figure 8.2 shows a little five-point scale I now use
to quickly gauge whether a particular person would be a good SRP:

Desperation.   Their need for new clients is just too obvious. They
come across with a hard-sell attitude or a quiet desperation, and as
soon as they discover you aren't going to buy from them they walk
away. There is no indication of reciprocation. A person in this category is *not* a good SRP.

Distress.   Their client base has been in decline and disarray for some
time, and they need to turn it around fast or else they will be in real
trouble. They may disclose their distress to you if they feel that they
can trust you or believe you might be able to help them. They may or
may not be a good SRP. It depends on how hard they are willing to
work or if they are biding their time until something better comes
along, such as a new job offer, retirement, or a buyout offer.

Deliberateness.   They have a solid and growing client base. They
actively seek out new clients, are open to new ideas and opportunities, and have a high rate of referrals. A person in this category is the
best person to have as an SRP.

226

1	2	3	4	5
Desperation	Distress	Deliberateness	Denial	Disinterest

FIGURE 8.2   Scale for gauging potential SRPs.

Denial.   They also have a strong client base, but it has tapered off over time and is focused on a few long-term clients who trust their advice implicitly. They are not actively seeking new clients and may only accept direct referrals. A person in this category is a good SRP to know because of their solid relationships with their existing clients. However, you may have to work harder to break into the inner circle of power because there is really nothing you have to offer them that they really need. They already have all the business they can handle, so they don't want your referrals, and they are in denial that they could ever need new clients. These are the people who are usually caught completely off guard if one of their clients leaves them. They then enter a short period of crisis in which they look for a new client to fill that need (because all of their clients are major clients). That is the only time when they are truly open to your referrals and may feel indebted to you if you lead them to a new client.

Disinterest.   These professionals have long established their client base. They have not had any new clients for years and work only on cases where the profit margin is extremely high. They actively turn away new clients and intentionally do not ask for referrals. A person in this category is typically not a good SRP. However, you may come across an individual in your field who is in this situation and would welcome the opportunity to pass off the referrals who come to them to someone else, but they must be absolutely convinced that your work is just as good as theirs (which is a hard thing to do).

Here are some other key indicators I use when looking for strategic referral partners:

- They have a good client base, but are actively seeking new clients.
- They spend time on marketing.
- They spend money on marketing activities.

- They are associated with a big-name firm with a good reputation.
- They have access to a key client list.
- They belong to an elite networking group.
- They keep being mentioned in conversations as knowing everybody.
- They turn up at more than two or three of the networking events I attend.
- They own their own firm or are a primary decision maker at their company.
- They do not primarily compete with my business.
- They are actively involved in their community or the business world.
- They have recently obtained some positive publicity for themselves or their company.

IDENTIFYING STRATEGIC REFERRAL PARTNERS WHO ARE CENTERS OF INFLUENCE

People who are centers of Influence (COIs) are the natural networkers of the world. These are the people who know everyone who is anyone. If the average person has a personal network of about 250 people, COIs have personal networks of three to six times that number. COIs don't network just to network; they have a purpose, a goal in their networking, and they network because they love to meet and connect people. They also clearly recognize the unwritten rule that building a deep, broad, and powerful network will pay rich dividends in the long run. You can't build authentic relationships with COIs when you're desperate for business. You must develop them before the need arises. Look for COIs outside of your industry. Here are some of the ways you can find COIs:

- You can meet them in elite networking groups.
- You can meet them when they speak at business conferences and seminars.
- You can find them in community leadership positions.
- You can contact them through recommendations from other COIs.
- You can read about them in trade magazines and business journals.
- You can find them through a published top-10 list or "Who's Who" list.

- You can contact them through venture capital firms.
- You can meet them through well-connected lawyers, business brokers, investment bankers, and stock brokers.
- You might meet them in the first-class section of an airplane.
- You can sometimes contact them through well-placed journalists and reporters.
- You can find them as members of prestigious clubs and organizations.
- You can find them on the board of a local nonprofit or for-profit company.

> SRPs can become a powerful weapon in your arsenal. Successful coaches always look for strategies that give them not only an edge, but also complete dominance over their competitors. One way to do that is through building strong relationships with multiple SRPs.

Everyone knows someone in their industry, but a strong network must be as broad as it is deep. Develop relationships with COIs in many different industries and fields, and don't limit your thinking. Remember, meeting people who are true centers of influence does not happen by accident. You must know who they are and then develop a plan to get to know them. When you meet these people, always walk away from every meeting with a reason to get in contact with them again. Follow up with them promptly and contact them on a regular basis via e-mail or voice-mail.

LEVERAGING YOUR MOST VALUABLE ASSET — YOUR TIME

When it comes to building relationships with SRPs, you are not only looking to receive referrals from them directly, but also to network your way into meeting some of their personal contacts. It has been a theme throughout this book that every person has a limited amount of time, energy, and resources. The major point you need to remember when identifying and setting up meetings with SRPs is that these relationships are among the most effective ways to leverage your most valuable

Rey Carr, PhD, Level III Peer Coach
Founder and President
Peer Resources Network
Victoria, British Columbia
www.peer.ca/peer.html
rcarr@peer.ca
(250) 595-3053

Rey Carr is the founder and president of Peer Resources, an international, nonprofit corporation focusing on providing training, resources and support information for new and experienced coaches on the subjects of peer coaching, coach training, and mentoring.

How did you first get started in coaching and mentoring?

I began to recognize that a lot of my friends often talked to me about their concerns, goals, and dreams. If I thought their situation warranted it, I would sometimes suggest they consider talking to a professional counselor. However, they usually rejected this idea outright or could not see the value because a counselor only "deals with problems." I started to understand that while a person can be troubled by not being able to realize their dreams, he or she doesn't typically see it as a "problem" in need of therapy. I decided to put the natural, friendship-based skills into practice and called it "peer coaching."

Tell us about your current practice.

The majority of my current work is educating people about the benefits of coaching, assisting them in finding a personal coach, and helping other coaches develop professionally. All my clients are people interested in doing their best and establishing best practices. The majority of my practice is through the Internet and via a toll-free telephone number. I occasionally provide in-person training workshops to help people discover how to put peer coaching into practice, and I offer a coaching service that specializes in helping people design, carry out and complete projects such as workplace activities, student theses or dissertations, or research projects.

What do you consider as one of your big secrets to success?

I believe one of the secrets to the success of the Peer Resources Network is our unique ability of taking a cooperative and inclusive approach to coaching. We are the only organization I am aware of that recognizes and advocates for *all* reputable coaching services and organizations. When a person contacts our organization we believe it is our responsibility to educate them about coaching and then help them make a decision about what kind of resource would be most useful for them personally. We open up the door to various opportunities for them.

The majority of our clients come through our internet web site: www.peer.ca/peer.html. We have designed the web site to function as a resource where we provide impartial, comprehensive reviews of what is available in coaching, including web sites, coach training schools, books, specific coaching opportunities, and much more. Most other major web sites only include information about themselves. We decided to take an all-inclusive approach. For example, on our web site we provide users with brief reviews of over 124 different coach training schools, not just the ones approved by our organization.

What were two mistakes you made early on in your practice that beginning coaches should avoid?

The first mistake I made was implementing major business decisions without talking it over with a trusted friend or associate. Not discussing it first with an objective party often resulted in a waste of my time and money. I believe this is an inherent danger in the coaching business. Most coaches work independently (as sole proprietors or solo entrepreneurs) and often treasure this independence, but the potential downside is impulsivity without adequate reflection. Coaching is both a business and a personal helping intervention. And while the two share some common factors, coaching interventions often benefit from spontaneity, but business decisions usually suffer from the same characteristic.

A second mistake was not seeking my own voice. While it is natural for beginning coaches to want to emulate their mentors or trainers, act as advocates for certain training principles, or act as disciples of a particular school of thought, the sooner coaches truly find their own center—their own voice—the more meaning and satisfaction they will find.

(Continued)

What do you believe coaching will look like in three to five years?

I believe more and more people will start using coaching in their work life, school life, and personal life. However, the trend will be "free" coaching; that is, as coaching becomes more well-known, coaching principles will become integrated into everyday practice. Managers, supervisors, and leaders will learn to use coaching as part of their everyday communication style. The professionalization of coaching will slow, with fewer people seeking certification. Coaches will increase the number of free clients they coach.

Peer Resources probably has the most comprehensive listing of coach training schools of any site on the Internet. Based on your experience, what are some critical questions coaches need to ask when evaluating coaching schools and making a decision of which one to attend?

If I were a coach looking for a coach training school or certification program, here are the top questions I would consider when making my decision:

- What are my personal coach training needs, wants, and preferences?
- What kind of training did other coaches go through who are doing the same kind of work I want to do in the future?
- How long has the school been in business and how financially stable is it?
- What are the qualifications and experience of the school's leaders and instructors?
- What do current participants and graduates believe are the positives and negatives of the school?
- How does the school track the progress of its graduates, and how does it ask for feedback from graduates about how the school impacted their work life?
- What percentage of recent graduates are actually working as successful coaches?
- Does the school have other information, such as a newsletter or free teleclass, it can give me to help me experience how it operates and the quality of its programs?

- What is the school's policy for returns or refunds of tuition (including reimbursement to me should the school cease operations)?
- How connected is the school to the professional coaching community?
- What is the school's system for resolving disputes, including a difference of viewpoint regarding the degree to which your previous experience counts toward completion requirements?
- Do other coaching schools have a reciprocal arrangement with the school for transfer of credit for courses and activities?

asset—your time. With the right connections and a clear picture of how they can best help you, SRPs can become a powerful weapon in your arsenal. Successful coaches always look for strategies that give them not only an edge but complete dominance over their competitors, and using strategic partners is one of the best.

SUMMARY

In this chapter we have focused on building relationships with strategic referral partners as a critical method of developing your business. More than 60 percent of top coaches report that developing these relationships is one of the top ways they consistently find new clients. Building strong, consistent relationships with SRPs allows you to leverage your time, but in order for this method to yield results, you must have SRPs who are in the right industries (ones built on trust), have a desire and a need for more clients, and are natural networkers. Make a commitment today to start reaching out to these people. Try to meet with at least two to four potential SRPs every month, and I guarantee you will see big results.

CHAPTER 9

15 Key Strategies for Finding Your First 10 Clients

The most difficult time for most new coaches is right after they have made the official decision to become a professional coach. They have talked about this new venture in an excited, enthusiastic manner to everyone they know, and probably have read several books on the subject, participated in a number of teleclasses, and searched the Internet for hours on end looking for ideas, answers, and examples of what other people are doing. Perhaps you can relate?

At some point after a new coach makes the decision to go into business, someone always inadvertently inquires as to how many clients they currently have. After stating that they have just started their practice, the question comes back to haunt them: "How do I find clients?" In my survey of over 300 coaches nationwide, 65 percent of first-year coaches have fewer than 10 paying clients! This chapter is designed to reveal the key strategies that first- and second-year coaches can use to quickly find their first 10 paying clients. In this chapter we will do the following:

- Discuss the top 15 specific strategies and techniques successful coaches use to find their first clients
- Help you think through the challenges and avoid the pitfalls new coaches face when deciding where to spend their time, energy, and resources in searching for new clients
- Identify which techniques you want to build into your marketing plan
- Create a detailed action plan using three of these strategies

As you study each strategy and technique, place a mark beside the ones that you find most attractive and feel the most open to experimenting with. This will help you with creating the action plan at the end of the chapter. Let's move right into the strategies.

STRATEGY 1: DEVELOP A MARKETING PLAN AND FOLLOW THE PLAN

As part of your marketing plan (you remember, the plan you meant to write last week but never got around to it), you should clearly outline the following points:

- Who you want and need to talk to
- A list of 100 people you can tell about your coaching services
- A comprehensive list of networking events you want to go to
- What coach training you want to take
- How many phone calls you want to make every week
- How many e-mails and letters you want to send out about your business
- How many face-to-face meetings you want to have to talk to people about how coaching can help them
- How many free coaching sessions you want to give away every month

The easy part is developing the plan. The tough part is sticking to it!

STRATEGY 2: WORK WITH 10 CLIENTS FOR FREE

Ask your friends, colleagues, business associates, or neighbors if they will let you practice coaching them for two to three months. This is a useful technique that has several benefits:

- It gives you real-life experience practicing your coaching skills.
- It helps you discover whether you really like coaching as much as you thought you would.
- It allows you to tell real prospects that you have had experience coaching people.
- Hopefully, at least a couple of the people you coach for free are in your target market. Thus, it gives you specific knowledge about how to best approach and help prospects in your target market.
- It gives you the chance to ask for testimonials that you can use in your marketing materials, if you do a good job coaching them and they receive benefit from it.
- Coaching them over a longer period of time (two to three months) rather than for just a couple of free sessions gets you through the introductory stage into the working stage where your client can experience real benefits from your coaching, and it gets you past the stage of feeling uncomfortable when you don't know what to say next.
- It gives you the chance to ask them for referrals.

Strategy 3: Give a Free Coaching Session to Prospects

Coaching works wonders for some people and not for others. There are many variables in this equation, including your personality, your prospect's personality, your respective styles of communication, the type of problem or challenge, your coaching style, your ability to relate to the client, and so on. Prospects are taking a risk when signing up for your coaching. You need to do everything you can to reduce or eliminate potential risks. One way to do this is to offer them a free, no-obligation coaching session.

There are two models coaches use with this technique. The first one is to use the free session to sell prospects on coaching. The coach explains who they are, their values, what coaching looks like, the benefits of coaching, and who should have a coach. The second model is to conduct an actual coaching session. I follow the second model because I believe that your best chance of converting a prospect into a paying client is when you are meeting with them face to face and giving them a free coaching session, which is why I always try to hold the initial free coaching session in person. I have found spending this valuable time talking about yourself or explaining about coaching to be much less effective than the second model.

For the free coaching session I recommend a four-stage model:

Stage 1: Collect critical information.   Take 5 to 10 minutes to find out information about your prospect: what they do for work, their background, what intrigues them about coaching, what some of their current challenges are, what they expect out of the coaching session, and what one specific issue they would like to focus on during this time. Some coaches have found an intake from to be helpful in clarifying the goals of coaching and providing a quick overview of the prospect.

Stage 2: Coach them.   You will have much better success in landing your prospect as a client if you work hard to identify a specific issue or challenge they are facing and, with their permission, coach them around that area. Here is where your coaching skills come directly into play. Use them in the most effective way you know how.

Stage 3: Commit them to action.   Your goal by the end of the free coaching session (usually 30 minutes to 1 hour) is to have a few tangible action steps your prospect can take away as a direct result of your coaching. The more specific you can make the benefits they receive from your coaching, the higher your conversion ratio will be. End the session with specific action steps and a concrete follow-up plan.

Stage 4: Close the deal. Leave 5 to 10 minutes at the end to talk about the process of coaching, your monthly fees, and your strong belief that coaching can make a real difference in their situation. Make sure to have your fees in written form so you can give your prospect something to look at while you're explaining how it works. A tip to remember: When talking about your fees, look your prospect right in the eye. If you look at the floor or at a piece of paper when telling them the price for your services, the unconscious result is that they don't believe you're worth that amount. Body language is very important during a sales meeting—and make no mistake, a free coaching session is a sales meeting. Your goal is to land the prospect as a paying client. At the end, directly and unashamedly ask for their business. I have converted a significant number of people who were on the fence just because I asked for their business. I ask for their business even when I don't believe they want the coaching, because I have misread people's body language before.

Here are the five questions, in order, that I use at the end of the free session to close the deal:

1. Did you find our coaching useful in working through that challenge?
2. Do you believe it would be helpful to you in the future?
3. Would you like to continue this relationship?
4. Which coaching package would you be interested in the most?
5. When would you like to start?

Please do not misunderstand, I do not believe in a hard sell, where you try to force the prospect to sign up even when they express no interest. I have never seen it work for coaching (or anything else for that matter). I do not believe in coercing people or manipulating them into making a decision they don't want. They will only cancel it the next day. I only work with clients who strongly believe they are receiving value from my coaching. As a rule of thumb, unless you have direct experience as a sales professional, a good goal for the first 30 or 40 free sessions you do would be to convert 20 to 30 percent of your prospects. Once you feel more comfortable with the process and have done a few dozen, that percentage should double. An experienced coach who gives free introductory coaching sessions with qualified prospects will convert 50 to 75 percent into paying clients. Part of that process is discovering how to quickly distinguish people who are serious from those who are not and offering the free coaching session only to the really serious people. You also become more confident in your coaching and can explain to prospects exactly how you can help them. Confidence is contagious.

Strategy 4: Tell Everyone You Know about What You Do and How You Can Help

Develop a clear, concise, and compelling paragraph about who you are, what you do, who you help, and what results your clients achieve. Start with all your friends, family, relatives, and business associates. Do not directly ask them for business ("Please be my client"); instead, ask them if they know of anyone who needs your services. Every few months, give them a brief update on how things are going and remind them of who your ideal client is, how you help, and the kinds of results your clients achieve. The more they know about you, the more attuned they can be when they meet a good prospect. Don't be shy about telling other people you come across, as well. You can never be sure where you will find a prospect. I have found prospects on a plane to Paris, on a cruise ship in the Caribbean, on the beaches of Mexico, at a conference in Toronto, and in a university in Kazakhstan.

Strategy 5: Speak to Every Group You Can

One of the best ways to find new clients is by speaking in front of a group of prospects on a topic of importance to them. If you are a career coach, develop a presentation on "Finding Your Dream Job" or "10 Tips to Take Yourself to the Top" or "Strategies for Successful Salary Negotiation Skills for Managers." If you target small-business owners, develop a talk on "How to Motivate Your Employees without Using More Money" or "Top 10 Steps to Launching a Successful Start-up."

Sandy Vilas
Chief Executive Officer
Coach, Inc.
Steamboat Springs, Colorado
www.CoachInc.com
www.coachu.com
www.ccui.com
(800) 48-COACH

Sandy Vilas is the CEO of Coach, Inc., which operates Coach U and Corporate Coach U, the two largest coach-training schools in the world, with over 8,000 students and graduates.

Tell us how you first started out in coaching.

Well, I first took a course on life planning from Thomas Leonard back in 1988. At the time I was a professional speaker and corporate trainer looking to expand my services. Two years after that course, I hired Thomas to coach me, and a year later I had over 70 clients. I continued to build my practice, and in 1996, I purchased Coach U from Thomas and cut my coaching practice back and refocused my attention on building Coach U.

Many coaches are struggling to find clients today. How did you build up a successful practice within a year?

There were several things I did which I still recommend coaches to do today. For the first 90 days after officially launching my coaching business, I held at least 8 to 10 face-to-face meetings a week, over breakfast and lunch, with prospects. During the course of our conversation I would ask them about their challenges, and when a particular issue arose, I would ask their permission to coach them around it. I always ended our conversations with something like, "Choosing a coach is a very personal decision. I'm not going to call you back to ask you if you want to hire me as your coach. If this is something you want to do, you'll need to call me." At the beginning I was converting one person for every three to four people I met with. Within six to nine months I was landing 50 percent of my prospects as clients.

(Continued)

Do you have any advice for new coaches trying to build a successful coaching practice?

Yes, here at Coach U we work hard to help our coaches build their business. Specifically, we tell them to:

- Have a full-practice attitude. Don't be seen as a needy person or desperate. That's a turnoff.
- Always give people the experience of being coached instead of just telling them about coaching.
- Come from the place that you are already a great coach, then get the skills to go with it.
- Know the 10 reasons why people should hire you.
- Create a list of 100 people you know, without a lot of judgment around it, who might be good clients. Don't include any friends or relatives. Start calling the list of 100 and set up in-person appointments, or phone appointments if they're located out of town. If you don't have a natural network already in place, it will take you a lot longer to build a successful coaching practice.
- Every day, determine your *single daily action*—What is the one thing I can do today that will guarantee the success of my practice? I determined that for me it was one-on-one conversations with prospects in person or over the phone.

What's one thing new coaches can do to speed up the learning curve of how to build a successful practice?

Interview 10 to 15 coaches who are currently making at least $100,000 a year from coaching.

Any words of advice for new coaches?

Coaching is the business of modeling. People hire you because they believe you have something they want but don't have. That may be strong leadership skills, an ability to communicate effectively, living a balanced life, or having your finances in order. Work hard to live a life that other people would want to emulate.

This is yet another good reason to be crystal clear about who your target audience is, because the more you can define the members of that audience, the more information you can learn about their biggest challenges and struggles. Your talk then becomes a tool to demonstrate to them that you know about their situation and can help them resolve it. Give examples and illustrations during your talks about clients you have worked with and how you helped them resolve their challenges. A few points to remember:

- Be sure you are speaking to the right audience. This will make all the difference in whether you land clients from your presentation.
- Don't bore the audience. Involve them in the presentation when appropriate, ask them questions, break them up into discussion groups, or give them a handout with some blanks in it.
- Don't practice your speaking skills on your target audience. If you are not comfortable speaking, join Toastmasters and learn how.
- Always give them a handout with all your contact information on it. If your content is good and the topic is pertinent to them, they may keep it. I recently landed a small-business owner as a client who heard a presentation I gave in a different state over a year ago. He had long since lost my business card, but had kept the informative handout I gave him on how to market his small business. Thankfully, I put all my contact information on my handout, and a year later he called me up to coach him.
- Know your speech. People are not attracted to speakers who read their notes. Be very familiar with your presentation, even memorize it, especially the opening and ending.
- Don't be afraid to give away good ideas, information, or resources. Sometimes we fall into the trap of believing that if we give away our "secret" knowledge, then people will not hire us because they will already know how to solve their problems. Actually, that could not be further from the truth. First, there is no such thing as secret knowledge. There is nothing you know that someone somewhere else does not know as well (perhaps even your competition). Second, giving away information and content reinforces in the audience's mind that you are a valuable resource and that there is probably a lot more where that came from. Third, there is a big dif-

ference between knowing how to do something and actually doing it. Part of the attraction of coaching is that it helps people to actually accomplish their goals, not just set them.

- Don't talk about coaching—illustrate it or demonstrate it every time you get the chance.
- If you are speaking to a group for free, ask for something in return: a list of everyone who attends that day, permission to contact all their members via e-mail, an invitation to write a follow-up article for their next newsletter, a testimonial from the group's leader, or all of the above.
- End the presentation by giving away a book or a free month of coaching; something that allows you to collect their business cards for later follow-up.
- Have a plan to follow up on every serious contact via phone. Send the rest of the audience an e-mail thanking them for attending and offering them a free coaching session.
- Follow up with everyone you need to no later than two to three days after the presentation.

Strategy 6: Find an Experienced Coach to Mentor You

First, a disclaimer: I believe there are a lot of coaches who take advantage of new coaches by promising them easy riches if they sign up for their coach training or variations of "I built a full-time practice in 60 days and you can too (if you pay me a lot of money)." Some organizations even certify "mentor coaches"—to which I would respond, doesn't every coach play a mentor at times with their clients? I have become increasingly skeptical of individual coaches whose only or primary clients are other coaches. I know there are sincere people and organizations out there who train coaches and help them succeed, but what I'm afraid of is that there is a growing number of coaches who can't find *real* clients and in desperation are feeding off their own kind and are simply spreading their ignorance around about how to build a successful business or live a better life. (Please don't send me hate mail about this. I personally know plenty of exceptions and recognize that there are many good people in the coach-training field.)

Second, I do believe that finding and working with a successful coach can be a big boost to your practice, especially if that coach has a strong background in sales or marketing, which are generally the two biggest deficits new coaches have. Seventy-six percent of coaches who make more than $75,000 a year from their practices have a coach. Most of the time new coaches hire a coach to help them build their business, not just support them in their struggles. The best coach to help you build a successful practice is one who has a successful practice. I strongly recommend you interview several coaches and ask them some pointed questions:

- *How many clients do you currently have?*
- *Describe a few of your typical clients. Who do you primarily target?* Look for coaches who have a large percentage of their client base in the area that you want to focus your practice on. For example, if you are doing personal coaching and want to move into business coaching, find a coach who primarily targets businesses and professionals.
- *How much time do you spend on sales and marketing activities in a given week or month?* Beware if they say they don't do much of either, because they will not be able to give you the kind of fresh expertise you need to help you build your practice. Not doing regular marketing activities is a sign of one of two things: Either their practice is not very successful, or it's so successful that they only need referrals to keep their business going. Neither of these situations will be very helpful to you as a new coach just starting out. In the first situation, they don't know how to market, and in the second, they haven't marketed in so long that they won't be able to relate well to your current situation.
- *Other than referrals, what is the best way you have found to find clients?* This can help weed out the coaches who either don't know how to market or who have built their practice entirely from referrals, which usually takes a long time.
- *How many other coaches do you have as clients in your practice?* What percentage of your practice is made up of coaches? A good rule of thumb is to look for a coach whose client list consists of less than 20 percent other coaches.
- *How long have you been coaching?*
- *What are your fees? How much do you charge per hour?*

- *Approximately how much do you make in your coaching practice?*   While many coaches may consider this to be an invasion of privacy, tell them the reason behind your question (you don't want to hire a part-time coach who only made $10,000 last year), and ask them for an estimate. The more successful personal coaches are making $50,000 to $80,000 a year, while successful business coaches are making $80,000 to $150,000 annually.
- *What do you consider your two or three strongest areas of expertise?*
- *Do you have a coach that you pay for services?*   The best coaches put their money where their mouth is. If they believe hiring a successful coach will make them more successful, they will do it.
- Tell them about your goals (want to write a book, build a business coaching practice, speak more, find 10 new clients in the next four months, go from part-time to full-time in the next six months) and ask them how comfortable they would be in helping you achieve that goal.

Listen for their responses. Do they give you a straightforward answer, or do you detect a hint of hesitation in their voice? I'm sure people will disagree with me about the process and the reasons for hiring a successful coach. Just to be clear, I do not believe that every person or organization who works with, trains, or helps new coaches to succeed is corrupt or dishonest, but as with any business decision, let the buyer beware. Just because the mantra of the coaching industry is "Get a coach" doesn't mean that everyone offering you their services is the best fit for you and your goals. Enough said!

Strategy 7: Develop Multiple Audio Logos

Audio logos, if you recall, are powerful, dynamic, one-sentence answers to the question, "What do you do?" The response you give is usually in the format of, "I help (*identify your target audience*) to (*state the results you achieve*)." For example, "I help small-business owners find new clients faster with less effort." One technique you can use to find new clients is to develop multiple audio logos for each of your target markets. If you have two primary target markets, find out what their top two or three challenges are and develop a separate audio logo for each one. This allows you to be even more specific and detailed when talking with a prospect.

STRATEGY 8: REFINE YOUR MARKETING MATERIALS

Unless you are a former graphic designer, I recommend you hire a professional to design your marketing materials. What kind of materials you need often depends on who you are targeting, but most coaches need at least sharp-looking business cards and a simple brochure. Whatever materials you finally decide on, make sure they answer all three critical questions: who you help (your target market), how you help them, and what results you achieve or what benefits your clients receive. Do not focus on listing every kind of client you work with or try to include a comprehensive listing of all your services. Focus on your primary target market, their primary challenges, and the top benefits and results they receive when you coach them.

STRATEGY 9: REFINE YOUR TARGET MARKETS

One of the biggest mistakes I see coaches make, both new and experienced ones, is having too big a target audience. The larger your audience, the more difficult it will be for you to reach them often enough to make an impact. As a coach, recognize that you are competing against thousands of other companies, products, and services that want the time, attention, and money of your target audience. Your target audience definition must be much more specific than just "people who are going through a midlife career transition." The time you spend in clarifying exactly who constitutes your target audience will be well spent. Be sure to do this in your very first month of business and reevaluate it annually.

STRATEGY 10: DEVELOP A LIST OF LOCAL NETWORKING GROUPS AND START ATTENDING THEM

The quality of networking groups varies greatly. I know people who spend way too much time attending networking groups that are a complete waste of their time. I believe there are only two reasons why you should regularly attend a networking group: (1) for your personal and professional development, and (2) to find new clients. Assuming that we are talking about the second kind of group, start out by making a comprehensive list of all the networking groups that meet in your area. You can find these using the Internet, your local research librarian, trade associations, and the local newspaper. Here are some questions to ask in your research:

- What kinds of people primarily attend this group?
- How often does it meet?
- What is the usual structure of the group?
- Is there usually a speaker? If so, what kinds of topics are covered?
- How much time is allotted for actual networking?
- How many people typically attend?
- What is the cost for attending?
- If I really want to become involved what other opportunities are there?
- What other activities does the group participate in?
- What are the time, place, and dates of upcoming meetings?

This should provide you with enough basic information to determine whether a group might be a good one for you to visit. Visit two to three times to confirm your impressions, then if it still seems right, commit to attending every meeting you can for the next four to six months. If you still have not found a good response among the group for your services after six months, mark that group off your list and move on. A good response would include several people who have taken you up on a free coaching session, with at least 20 to 30 percent of them being converted into paying clients. There are far too many networking groups in most cities to waste your time attending one that does not give you a solid return on your investment.

Strategy 11: Get Out of the House

Too many coaches spend too much of their time in their offices, on their computers, trying passive marketing techniques. Set a goal to go to a certain number of networking events per week or per month, to meet a certain number of new people in your target audience, to give a certain number of free coaching sessions, and to make so many sales calls per week. Stick with your goals and look to expand them every two to four months. No matter how much you want to believe it, clients will not come to you just because you believe you are a great coach. You must go find clients, and to do so you have to go where they are, and unless you have a *very* big living room, you will not find many inside your house. Get out of the house!

STRATEGY 12: FIND SOMEONE TO HOLD YOU ACCOUNTABLE

Good coaches practice what they preach. In order to accomplish your goals, you first have to set goals that are specific, measurable, achievable, realistic, and timed (SMART), then follow through on them. If you are having trouble following through on your goals, find someone to hold you accountable (other than your significant other). Ask another new coach to exchange coaching services with you—you coach them one week, then you switch places. Find another small-business owner and get together on a regular basis to exchange target goals and achievements.

STRATEGY 13: NETWORK WITH SUCCESSFUL COACHES

Find a few coaches who have built successful coaching practices and spend some time with them. Most of these elite coaches don't visit the traditional local coaching groups, so you will have to find another way to seek them out. When you find them, offer to buy them lunch. You can ask for their advice, but don't try to simply pick their brains for free. That's insulting and a big turnoff. Many successful coaches are willing to share a few "insider secrets" that may help you or turn you on to a couple of good resources. Perhaps you're struggling with a particular issue and don't quite know how to handle it—other coaches may be able to give you some good ideas based on their experience. Ask them what books, associations, conferences, or resources they would recommend you look into. Then be sure to thank them for their advice, perhaps even buy them a small gift. Periodically keep in touch with them, telling them how their advice helped.

Strategy 14: Interview Professionals, Business Colleagues and Associates in Your Target Market

Set up interviews with appropriate professionals and associates and ask for their advice in determining who the best targets for your services are and what specific ways they would recommend that you use to reach these people. Develop a list of half a dozen questions you can ask them to best elicit advice, but do not ask these people for their business. You are coming to them as one business owner to another asking for advice, not as a salesperson looking for another account. Be very clear about this before you meet.

Strategy 15: Practice Answering the Hard Questions and Overcoming Common Objections

Some of the hard questions and objections prospects will ask you include the following:

- *Why should I hire you?* To properly answer this question you have to know a little bit about the person you're talking to, which is why you should always try to ask the person a few questions about what they do, what their biggest challenges are, and how things are going for them before you disclose too much information about yourself and your services. You want to use the information they have told you to customize your response, but what do you do if you don't have enough information about them to solidly answer their question? One technique I have used is to confront their objection head on: "I don't know if it makes sense for us to work together or not. I would need to know a lot more about your particular situation and the challenges that you're facing, and you would need to know more about me and the results I help people achieve before either of us would be able to answer that question. How about we get together this next week for some coffee and talk a little more in depth?" That kind of nondefensive and honest response can be very disarming. At the same time it can also be used to distinguish people who are really interested but want more information from those who are simply "kicking the tires" or testing you.

- *How much do you charge?* Your response to this question depends on when it comes up. If it comes up early on in the conversation, the only response you can give is, "It totally depends on the situation." If the person presses a little more, ask them to give you a specific scenario. Often they will give you an illustration about themselves or an event at their company. I have found that most people who ask this question early on are not really seriously interested; they are either just being curious or casually wondering if they could ever afford your type of services. At that time it is best to try to avoid answering the question, but if you are pushed into a corner where you feel you need to give a response, only give a large range. "Well, assuming I was to coach you one-on-one it could be anywhere from $200 to $800 a month, but if you're really interested we should get together so you can experience the power of coaching." If this question is asked toward the end of a long, involved conversation or at the end of a free coaching session, you should take the question more seriously. Whenever you give a free individual coaching session you should have a one-page information sheet you can hand out that details your regular services and the associated costs. If the prospect is asking you for a quote on a particular project, say a management coaching seminar for 10 of their managers, it is absolutely appropriate to say, "Let me think about that. I'll work you up a quote by tomorrow afternoon."

- *You charge* how much? *Wow, that's a lot. How come it's so much?* Possibly the best response to a comment like this is to provide a real-life illustration of how coaching can help. Here's one I've used: "Well, it's all a matter of perspective. For example, if I worked with you for four months on advancing your career and as a result you received a $30,000-a-year promotion, would the $2,500 you paid me be worth it?" Or if you're talking to the owner of a small manufacturing company doing $10 million a year in business, perhaps you could say something like, "Well, let's say I came in and coached you for the next six months and as a result you increased your personal productivity by 20 percent, which meant that you could significantly reduce the number of hours you personally worked every week, while helping you to find ways to increase your annual revenues by $1 million to $2 million—would it be worth the $1,200-a-month investment?" Usually, a powerful example like this will help them to put it in perspective.

The best examples come from actual results you have achieved for former or current clients, because invariably a sharp prospect will ask you, "Is that what you can do for me?" or "Have any of your clients ever achieved that?" A variation on this is to create a value proposition for them: "If you were able to accomplish that goal you mentioned in half the time, what would that be worth to you?" or "You mentioned you've been trying to write your book for the past two years, but just can't seem to finish it. What would it be worth to you if I could help you finish it in the next 60 days?" Using a real situation they have disclosed and creating a vision of how you can help them achieve their goal faster than they can on their own can be a powerful motivator for them to take the next step—sign up for a free introductory coaching session. The point to remember here is that when a person states an objection to your prices, it is a good sign that you have failed to convince them of the value of coaching, not that they can't afford it.

- *Who have you worked with before?* What they are really asking is, have you worked with anyone like them before? If you have, respond by giving them examples of clients who are similar to them in position, title, industry, or field. If you have not, give them a brief description of who you typically work with in a way they can relate to: "I usually coach stressed-out business professionals who are very busy, but still want to accomplish ambitious goals."
- *How is coaching any different from consulting or counseling?* See Chapter 11 for some ways to distinguish yourself.
- *What kind of background do you have?* This person is probably asking, can you relate to me and do you know where I'm coming from by personal experience? Do not go on and on telling them everything about yourself. Focus on the major areas that highlight what makes you a great coach for them. Since I target business executives and small-business owners I usually say something like, "I have a background in consulting and psychology, and have owned and operated four small companies."
- *Why do I need a professional coach?* The best response is a nondefensive, nonassuming one, like, "I don't know if you do. Why do you

think you need a professional coach?" Here's another approach: "A lot of people don't need a coach. Only people who are really serious about taking their career, life, or business quickly to the next level need a coach." And here's another common response: "Even Michael Jordan, the best basketball player in history, didn't reach his full potential until he was coached by Phil Jackson."

- *What kind of results can I expect?* Here is where doing your homework beforehand will pay off. You need to keep track of how your coaching helps clients. The easiest way to do this by asking them for a testimonial or letter of reference. You can also offer general guidelines as to the kinds of results coaching achieves, including the following:

  - Accomplishing your goals faster
  - Creating the life you've always dreamed of
  - Discovering more effective ways to build healthy relationships
  - Developing better work-life balance
  - Gaining a deep understanding of your core strengths and growth areas
  - Taking your career to the next level

  But do not make the mistake of just throwing out a bunch of unrelated results. Instead, focus on the area you believe this person is most interested in: career development, work-life balance, running a business, or better relationships.
- *I've never heard of coaching. What is it?* See Chapter 1.
- *I don't have time for coaching, I'm too busy.* Give this person a response that states that you understand where they are coming from, along with an example of how you were extremely flexible with a current or former client you worked with who had an extremely demanding schedule, and how they were able to use coaching to increase their time-management skills and free up several hours a week for time with their family or to be alone. Also, point out that coaching is perfect for the busy person because it can be done either in person or over the phone at their convenience. This kind of response usually comes from someone who doesn't see the value that coaching can bring to their life, so if the conversation continues, concentrate more of your time on illustrating the value and benefits to them.

> The most valuable commodity you have is your time. You must invest it wisely for it to produce a good return. Don't waste your time following up with people who are not interested. Only follow up with people who express at least a minimal level of interest.

- *I'm not ready to make a decision right now. Call me up in a month or so.* This is one of the more difficult responses you might encounter, because it can be very difficult to determine whether the person is truly interested or just trying to get rid of you. If they are not interested you want to know, because you don't want to pester them, and you don't want to waste your time chasing down people who just don't want what you have. Let's face it, coaching can be very valuable to many people, but not everyone wants or needs a coach. There are so many people out there who *do* want what you have to offer that you can't afford to waste your time on people who don't. The most valuable commodity you have is your time. You must invest it wisely for it to produce a good return. A good coach will work quickly to distinguish people who are truly interested from those who are not. This is just plain old good time-management skills.

    One of the easiest ways for you to do this is to give them permission to say, "No thank you." This is contrary to what a lot of sales courses and books will teach you—"Ask prospects a series of questions that almost everyone says 'Yes' to because it will make it easier for them to say 'Yes' when you ultimately ask them for their business." I call this sales technique "dialing for dollars" because it is commonly used on telemarketing calls—the caller asks a series of "idiot-proof" questions—questions only an idiot would say "No" to. For example: "Stephen, do you want to save more money on your telephone bill?" or "Would you like a free vacation to Hawaii?" or my favorite: "Mr. Fairley, you have been selected to win a (*you fill in the blank*). All I need to do is get your correct address and credit card verification and I'll send out your prize information right away." I mean really, how stupid do these people think we are?

    When you're selling coaching, you're selling a vitally important relationship, not some cheap get-rich-quick scheme. Why would you use idiot-proof questions to try to manipulate someone into buying something they don't want? A much better way is to treat people as highly intelligent human beings who have freedom of choice. One way you can do that is by giving them verbal permission to say "No thank you." If someone says they are not ready to make a decision, but asks you to follow up with them in the future, it's perfectly acceptable to come right out and say, "It's okay to say you're not interested in coaching because I don't want to waste your time or mine by following up with you if you're not really interested." Here are a couple other ways you could respond: "Is it that you're interested in coaching, but don't want to make a decision right now, or are you just not interested?" or a softer approach, "I send out a monthly newsletter by e-mail that covers current topics of interest to business professionals. Would you like me to put you on our mailing list?"

- *Send me some literature on your company.*   Most of the time the person asking this question is not really interested in what you have to say and is politely disengaging from the conversation. If you understand this perspective, it makes your choice of response a lot easier. Here are four that come to mind:

  - Everything about our company is on our web site, which is listed on my business card.
  - Is there a particular question you have about our company that I can answer?
  - We have found that most people who ask for literature are simply being polite and are not truly interested in coaching. And if that's the case, it's okay, because we don't want to waste anyone's time who isn't interested.
  - We typically don't send out literature because, as you know, most of the time it simply ends up in the trash. But if there's a specific question you have, I would be glad to answer it.

The point here is not to be argumentative, insensitive, manipulative, demanding, or sneering, but open, honest, polite, and honoring people's God-given right to say, "No thank you." Business professionals and busy people will appreciate your giving them a way out. This also sets you apart from people who use strong-arm tactics and the never-take-no-for-an-answer salespeople they are used to dealing with.

Action Step

Finding your first 10 paying clients can be a long, trying, and even discouraging experience, unless you know how to do it, create a plan, then implement the plan. In this chapter we have focused on 15 strategies successful new coaches use for finding their first 10 clients. Remember the first one — develop plan and follow it? Well, here is where you start developing your plan.

Step 1.   Go back through the chapter and circle each of the 15 strategies you want to use that you are currently not using.

Step 2.   Of the ones you marked, write down the top three strategies you will commit to starting in the next 30 days and the specific plan you will follow for implementing each one. Provide as much detail as possible.

Step 3.   Provide some measurement about how you will know if you have been successful at using each strategy and when it will be time to add more strategies onto your plan. For example: "I will visit three different networking groups per month until I find the two best groups for me to continue participating in. I will establish my connections with people in those groups for six months before adding any more groups."

CHAPTER 10

Why Most Marketing Fails: The Top 10 Marketing Mistakes Beginning Coaches Make

Every coach who starts a coaching practice fully intends to succeed, yet many still fail. Why? Is it a lack of knowledge? Their inability to implement? Or a lack of effort? Unfortunately, there are no easy or simple answers, but in this chapter we will cover the 10 most common marketing mistakes beginning coaches make, any of which can result in the death of your business. Some of the areas include:

- The biggest false belief held by many in the coaching community
- The four fundamental functions of every successful business
- Why knowing the difference between active and passive marketing techniques is vital to your success
- How to evaluate your networking efforts
- Why you should not talk about your services
- The 10 critical questions to determine whether to outsource a project or do it yourself

MISTAKE 1: BELIEVING IN THE MYTH OF THE FIELD OF DREAMS

One of the most common mistakes I see coaches make is buying into what I call "the myth of the field of dreams." If you recall the movie then you will likely recognize this phrase—"Build it and they will come." When applied to starting a business, it's the false belief that if you start your coaching company and tell your friends and family about it, then it will grow all by itself. All you need to do is sit around and wait for people to line up at your door. This false belief is sometimes propagated by people under the "laws of attraction principle"—live an attractive lifestyle and prospects will come to you with no effort on your part. Unfortunately, reality indicates that it just doesn't happen like that, unless your close friends or family members are the Gateses, the Bushes, or the Buffetts. If it did, everyone who started a business would become successful, but year after year 40 to 60 percent of start-ups fail. "Officially" starting a coaching practice can take little more than the idea and $200 for some business cards and a phone, but building and growing your practice to the place where it provides a constant stream of revenue and satisfaction takes a lot of time, energy, and resources. For 98 percent of all successful coaches, building their business is something they did over a period of months and years, while expending a lot of energy and pouring all their resources into it. The other 2 percent who built it in less than a year experienced a series of fortunate breaks that launched them into the big leagues or left their regular job with a large coaching contract already in hand. Make no mistake, the majority of small businesses fail within four years. There are two important questions you must ask yourself before starting your coaching business:

- What are the top causes of business failure?
- What will you do differently to significantly increase your chances of success?

I've mentioned this before, but according to the Small Business Administration and *Entrepreneur* magazine, the two most common causes for small business failure are:

- *Undercapitalization*—lack of available funding when starting
- *Lack of revenue stream*—inability to generate revenues by finding new clients

ACTION STEP

Write down four specific things you will do to counteract these causes which will significantly increase your chances of success.

MISTAKE 2: FAILING TO FOCUS ON ALL FOUR FUNCTIONS

There are four fundamental functions of every successful business, and every business owner has to work hard to ensure that all of them are adequately covered:

- *Entrepreneurship and managerial functions.* These involve creating and implementing strategic plans of what you want your business to become, managing projects, and ensuring that everything gets done on schedule.
- *Administrative and operations functions.* These involve the day to day tasks such as paying the bills, returning e-mail inquiries and phone messages, and an assortment of repetitive tasks.

259

Jim Rohrbach
Success Skills Coach
Niles, Illinois
www.SuccessSkills.com
(800) 572-2770 ext. 1-2633

Jim Rohrbach is a success skills coach and a master at teaching other people how to market and sell their services.

You were coaching way back in 1992, when most people didn't even know it existed. How did you get started, and how have you been able to maintain a thriving practice for this long?

When writing my book, *Business Success Skills*, back in 1992, I called myself a "success skills coach," the same term I use to this day. I only work with small-business owners, entrepreneurs, and sales professionals now, and about 70 percent of my business comes by referral. When talking to business owners, I always tell them, "If it were easy to have a business of any kind, even a coaching business, than everyone would be doing it and it would be the equivalent of flipping hamburgers at McDonalds." I'm convinced there hasn't been a single business owner ever who didn't spend *at least* one night completely wide awake asking the question, "What in the world was I thinking? How am I going to make this work? I must have been out of my mind!" Yet, they get up the next morning and get back to work. How did I acquire this particular piece of "wisdom?" Answer: I've been there!

If 70 percent of your business comes from referrals, where does the other 30 percent come from?

About 10 percent comes from presentations I make to business groups—when I first started I spoke everywhere. When presenting, I'm always looking for the 1 or 2 people in a crowd of 100 that want to work with me one-on-one. The other 20 percent of my clients come from online leads—I'm a guest columnist and discussion board leader on a daily e-zine called horsesmouth.com.

What's one piece of advice you would give to a new coach just starting out?

Learn the business part. You must take yourself seriously if you're going to have a successful coaching practice. You need to learn marketing skills—which is *attraction,* as well as sales skills—which is *enrollment.* So marketing is what you do to get yourself in front of prospects—this includes speaking engagements, networking, seminars, teleclasses, and so on. Sales is what you do (and *don't* do, which is talk a lot!) when you're one-on-one with a good prospect to turn him or her into a paying client. It takes both to be successful in the long run.

A lot of coaches have difficulty with the sales aspect of building their business. Any tips?

Absolutely. The number-one tip is: Learn to conduct a consultative interview. A consultative interview consists of a series of powerful questions asked in a logical sequence that helps prospects to identify their need for coaching, their ability to invest in coaching, and their ability to move forward in making a decision to sign up for coaching. (Note that during this type of interview, you do not coach.)

The second tip is to define the gaps by asking "gap questions." Gap questions help your prospects to define: Where are they now? Where do they want to be? What are the obstacles holding them back? What are the key areas of improvement they need to work on to get to that next level? With each question, the prospects talk about the gaps between where they are and where they want to be. And in this manner, you help them come to their own conclusions about why they need you as their coach.

The third tip is to make sure you walk your talk. To be a good coach, you need to be a person of integrity and have it reasonably together mentally, physically, emotionally, and spiritually. For example, if you're going to do business coaching then you need to know how to run your own coaching business. Or if you want to be a relationship coach, you can't be a hermit living in a cave on a mountain top.

- *Sales and marketing functions.* These include tasks that involve building relationships with prospects, telling people what you do over and over again, finding ways to effectively reach your target audience, convincing people of the value of coaching, and landing new clients.

- *Technical or service functions.* These involve actually doing the work of coaching, consulting, speaking, or training.

Most people who start their own coaching practices are technicians—the people who really just want to do the actual work of coaching, which is great and necessary. However, technicians typically underestimate the difficulty of the other three roles—that is, starting, building, and maintaining a successful practice. They also typically overestimate their ability to market and sell their services. Other than the actual decision to start the business, the sales and marketing aspects are the most important function of your business. If there is no sales and marketing, there are no clients to service. If there are no clients, there is no revenue. If there is no revenue, there is no business. It is all a big cycle, and that cycle starts and ends with sales and marketing. To be successful in your coaching practice you must accept that you are the chief marketing officer (CMO) as well as the vice president of sales. There is just no getting around it. If you don't market yourself and sell your ability to help people change, you will never get clients. Period. As much as you want to "just do coaching," you will spend the majority of your time in the first two years doing sales and marketing. You have three choices if this is not an area of strength or interest to you:

- Do whatever it takes to make it an area of expertise.
- Find a partner or two who are strong in sales and marketing.
- Outsource it to someone outside of your company who is strong in these areas.

Action Step

The life of your business depends on your ability to identify and convert prospects into paying clients on a regular basis. Of the four critical areas, choose the one you consider your greatest strength. Now write down a brief plan for how you can adequately cover the other three areas.

MISTAKE 3: USING PASSIVE MARKETING TECHNIQUES VERSUS ACTIVE MARKETING TECHNIQUES

Some years ago when I first started out in consulting, I met with a marketing coach to talk about targeting my ideal client more effectively. She asked to me give her a comprehensive list of every marketing activity I was doing. After looking at my list her first reply was, "Stephen, everything you're doing is passive." At first I didn't understand, but as she explained I saw a theme emerge. I was constantly busy doing marketing activities, but they were all passive or reactive ways to try to find clients. I was waiting for people to come to me instead of going out and finding them.

We worked hard to rebalance my marketing efforts to include both passive and active marketing strategies. Like many coaches, I was reluctant to get out of my office, meet people, and talk with them face to face about how I could help them. Where would I meet them? What would I say? Would I sound stupid? How would I react if they weren't interested in coaching? Of course, if the truth was told, I was just nervous and didn't want to experience rejection.

Here's a brief list of passive marketing activities and their alternative active marketing activities:

Passive Marketing Strategies	*Active Marketing Strategies*
Sending out direct-mail letters, postcards, or flyers announcing your company, services, web site, or a new workshop you're offering	Calling everyone you send the direct-mail pieces to until you reach them and asking them to attend or sign up
Sending out e-mails inviting people to take advantage of your free coaching session	Getting people to commit to a face-to-face appointment
Researching area associations that you can speak to	Calling a list of 10 organizations a month and inquiring about speaking opportunities

Creating a speakers package you can send out to meeting planners

Following up with a meeting planner's request for information about you and asking them to let you speak to their organization

Developing and practicing 3–5 key presentations and speeches so you can give them comfortably and at a moment's notice

Giving your key presentations as often as possible to people in your target market

Reading books and trade magazines to find out what the current industry challenges are

Cold calling the decision makers at specific companies that you have targeted because of my research

Redesigning the company web site

Tracking visitors to your web site and personally inviting them for a free coaching session

Writing and sending out a sharp looking e-zine to your target market

Sending a personalized e-mail invitation to each person on your list asking them to act on the offer in the e-zine

Following up with e-mails that come to you from your web site

Sending out targeted e-mail campaigns that drive people to your web site or give them a limited time offer and ask for action

Returning voice mails promptly

Trying to always pick up the phone and personally call someone versus sending out an e-mail

Refining your unique selling proposition (USP)

Asking people directly to hire you as their coach

Doing competitive analysis on competitors

Contacting potential SRPs by phone and trying to set up face-to-face meetings with them

Modifying your coaching packages to offer more choices to prospects	Using your coaching packages to upsell clients into longer or bigger engagements
Writing or reworking the company brochure	Handing out your brochure to hot prospects you meet at a networking event
Participating in teleclasses, seminars, and coach training	Giving a teleclass, seminar, or workshop
Practicing your coaching skills on nonpaying clients	Giving free coaching sessions
Attending nonproductive networking events	Attending productive networking events
	Following up on top prospects via voicemail within 24 hours
	Following up on every viable contact you meet via e-mail or voicemail within 48 hours

ACTION STEP

1. Write down a comprehensive list of every marketing activity you have done in the past six months.
2. Examine that list and determine what percentage of your recent marketing activities are *active* versus *passive:*

   ____% are *passive* and ____% are *active*

3. List six specific things you can do to increase your *active* marketing activities over the next three to six months. Be as specific as possible.

MISTAKE 4: RELYING TOO MUCH ON A NATURAL NETWORK

Everyone has a natural network made up of friends, family, relatives, close business associates, church members, and old high school and college friends. One of the first things you should do when starting out in business is to develop a consistent way to clearly and concisely tell all of them what you are doing, who you help, and what results your clients achieve. However, a common mistake is depending too much on this natural network to find you business. No one is responsible for finding you new clients except you. You must work hard to expand your network outside of your comfort zone. Your plan should include several different kinds of active and passive marketing strategies. As you go through this book, make sure to note the specific ones you want to use.

Another thing to consider is that when a person hires you as their coach, it is not so much because of who you know or who knows you (that will only get you the initial introduction); it is because of who you are—your persona, your authenticity, your personality, your intelligence, your lifestyle, your experience. Regardless of how well your friends and family know you and love you, they cannot completely convey to prospects what you do, how you do it, or how effective it is. That is your responsibility.

Mistake 5: Networking Too Much or in the Wrong Places

Recently one of my partners, Tom Horne, was talking with a consultant about her marketing efforts and how effective they were. She mentioned that lately she had been a little frustrated because her efforts were not producing results as she had hoped. Tom asked her to tell him some of the top ways she was marketing herself. After listing a couple of common things, she began talking about all the different networking groups she belonged to. This consultant belonged to more than 30 different networking groups! That's about one meeting a day, assuming each group met only once a month. No one person can adequately cover 10 different networking groups, much less 30. I'm a firm believer in getting out there and networking, but you can experience too much of a good thing. I commonly meet coaches who spend a great deal of their marketing time and resources on attending various networking events. I see three problems with this consultant's hypernetworking efforts:

- First, she was going to so many different groups she probably didn't have time to do any other kind of marketing activity. Networking is one of the less effective ways to find new clients for coaching or consulting, because so much of it depends on the group you join, what kind of person regularly attends, how often you go, and especially how much time you devote to following up on the leads you obtain.

- Second, there is no possible way one person can properly follow up with every single prospect from 30 different events. If you meet an average of 20 to 30 people at a networking event and only go to 5 events per week (20 events a month), and 10 to 15 percent of the people you meet are somewhat interested in coaching, that still means you have 40 to 90 new people every month to develop and implement a marketing plan for. This doesn't even count the 120 to 270 people you met over the past three months and have to maintain regular contact with via phone, fax, e-mail, voicemail, or in-person meetings. Remember, there are times when more is better. The smaller your target market, the more time you can spend developing a closer relationship with each one of your prospects — and given that it takes seven to nine "meaningful touches" to move a person along in the sales cycle to the point where they want to hire you, the more time you spend with each viable prospect, the higher your conversion rates will become.

- Third, she more than likely could have stopped attending 80 to 90 percent of those groups and still found the same results. You have to be picky about the networking groups you join. Many are time wasters because your ideal client doesn't regularly attend, or they are held at a bad time for you or a long distance away so you don't regularly attend. There is nothing wrong with trying out a couple of different networking groups to see the results, but find a way to measure your results to help you determine whether a particular group is worth the effort of maintaining your membership. Track the exact number of ideal clients you meet versus how many meetings you attend, how many of those ideal clients were interested enough in coaching to return your calls or e-mails, what percentage resulted in face-to-face meetings, and precisely how much work you obtained as a direct result of those meetings. Set a goal for every group each year, and if you don't reach it after a year, go find a different networking group that better meets your needs.

MISTAKE 6: NOT TESTING AND RETESTING MARKETING EFFORTS

You often wonder why people seem to make the same mistakes over and over again, yet if you do not take time to test your marketing efforts you will likely fall prey to the same error. Today's Leadership Coaching is the fourth small business I have either started or owned, and in the course of doing business at these companies I have planned and implemented many different marketing campaigns. Some have been successful; others have been a complete waste of time and money.

To be successful, you must approach each marketing activity with a specific goal in mind. For example, if you go to a networking event with more than 100 people in attendance, you should be able to talk to at least 10 to 20 people during the course of the event, walk out with three to five decent prospects, follow up on all of them within 48 hours, obtain one to two face-to-face meetings or free coaching sessions, and walk away with one client 50 percent of the time. These are specific goals that help you determine whether that particular networking group is worth your time and effort or you should look elsewhere.

Perhaps you want to send out a direct-mail piece to offer prospects a discount on your new book about leadership. You purchase a list of 4,000 people who are in your target market. The direct-mail piece is exceptionally well done, and so you receive the typical 1 to 3 percent response rate (40 to 120 people). Of those people who inquire about the book, you should be able to convert 20 to 40 percent into buyers (8 to 48 people). Of the ones who actually read the book and find your concepts stimulating, perhaps 10 percent will call you for a consultation to see how your leadership concepts could be applied in their organization (one to five people).

Go into each marketing activity with a goal that you can measure in mind. If you reach the goal, keep doing it! If you don't reach your goal, analyze why not. Here are several possible reasons to look at:

- Your goal was not realistic.
- The approach you took was not appropriate (you only used postcards instead of adding personal phone calls).
- The campaign was not carried out according to plan.
- You didn't have a strong call to action (reason why they should call you now).

- The timing was poor (e.g., direct e-mails sent on Tuesday are read five times as often as those sent on Monday or Friday).
- You did not have enough meaningful touches that connected with your target.
- It was not the right target audience for your product or service.

Try to eliminate each reason before giving up on your activity. Perhaps you missed something that you considered small, but was critical to the decision-making process of those in your target market. In the end, try to measure your marketing efforts and look for the one or two things that give you a 5- or 10-times return on investment. Focus the majority of your efforts on those activities and look for ways to drop the bottom 20 percent that take up a lot of your time, energy, or money but fail to consistently produce results.

MISTAKE 7: TARGETING THE WRONG MARKET

When getting started in coaching, it is very common to think of your goal as "helping people achieve the life and business they desire" or something similar to that. As your initial thoughts about how easy it will be to attract clients don't quickly come to fruition, you may start to grow nervous and wonder exactly who you do help.

One of the most common mistakes I see small-business owners make is to target too big a market or one that does not meet the right criteria. Your ability to quickly and explicitly identify who your ideal target is will pay early dividends when it comes to saving you time, energy, and money. The more specific and narrow you can make your description of your ideal market, the better off you will be when it comes to easily identifying prospects in a crowd, recognizing prospects when you meet them at networking events, selecting which networking groups to participate in, and determining which organizations you want to speak at.

When defining your ideal client, keep in mind these three simple criteria: *need*, *want*, and *afford*. Your ideal client must meet all three in order for you to do business with them. They must *need* you, because that is something you will find very difficult to create if the need does not already exist. Now, they may not be able to clearly articulate that they need a *coach*, but they recognize that they need help with things that you, as a coach, can provide. They must also *want* you. This is where it gets more personal, because once you have identified yourself as someone who can assist them, they must recognize that they truly want you personally rather than someone else. Finally, they must be able to *afford* you, and that's the difference between making a sale and being a missionary. If they do not meet all three of these criteria, there is no common ground on which you can build a coaching relationship (unless you are interested in doing pro bono work).

Any market that is not specific or that does not meet all three criteria is the wrong market for you. You should be able to quickly and precisely tell anyone exactly who is in your target market. If you can't do that right now, go back to Chapter 2 and go through the action steps until you can. Be deliberate about choosing target markets that you have experience with, that you are passionate about, and that you have broad and deep knowledge about with regard to their specific challenges and issues.

MISTAKE 8: FOCUSING ON SERVICES AND FEATURES INSTEAD OF BENEFITS AND RESULTS

Another common mistake coaches and service professionals make is to spend a lot of time developing and talking about all the different services and programs they offer and the specific features or details of each one. Although it is important to offer them to prospects, please understand that prospects simply do not care what specific services you offer. They only truly care about one thing—can you help them resolve their particular challenge or problem? It is fairly common to see brochures from a coaching or consulting company with long lists of all the different services they offer or a service description paper that lists the three primary services a company offers followed by mind-numbing details about the features and details of each service. Prospects only give you a limited amount of their time and attention, and it will be best spent by briefly identifying who you work with, and the primary challenges you help clients with, then spending the majority of your time on the benefits and results you achieve for clients. Here are two different examples of how this could look:

> Prospects only care about three things:
> - Benefits
> - Value
> - Results

MODEL 1: TYPICAL SERVICE-BASED MODEL

Here at Today's Leadership Coaching, we provide:

Small-Business Coaching	Executive Coaching	Mid-sized Business Coaching
Leadership Development	Management Coaching	Management Training
Performance Coaching	Conflict Coaching	CEO Coaching
Business Development Coaching	Family Business Coaching	Corporate Coaching

MODEL 2: BENEFITS AND RESULTS MODEL

Here at Today's Leadership Coaching, we use executive coaching and leadership development programs to help small businesses develop leaders who deliver results.

What kind of RESULTS do our coaching clients experience?

- A business that produces better results faster with fewer resources
- Enhanced leadership performance in times of transition
- Significant increases in employee performance and productivity
- Discovering how to use their competitive edge for maximum impact

Assuming you are a small-business owner looking for assistance in growing your company, which one do you find more attractive, Model 1 or Model 2? Most people would say Model 2 because it focuses on the needs, challenges, and results of the small-business owner, as compared

271

to Model 1, which focuses on the services of the company, even though many of the same words are used.

ACTION STEP

For your two primary target markets, list the services you provide and the benefits and results they receive from those services. Here's an example:

Target Market: Small-Business Owners	Benefit (immediate effect of your coaching)	Results (ultimate results of implementing the benefits)
Service 1: New business development strategies—help them find more clients faster with less effort	• Spend less money on ineffective forms of marketing • Find the best ROI for their marketing dollars	• Increase their profits • Increase their time by automating the marketing processes

What are four specific ways you can use these statements in your active and passive marketing strategies? Write them down.

MISTAKE 9: TRYING TO BE COMPLETELY SELF-SUFFICIENT

One of the keys to being successful in any business is to recognize your strengths as well as your weaknesses. Many coaches waste too much of their precious time, energy, and potential profits by trying to do everything for themselves as a way of saving some money. Here are a few common examples:

- Developing their own corporate identity package (CIP)
- Printing their business cards off their home computer
- Refusing to upgrade their old computer
- Spending weeks trying to design the perfect brochure
- Learning how to build a web site from scratch
- Trying to understand all the intricacies of marketing and selling their services simply by reading a book or going to a seminar

I am not advocating outsourcing every aspect of your company, but unless you have specific experience in certain areas, you will not be able to represent yourself and your services in the best possible light without the help of an experienced professional. When pointing this out to beginning coaches, I have heard such reasoning as, "I am not targeting businesses or top professionals, but regular, everyday people, so I don't need a real professional image." That sounds great, but the logic is flawed. People who are attracted to coaching and can afford it (remember the three criteria: need, want, and afford) are not everyday, run-of-the-mill people. Coaching is not ubiquitous, yet. Currently, it is rather an anomaly to have your own personal coach. Most of the people who hire a coach fit this profile:

- They are in the upper two-thirds of the socioeconomic echelon (at least $80,000 annual income).
- They are either white-collar professionals or live in a white-collar household.
- They are more likely to be college educated.
- They are rather sophisticated in their buying habits.
- They tend to be image conscious (they want the best they can afford).
- They are ambitious in wanting to achieve their goals.
- They tend to be rather driven, enough to seriously invest their money to ensure their success—however they define success.

They want to work with someone who has a professional image. This image is created from every part of the successful coach, from their personality, to their marketing savvy, to their web site and business cards. Let's examine how working with an experienced professional can give you a competitive advantage in terms of officially launching your business; creating a business image; designing your business cards, brochures, and web site; developing dynamic audio logos that rapidly attract your target market; building a solid sales and marketing plan; and implementing your strategies faster than you could on your own. See Table 10.1.

Doing all of these projects yourself can feel empowering and sounds like a great way to save money, and at times it is, but evaluate each project carefully and use your precious time, energy, and resources to obtain a maximum return on investment. Saying yes to one thing always means saying no to something else. Try never to say yes to things that keep you from practice-building activities.

TABLE 10.1 Handling Start-up Tasks Yourself versus Outsourcing Them

Method	Costs	Time Frame from Idea to Official Business Launch	Secondary Impact	Primary Impact
Doing it yourself	Minimal	Realistically, 4 to 9 months before all tasks are completed and plans are fully implemented	You struggle to find more than a few clients at a time; can become discouraged and wonder if you made the right decision.	You lose time and energy during the critical start-up phase and spend most of it getting ready to find clients, rather than actually finding new, paying clients.
Working with various experienced professionals	60–200% greater than doing it yourself	Varies greatly, but can be done in 2 to 4 months	You can focus on the critical parts of your business like finding more clients faster and landing new business, using less energy and time.	You reduce your official launch time by 50–60%. You can focus on building your business and finding new clients now, rather than expending all your time and energy on getting ready to find clients.

ACTION STEP

How do you know when to outsource a project or do it yourself? Answer these 10 questions when considering whether to hire a professional for assistance:

1. Have you ever done this before?

   - *If no:* How much time, energy, and resources will you have to spend just in order to learn how to do it? How steep will your learning curve be?
   - *If yes:* Is this something that you enjoy doing and are able to do with relative ease, or is it something that you will find dreadful and difficult?

2. Realistically, how long will it take you to get this to where you are very satisfied with the results? (This question is especially important if you have any perfectionistic tendencies.)

3. Exactly how much will it cost if you hire this out? (Don't assume you know, as you may find the actual costs to be much higher or lower than anticipated).

4. If you spend the money to outsource part or all of this project, what other projects will you have to put on hold? If you spend your time and energy doing this project yourself, what other projects will you have to put on hold?

5. Does this project have a direct impact on your ability to launch your business, find more clients, or land clients faster or more efficiently? (In general, the more a project impacts an important business function, the more you should consider hiring an expert to help you with some or all of it.)

6. Does this project have a direct impact on how others will view and perceive your business?

7. What does your trusted advisor think? What would you tell your clients if one of them asked you for coaching on this?

8. When you think about doing this project, does it feel energizing or draining?

9. Do you want to do this project yourself because you believe you can do it better or faster, or do you just not want to spend the money?

10. Knowing your time and skill set limitations, what would be best for your business in the long run, from an objective point of view?

MISTAKE 10: STARTING OUT WITH A LACK OF FUNDING OR MARKETING CAPITAL

Take careful stock of how much actual money you have to start and build your business without counting on any additional revenue from your new coaching practice. The greatest outlay of cash will come in the first 12 to 18 months. You should have enough money to cover all your business expenses, marketing expenses, living expenses, and unanticipated expenses for at least 12 months. The most powerful aspect of money is that it creates opportunities. The more money you have available, the more opportunities you can pursue. You are also less likely to make "live-or-die" decisions or impetuous choices when you have multiple opportunities. Your marketing plan must include projected expenses for all your activities (for a detailed list of first-year budget items, turn to Chapter 4). Take your expected annual total costs and multiply them by a factor of 1.3 to 1.6 to give you a rough estimate of how much you will actually need that first year. There will always be unexpected problems or unanticipated opportunities you want to pursue that are not accounted for in your plan. About 60 percent of your budget should be set aside for sales and marketing activities. The new coaches who have built their businesses the fastest spent about $200 to $500 per month on sales- and marketing-related activities for the first year.

> Money creates opportunities. The more money you have available, the more opportunities you can pursue.

SUMMARY

In this chapter we have focused on the 10 most common marketing mistakes beginning coaches make. In each section we have discussed specific ways you can both avoid these mistakes and remedy them if you find yourself in the middle of committing one. Take a few minutes and scan the chapter again. Note each mistake you believe you are most likely to commit in the coming year, then write down one to two ideas you can use to help you avoid this situation. Use this chapter in developing your SWOT (strengths, weaknesses, opportunities, and threats) analysis, as discussed in Chapter 6.

Although experienced coaches often make the same mistakes, they usually find ways to make new ones, so here are the top 10 mistakes I have seen experienced coaches make:

1. Working their referral networks inconsistently instead of finding multiple ways to keep in touch with all their referral sources on a consistent basis (every four to eight weeks)
2. Failing to keep on marketing when they have enough clients to keep them satisfied instead of consistently investing 10 to 15 percent of their time on marketing
3. Failing to develop solid relationships with multiple referral sources because you never know when your best source of new clients will dry up
4. Failing to reinvest their profits back into their company to further grow their business
5. Falling back on just being a technician, instead of building a company
6. Surrounding themselves only with other technicians who do the work instead of rainmakers who bring in the work
7. Relying on what worked in the past to get them through their current slump instead of rapidly responding to the ever-changing markets by modifying their packages, pricing mix, or services
8. Failing to develop multiple revenue streams by offering products, other services, consulting, or training events
9. Staying in the niche they are most comfortable with instead of expanding their efforts once they have established a solid base
10. Becoming too protective and running their business out of a fear mentality instead of running it from an abundance mentality

From Counseling to Coaching: Constructing a Connection, Bridging the Gap, and Defining the Differences

This book would not be complete without a section on making the transition from a professionally regulated field, such as psychology or counseling, to coaching. While it is outside the scope of this book to deal with this issue in full, I do believe it is important to discuss some of the major differences you will have to confront, plan for, and overcome if you are to be successful in the field of professional coaching. For our purposes here, I will use the example of psychology because it seems that the majority of coaches making the transition from other professional fields are coming from the mental health or psychology field. In this chapter we will discuss the differences in the following areas:

- How you market and sell your services
- How to talk about your experiences as a psychologist or counselor
- The biggest areas of change from counseling to coaching

DEFINING YOUR TARGET MARKET

In psychology it's pretty easy to define who your target market is: someone who meets the diagnostic criteria or comes close to it. There is no handbook telling you who "qualifies" as a legitimate coaching client. It is entirely up to you to define who your target market is, and because of your background, you probably have not had much experience or interest in defining a target market. However, this first step is critical to your success in coaching. "Adults in general" will not cut it. You must be absolutely crystal clear about who your exact target market is, because it is only then that you can talk about how you can help potential clients in a compelling way. See Chapter 2 for more help in defining your market.

CLARIFYING THE PROBLEMS YOU HELP PEOPLE WITH

Though this may seem like an obvious statement, many professionals miss the point that they are really helping people with completely different problems and challenges when coaching them rather than conducting psychotherapy. If you talk to typical psychologists turned coaches and ask them what they do, it seems they use the same phrases and descriptions as they did when they were talking to people about their therapy practices. You must think and talk differently. You are no longer dealing with depression, anxiety, and intrapsychic dysfunctions. Instead, you are working with people's goals, dreams, passion, and vision. The distinction must be clear in your mind and in your speech. In coaching, you are no longer the aloof expert with all the power; your goal is to create a partnership with your clients. Your clients are people not to be coddled or protected, but pushed to dream and achieve. Remember this focus when creating your brochures, giving your presentations, marketing your services, and talking with prospects.

THE TYPICAL SALES CYCLE

Possibly the biggest difference between traditional psychotherapy and the current coaching movement is the typical sales cycle—the process whereby suspects become prospects and prospects become paying clients. In my personal experience, by the time people make contact with a therapist, they are way past the point of being advised that they might need some help. In all likelihood, they have long exhausted all their personal resources (friends and family), and they have already made the decision that they need professional help. They don't need much convincing; rather, for the professional it's a matter of screening them for appropriateness (e.g., active suicidal ideation, substance abuse, need for psychological testing, age group, and insurance status). There is little to no formal "selling" involved. You talk with the client over the phone, set up an intake session, have them fill out some paperwork, conduct the intake session, and either set up the next appointment or make a referral.

Nothing could be further from the truth when it comes to the sales cycle in coaching. The sales cycle in coaching will be as smooth and straightforward as in counseling in only a very small percentage of cases. More often than not, it is long, involved, and rarely clear cut. Let me illustrate. In most cases, the prospect you are approaching is not asking around for a good coach they can go to, because they don't even know what professional coaching is, much less how a professional coach can help. So your first task becomes one of basic introduction and education. After you explain what a professional coach is, if they are still interested, they start asking you questions like, "What kinds of things do you coach people on?" The temptation here is to list as many things possible in the hope that one or two items will connect with them, but this would be a mistake, because you would be trying to sell coaching and your services. You should never try to sell coaching or your services. First, people don't care what services you provide. Second, coaching is a tool. It's only the process you use. When talking with prospects, you should always focus on selling the results your clients achieve, the benefits you give, and the value you provide. If you pass this initial questioning by interested prospects with flying colors, then the real dance begins. You may go through several e-mail and phone contacts to get them to the point where they are ready to meet face to face for a coaching session. During the coaching session, you again are exposed to some difficult questioning (especially after they find out how much you charge), and if you're lucky they will make the decision then and there. Otherwise, there may be a period of ongoing debate and dialogue about the same issues you have already explained (how you can help, how long you work with people, who your clients have been, what the typical results are, and so on) before they make the decision to move forward or not. This whole process from start to finish often takes a few weeks for individuals. Now, if you are targeting businesses, this is often just the first level, and the larger the business, the more levels there are. It is not uncommon for a midsized company to spend four to eight months researching, asking questions, receiving proposals, and interviewing before they make the final decision to move forward or not with a given coaching project.

> Never sell coaching. Coaching is only a tool, the process you use to reach your goal. Always focus on selling the results, the benefits, and the value.

It can be difficult for psychologists to grasp that there is no "typical" sales cycle in coaching because there are so many variables it depends on: your target market, the total cost, your experience, the strength of your references, your sales ability, your proposal-writing skills, and so on. Just remember, it is totally different from the sales cycle you are used to in your professional field.

CONFIDENTIALITY

Even though I believe that professional coaches should have a standard of confidentiality, and many professional organizations are implementing one, the industry standard is not anywhere near the one followed by mental health clinicians. I remember the first time I unexpectedly met one of my current clients at a networking event. I was completely caught off guard when he started introducing me to people as his coach, and I wasn't sure if I should say something to him or not. Unfortunately, there is still a stigma in our society about seeing a mental health therapist, and most people would rather die than introduce someone as their therapist in public. However, the most common way professional coaches find new clients is through direct referral from current and former clients (32 percent). There is also the small matter of client testimonials: It can be ethically risky for a therapist to either ask for or use, testimonials, but it is critical for professional coaches to both ask for client testimonials on a regular basis and use them in all their marketing materials.

COMPETITION AND DIFFERENTIATION

The competitors of clinical psychologists are well defined—other psychologists, social workers, master's level therapists, community mental health centers, treatment that relys solely on prescribed psychotropic medication, and that's about it. The competition for the kinds of services a coach provides can come from many different sources: other coaches, psychologists and other mental health therapists, spiritual leaders, organizational development experts, human resource agencies, thousands of consultants looking for alternative revenue streams, motivational speakers (for example, Anthony Robbins has added personal coaching to his team's repertoire), internal HR departments, intensive seminars and interactive workshops, and self-help resources (books, radio and television programs, and support groups), just to name a few. You must be familiar with the pros and cons of each of these in order to know how to best differentiate yourself from your competitors.

When conducting psychotherapy, there are very few ways to truly distinguish yourself, at least that you can easily explain to the average layperson. The most recognizable difference is whether you prescribe

Shirley A. Maides-Keane, PhD
President
Maides-Keane Associates, Inc.
Oak Brook, Illinois
www.m-kassociates.com
mka@m-kassociates.com
(630) 990-1919

You have a strong background in psychology. How did you first get started in coaching and consulting?

If I go back to the very first time I did coaching, I would have to say it was with a client in 1980–1981. This individual had initially sought psychological treatment for her career dissatisfaction. After treating the underlying depression, she continued to work on life-planning and career-planning issues. In short, I coached her from music teacher getting an MBA at Northwestern while working in a publishing company into a career that has taken her to the top of the classical music business as business director for the most renowned orchestra in the world. In 1981, when I established a psychology practice on Michigan Avenue in Chicago, I found myself working more as a coach than a therapist. I had a CEO as a client who wanted to work on setting up an effective family structure with his new wife and children, a businessman who needed coaching beyond nonproductive habits that were creating problems for him in the workplace, two business associates who asked for help in working out their communication issues, and so on. Essentially, coaching has always been a part of my professional work. I called this part of my practice "consulting" and ran it side by side with my clinical practice for almost two decades. Then in 1999 I began to separate the consulting practice from the clinical practice and shift my focus to the consulting work.

Tell us about your current coaching and consulting practice.

My current coaching practice is evolving into specialty niche areas. I am focusing on professional service firms (accountants, attorneys, consultants, etc.) and family businesses, and continuing to work with companies that have been clients for years. In the last year I have developed a web site, created a general brochure, begun public speaking engagements, and put together a marketing plan for 2003. I am expecting 2003 to be a pivotal year in the evolution of my coaching/consulting practice.

What is one piece of advice that you would give to a psychologist or therapist just starting out?

It seems to me that self-reflection and clarification about what one has to offer as a coach are critical to moving into a successful practice. The clearer you are about what you can offer, and who you would like to offer it to, the better your chances of getting going effectively. I think some sort of mentoring or coaching for the coach is important to assist in your self-assessment, and I would encourage someone new to the field to establish such a relationship.

Even though you've been in practice for more than 25 years, what were two mistakes you made early on in your coaching and consulting practice that beginning coaches should avoid?

The first mistake that I made had to do with forming nonproductive relationships with organizations promising to deliver business. I would caution beginning coaches to be very careful about investing in procurement services or affiliations that require a substantial financial investment.

The second mistake I would caution new coaches about is spending too much time with organizations that do not generate business for you. It is very easy to get involved in organizations that have great promise for your business only to find that after a year or so of heavy involvement on your part you have no new business to show for it. Stay aware of where you find business and allocate your time accordingly.

medication, but even that line is becoming blurred. The common distinctions used are the following:

- Who you work with (children, adolescents, adults, or the elderly)
- How long you typically work with people (less than six months, more than six months, or it all depends—which is the most common answer)

- Your theoretical orientation (cognitive-behavioral, psychodynamic, or eclectic—and good luck explaining the real differences to a client in emotional pain beyond a superficial level)
- Any specialty area (substance abuse, domestic violence, gay and lesbian issues, etc.)
- How much you charge per session
- What insurance you accept (the most important distinction of all to the average layperson)

In coaching, not only can the distinctions be greater, they must be a lot clearer if you are to land many clients. For each category, you must be able to clearly and concisely distinguish and differentiate yourself, your services, and your results from your competitors. For more help with this, turn to Chapter 7.

Setting Fees

In most areas, fees for the practice of psychology are set either by community standards or, more likely, by what insurance companies will pay. At the time of this writing, here in Chicago, the standard clinical psychologist charges about $120 per hour. On the East and West Coasts the rates are slightly higher, at about $150 an hour. To go much above or below that is just not done by anyone except an elite few. However, the variation of fees for coaching is enormous, ranging from a low of $20 to more than $750 per hour. Let's get even more specific: In my survey, 59 percent of all coaches charged between $75 and $175 an hour (mean = $162, median = $150). Among personal coaches, the average was $132 (median = $100) with a range of $25 to $400. Among business coaches, the mean was $213 (median = $200) with a range of $50 to $750 per hour. As you can see, there is even a large difference between personal coaches and business coaches. I have worked with several psychologists as they made the transition into coaching and have found that every single one of them struggled with charging an appropriate amount based on their years of experience and ability to make a significant impact on their clients' lives. Research indicates that in coaching and consulting the more experience you have the more you charge, yet psychologists never seem to want to charge more for their coaching than they do for their counseling, which is a big mistake. Often my first piece of advice to a coach who comes to me for marketing assistance is "Raise your rates by 25 to 50 percent and then land your next prospect at the higher rate." Virtually all of my clients have successfully landed their next client at that higher rate (of course, there is much more to landing new clients than simply raising your rates, but you understand my point). This exercise in raising their rates seems to be very freeing for these clients, because for far too long, in my opinion, psychological services have been significantly undervalued, but mental health professionals have grudgingly come to accept this. The direct experience in interpersonal relationships and intrapersonal transformation that a typical psychologist has is very valuable to clients, and coaching is one area where they can actually be paid a more accurate rate based on their experience, abilities, and education. Of course it is not appropriate for a psychologist to coach a client at the same depth as they would perform psychotherapy.

Another major difference when setting fees is how you charge. I am not aware of any psychologist or therapist who charges a monthly, quarterly, or per-project fee. In fact, it is quite difficult for me to imagine a psychologist saying to a prospect, "I will charge you $3,500 to help you overcome your marital difficulties." However, charging monthly or project-based fees is commonly done in coaching; 52 percent of all coaches charge by the month, 20 percent by the hour, and 13 percent by the project. In business coaching, it is very common to write up a proposal based on conversations with the prospect, and determine one price for the entire project.

EDUCATION VERSUS EXPERIENCE

In the professional world, your education is everything—which school you went to, the degree you obtained (PhD, PsyD, MD), and whether your internship was accredited. In real life, your prospects won't care about any of these things. They probably will not ask about your academic education. In fact, you may even find your degrees to be a hindrance to landing some clients, because people don't want to be stigmatized by going to a psychologist or therapist who moonlights as a coach. I have come across many brochures, web sites, and business cards listing all the educational degrees from academic institutions a psychologist turned coach has acquired. What these people fail to understand, or perhaps *accept* is a better word, is that none of this matters to prospects. All their prospects really care about are these questions:

- Have you ever coached anyone in their particular situation, industry, or position?
- What were the results?
- How do they know you can help them?
- Will they get an excellent ROI on their investment in coaching?

So in your marketing materials and your conversations, do not focus on your education, but on your experience and the results you obtain for clients.

Major Ways to Find New Clients

Since this whole book is about marketing, I won't try to reiterate all the various points, except to say that the big difference here is that most psychologists and mental health therapists find clients primarily through passive means. In other words, they sit back in their offices and let clients come to them. In contrast, most coaches starting out must be very active in finding clients. They must get out of their offices on a consistent basis and actively seek out clients, and when they find them, they must directly solicit their business, which is anathema to the psychologist. There are few things that will kill your coaching business faster than just sitting at home waiting for the phone to ring. Regardless of how easy it sounded in that last teleclass you took on "How to make a lot of money coaching people—in less than 60 days without leaving your home," it just does not happen. Check out Chapter 9.

Discovering Your Strategic Partners

The primary differences here are who your best referral sources are and how you describe your ideal client to them. Common referral sources for most psychologists include other mental health professionals, medical doctors and psychiatrists, school system personnel, lawyers, church leaders, and hospital personnel. A single well-placed source can quickly produce more than enough clients to keep a single therapist busy for years to come. The list must be much wider for most coaches, including

Patrick Williams, EdD, MCC
Chief Executive Officer
Institute of Life Coach Training
www.LifeCoachTraining.com
Pat@LifeCoachTraining.com

Pat Williams is CEO of the Institute of Life Coach Training. He is a leader in the profession of personal coaching and the author of the recent book, *Therapist as Life Coach: Transforming Your Practice* (W.W. Norton, 2002).

Many people have called you the "ambassador of life coaching" since you were one of the first leaders in the field. Tell us about how you got started.

I started coaching as part of my psychology practice. I was constantly looking for new and innovative ways to use my skills outside of the office. In the late 1980s, I led several corporate training events using a weekend "executive bootcamp" and found I really liked it. In fact, I liked it so much that I wanted to go full-time in coaching and did so in 1996. At one point in my practice, I had over 40 coaching clients, 30 individuals and 12 executives in two groups. I also spent some time teaching at CoachU prior to starting the Institute of Life Coach Training, which focuses on helping mental health therapists make the transition into life coaching. We just graduated our thousandth student and our goal is another thousand in the next two years.

There is a growing number of professionals in the counseling and psychology fields who are transitioning to coaching. Any thoughts on that?

Well, my first thought is that there is not a really defined *field* of coaching, like there is a field of psychology. Coaching is too new and still in its infancy. Some of the potential conflicts I see between coaching and counseling are these:

- There is a small, but growing, effort to change the definition of psychology to include coaching. If this takes hold, it will cause confusion on both sides.

(Continued)

- A major distinction in my mind is that in coaching a client doesn't need or want to be diagnosed, as they do when seeing a psychologist.
- Some coaches are also confusing people when they advertise themselves as "ADD coaches." I believe it is best not to coach someone with a psychological disorder.

However, I do believe therapists can make great life coaches because they are skillful listeners; they have the gift of reframing, the ability to suspend judgment, and a gift for seeking solutions and thinking of new possibilities. After being a therapist for so long, the biggest mistake I made starting out as a life coach was not having an ideal client profile. Not spending time clarifying who I wanted to coach meant I wasn't as focused, and I ended up coaching clients who were very similar to my former therapy clients, which I didn't want.

What is one piece of advice you would give to a new coach just starting out?

A key tip I often tell new coaches is "Quit being a secret." In coaching, you will be hired for who you are, not just what you do; it's the persona you present. Make marketing a natural part of who you are. Eventually most conversations you strike up with people move around to "What do you do?" When you answer that question in a powerful and convincing way, that is marketing, because all the marketing strategies in the world won't work unless you are passionate about your coaching and you are able to clearly and concisely explain what you do.

Second, remember that coaching is about living the life, not the lifestyle. Right now there is too much emphasis on making a lot of money in coaching. Don't get me wrong, there is nothing wrong with making money, but coaching is about more than just making money. I tell people who are concerned about the money that it is possible to make a six-figure income, but a beginning coach shouldn't expect that. For therapists coming into coaching, I ask them, "What are you charging as a therapist? $100 per hour is average, with the East and West Coasts averaging about $150 per hour, but with insurance and managed care you never get that. In coaching, that's just the starting point, and many coaches charge a lot more than that."

What do you believe are the future trends in coaching?

Right now, coaching is primarily a baby-boom profession. Most coaches are baby boomers, as are their clients. In the future, I believe coaching has the potential to permeate our society so that it will be available at all levels of society, not just for the rich and powerful. Coaching can become a paradigm of communication — a way for people to relate in a healthier way than we currently do, rather than just a tool we use to help our initial results become sustainable over time.

doctors, lawyers, accountants, church leaders, trainers, community leaders, career counselors and recruiters, consultants who do not coach, board members, graduate professors, and bankers, to name a few. Mental health counselors tell referral sources something very similar to what they would tell prospective clients, and they let the sources fill in the rest of the details about what they do. Coaches must be more deliberate in drawing a picture of who their ideal clients are, because most referral sources are not too familiar with professional coaching. They do not have a common knowledge base from which to draw. For example, you may hear a business marketing coach describing their ideal client to a small-business lawyer as "the owner or CEO of a small business with at least 20 employees and $10 million in revenue who talks to you about their challenges in finding new clients, the high cost of advertising, and an overall decrease in their quarterly revenues." Study Chapter 8 for more specific information.

SELF-CONFIDENCE

I recall a graduate psychology professor of mine saying he didn't really feel that he knew what he was doing until he had been in private practice for about 10 years. Being a very humble man, I was sure he was grossly exaggerating at the time or was simply expressing some of the long-gone self-doubt that every professional has at one time or another, but then I recalled that he had obtained his doctorate from the PhD program at Vanderbilt when he was still in his early twenties. To place this in perspective, it has been my observation that psychologists get most of their healthy self-confidence from four areas: strong academic training, extensive knowledge about mental health, direct experience treating a given diagnosis, and personal life experience. If they lack confidence in any one area, such as their age (direct experience), they typically try to overcompensate in the other areas. When a layperson enters the psychologist's office, chances are quite high that the average therapist knows far more about a given disorder than the client. This knowledge gives the psychologist a sense of security.

> Being a consultant is about being the expert—having all the right answers. Being a coach is about being a partner—asking all the right questions.

The difference in coaching is that ultimately the client, not the coach, is the expert. Herein lies the startling difference. Being a consultant is about being the expert—having all the right answers. Being a coach is about being a partner—asking all the right questions. In order to be an effective coach you do not have to have all the right answers, but you must have the self-confidence to ask the right questions at the right time and believe that those questions can help your clients find their way through the maze surrounding them. No client will ever hire you if your reply is, "Well, I don't have much experience in this area, but I think I can help you." This is doubly true for business coaches, who often mix their coaching with consulting. You must have enough self-confidence to believe that what you offer is extremely valuable and can have an incredible impact in your client's life if they chose to apply it. No self-confidence equals no clients. This leads right into the next area.

TIPS FOR MAKING THE TRANSITION

- Deemphasize your educational credentials, instead emphasize your experience.
- Make up separate business cards with your coaching title on them.
- Don't mention your current psychotherapy practice anywhere on any of your marketing materials.

- Stop focusing on your services. Do not create a long list of all the different problems you coach around.
- If you are thinking about becoming a business coach, immerse yourself in business magazines, business books, and top periodicals.
- Stop going to the networking events your peers attend.
- Start going to the networking events your prospects attend.
- Talk to your current referral sources about your transition and what that means to your relationship with them.
- Set aside a specific amount of time every week to work on your coaching practice.
- Find a marketing coach to help you clearly understand the process and work with you during the transition.
- Develop a timeline for making the transition. It takes most professionals one to two years to complete the transition.
- Read good books on making the transition.

SUMMARY

Leaving your professional field can be a difficult decision to make. After all, you spent so much of your time, energy, and money obtaining the academic credentials and fulfilling all the licensure requirements to practice. The reasons to change or modify career paths vary from person to person, but for many professionals in the field of psychology and mental health, coaching is a breath of fresh air. No managed care. No late-night hours. No constantly ringing pagers. No suicidal or borderline clients. And the hourly rates are much higher. I'm not here to try to convince you to change, but if you are considering the change, I recommend that you work through each area mentioned in this chapter. Most professionals make the change over a period of months or even years; some complete it within a couple of months. Whatever your decision, be clear about your choice, develop a solid plan, and work the plan.

CHAPTER 12

Harnessing the Power of Internet Marketing, E-zines, and Web Sites

When it comes to using technology in your coaching practice, I believe there are two types of coaches—those who effectively use the power of the Internet and those who will be left behind. The Internet is not a fad. It is not a trend. It is a reality, and as technology becomes more and more entrenched in our society, prospects will not ask you *if* you have an e-mail address, they will assume you have one. They will not ask *if* you have a web site, they will ask you what the address is. To a large extent, we are already there. Having a presence on the Internet is now so inexpensive and relatively easy to accomplish that not having one signifies that your company is either brand new, illegitimate, or a fly-by-night organization. Is this the kind of image you want for your company? Obviously not. The downside of not having an Internet presence is magnified when it comes to the upside potential in terms of automating your business, educating your prospects, selling products, supplementing or even supplanting costly printed material, and providing value to prospects and clients.

In Chapter 4, we talked about the five basic costs associated with having an Internet presence: domain registration, writing your text, designing your web site, hosting the site, and maintenance costs. We are now going to cover each of these items in more depth. We will also be talking about these points:

- The dos and don'ts of web sites
- How to design your homepage
- Basic Internet marketing strategies
- Four steps to making money through your web site
- Electronic newsletters, commonly known as e-zines, one of the hottest marketing techniques in the coaching field right now

When thinking about using the power of the Internet to drive new business to your coaching practice and service existing clients, here are some important questions to answer:

- How can you leverage the power of the Internet for maximum advantage?
- What are the specific ways the Internet can make your life and business easier?
- What are your competitors doing on the Internet?

- How is the Internet changing the behavior of your clients and prospects, and how does that impact what you do with the Internet?

Launching Your Coaching Web Site

Domain Registration

The first step in having a web site is to register a *domain name*. A domain name is the name you type into your Internet browser to go to a web site. For example, www.yahoo.com, www.msnbc.com, and www.TodaysLeadership.com are all domain names. Registering a domain name is a very simple process. Go to one of the hundreds of web sites that register domain names and follow their easy process. If you don't know of any, go to your favorite search engine and type in the phrase *register domain name,* and you will find hundreds of them. In fact, many of them will even give you a simple, one-page placeholder until you get your regular web site up. This is also where you are able to set up your e-mail address. The company you register the domain name with usually has a web-based interface you can use to set up any e-mail address from your domain name, for example, Stephen@ TodaysLeadership.com or Info@TodaysLeadership.com. The cost to register a domain name is $10 to $35 per year, but the more expensive ones typically don't give you anything more than the cheap ones do.

If you use Microsoft Outlook you can easily set up your e-mail account so it looks as though you are mailing from that e-mail address as well, but good luck if you are using AOL or a free web-based e-mail program like Yahoo! or Hotmail, because as of this writing none of them allow you to do this. In fact, if you have been using the Internet for more than a couple of years and are still using one of these, now would be a good time to switch to a regular Internet service provider (ISP). The many advantages are beyond the scope of this book, but suffice it to say that having an e-mail address ending in .aol, .yahoo, or .hotmail does not look professional, not to mention that it opens you up to receiving more spam than your competitors.

Here are some tips when registering a domain name:

- Your web site name is a critical choice. Be careful about your choice. Make it short, memorable, related to your business, and hard to misspell. Some bad examples would be www.this-is-my-coaching-and-consulting-practice.com (too long) or www .billslifeline.com (easy to misspell).

- Try to get one that ends in .com rather than .org, .net, .info, .us, or any of the new ones. The .com extension is the most commonly accepted one for businesses. There are many new domain name extensions (commonly known as *TLDs* for top-level domains) now available, but they are not commonly recognized (e.g., .info, .biz, .ws, .tv, and .us).
- All of the good, straightforward .com domain names are long gone, so you will have to be a little creative.
- There are several good web sites that give you alternative domain names. For example, instead of TodaysLeadership.com, which is already taken, they might recommend eTodaysLeadership.com or MyTodaysLeadership.com.
- Try to make the name short, less than 20 letters long.
- Try to use your entire company name or part of it when possible. If it is not available, use a name that describes what you do.
- If you want to look professional, you must have a professional-looking e-mail address, for example, Stephen@TodaysLeadership .com. Regardless of how attached you are to your AOL or Yahoo! account, if you want to look like a professional, you must have a professional e-mail address. In all likelihood, you received several free e-mail accounts when you registered your web site domain name, and all you have to do is activate them. If you don't know how, ask the company you registered your domain name with. Think of this as another way to advertise your web site.
- Don't use your own personal name for your primary company domain name. There are certain exceptions; such as if you are a well-known person or you are promoting yourself as a professional speaker (see www.StephenFairley.com as an example).

DEVELOPMENT OF TEXT AND LAYOUT

You can probably do much of the actual writing of the web site content, especially if you have spent time developing a solid, professional brochure that focuses on the benefits and results you offer, because much of the text can be very similar. Good copy is good copy is good copy—whether it is found in a brochure, in a newsletter, or on a web site, you need to have solid copy that emphasizes the results your clients achieve, your experience, who you help, and your credibility and creates a sense of trustworthiness. Though there are hundreds of ways people section off and divide up their web sites, most revolve around some combination of these four areas:

- *Homepage.* This is the first page you come to when you enter in a domain name.
- *Services.* This describes what kind of services you provide and the programs you offer.
- *Clients.* This page describes your typical clients, mentions who some of your former clients have been, and presents some client testimonials.
- *About Us.* This page gives a company overview and biographies of the owners.

There are a number of rules to remember when writing the copy for your web site:

- It has to immediately attract your target audience.
- It must focus on the benefits and results you offer, not your services.
- Each page should start with an attention-grabbing headline that clearly states the point you are trying to make on that page in a compelling way.
- Each page must begin to build the case for why people should contact you.
- There must be a call to action—why should they call you and why should they call you now?
- It must be creative, but not so clever that it drives your target away.
- There must be a component of educating visitors as to what coaching is and how it helps.
- It must be clear, concise, compelling, contagious, and communicative, speaking to your target group at their point of pain.
- You have only 7 to 10 seconds to catch visitors' attention before they go to another web site.

- Most people will only view your homepage, so make sure it is your best work.

If you do not have experience writing persuasive letters, direct-mail pieces, or presentations, I recommend that you either read a few books on how to do so or work with a professional who does have experience. As you write your text, focus on who your target market is and try to get inside their minds by answering these questions:

- If you were looking for a coach on the Internet, what kind of coach would you be looking for?
- How would that coach describe what they do?
- What is the real motivation that is driving you to search for a coach on the Internet?
- What kinds of benefits should you expect from coaching?
- What specific results typically come from coaching?
- Why should you hire this specific coach versus another?
- How does coaching work?
- What are the goals that you want to accomplish?
- Who has this coach worked with before?
- How do you know they can help with your situation?
- Why should you contact this coach now rather than wait a few more months?
- If you're interested, what's the fastest way you can contact this coach?

If you answer each of these questions in the text on your web site, you will be way ahead of most of your competitors.

ACTION STEP

The best way to get a feel for how others divide this information up and see what appeals to you is to spend some time looking at various web sites put up by other coaches, consultants, and potential clients. Assume that you are a member of your target audience and something causes you to seek out a professional coach for some assistance. Define what that problem or challenge is, then go to your favorite search engine (www.google.com is the best one) and do individual searches for *personal coach, business coach, professional coach, consultant,* or whatever title you use to describe what you do.

Here are some questions you can use to evaluate the web sites you come across:

- Write down the names of the web sites you are most impressed with for later reference.
- Trying to remain in a mind-set similar to your target audience's, which sites immediately attract you? Why? Be as specific as possible.
- Which ones immediately repel you? Why? Again, be as specific as possible.
- Which ones seem to draw you in right from the first page and make you want to find out more?
- What characteristics would be attractive to your target audience?
- What features do you find attractive?
- If you could imitate one idea from each web site, what would that be (other than the actual text)?
- How easy is it to navigate and find your way around the web site?
- What do they do to make it easy to find exactly what you're looking for on the site?
- What kinds of things do they emphasize (features, benefits, biography, services)?
- How do they communicate trust to their prospects?
- Can you quickly and easily identify their target markets? What are they?
- What colors and type of layout do the ones that attract you use?
- Write a description of the web site you want, using as many descriptors as possible.

Now that you have conducted some basic research, and hopefully clarified some of your thinking on the subject, it's time to develop your ideas and concepts even further. These questions will guide you:

- Write down the top three goals for your coaching web site (e.g., provide an online presence for your coaching business, help increase your credibility among your prospects).
- What is the primary purpose of your web site (e.g., to be an online brochure, to attract small-business owners, to make money, to get people to sign up for a teleclass, to sell your new e-book)?
- Who exactly makes up the target audience you want to appeal to with your web site?
- What kinds of questions can you ask visitors to quickly qualify them as good prospects?
- What exact information do prospects need in order to feel compelled to pick up the phone and call you?
- How will your web site lead prospects through the decision-making process?

The easiest way to conceptualize how a web site works is to visualize it as an organizational flow chart. Figure 12.1 shows an example of a well-developed executive coaching web site. The lines represent a direct link from one page to another. Notice how each level becomes more and more specific, guiding prospects toward the information they want based on preselected criteria. Unless you plan on coding the web site yourself, I suggest you start talking with your web designer at this level, instead of waiting until you have already written all the text. You can save yourself a lot of time and trouble by bouncing your ideas off your professional web designer, who can help you avoid some of the common problems and mistakes that beginners make, as well as give you some great and innovative ideas that you can build right into your web site layout.

DESIGNING YOUR WEB SITE

Thanks to the wonders of technology you now have a couple of choices when it comes to actually building and coding a web site: You can hire someone to do it or do it yourself. Building and coding the web site, which is the actual process of putting your text into a format an Internet browser can read, such as Hypertext Markup Language (HTML),

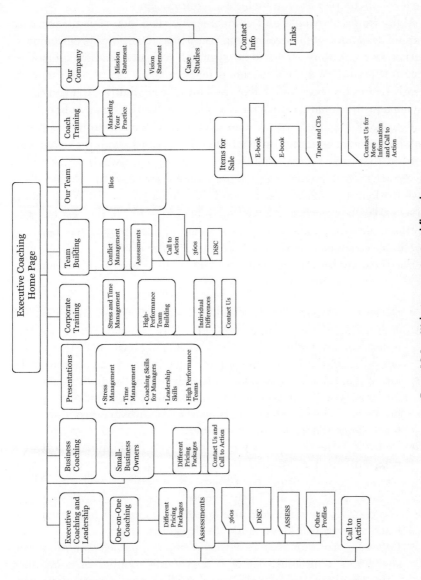

FIGURE 12.1   Web site organizational flow chart.

along with designing the navigational system and connecting all the links within the web site, can be relatively easy or difficult depending on the level of complexity you include in your design.

Many kinds of people and companies do web site design, including graphic designers, web development companies, computer programmers, marketing consultants, PR and ad agencies, web site hosting companies, your uncle, and your neighborhood teenage whiz kid. Rates can vary greatly from a few hundred dollars well into the six figures. In most cases, having a professional design a basic web site will cost you anywhere from $500 to $3,000, more if you use an experienced local person, less if you look for someone over the Internet. If you're serious about the image you present, I strongly recommend that you hire a great web designer with a solid track record of working with professional service firms. Personally, I have worked with Angela Nielsen at NIC Media (www.NICMedia.com) on several web projects and have found them to be one of the best web site development companies I have ever come across. Angela has been an invaluable strategic partner as my business has grown.

For those ambitious do it yourselfers or for those with not enough money, there are three options:

- *Option 1.* Learn HTML, which is the most difficult and time con-suming of the three choices and probably is not worth your effort unless you are technically inclined. Learning basic HTML codes is not difficult, but being able to put it all together in a coherent fash-ion so that it looks great and reads well is a challenge. If this option intrigues you, visit your local library and check out a couple of books on HTML. There are also several software programs that teach you HTML on your computer.
- *Option 2.* Become proficient with a web development software program, such as Microsoft FrontPage or Dreamweaver, which will guide you through the process of designing a web site. Many of these programs are fairly simple—if you can learn Microsoft Word or PowerPoint and use a mouse to cut and paste, you can learn to use a web development software program.
- *Option 3.* You can use one of the hosting companies that offers web site design templates. There is a growing number of companies offering several dozen templates that allow you to manipulate var-ious aspects of your web site, such as the layout, colors, graphics, font type, and navigational system. You pay a monthly fee and they

allow you to use their template and provide web site hosting for you. While this may seem like an obvious choice, the downside is the limited number of options. The templates are great if you are not too picky, but they can become a real hassle if you love endless choices and are a perfectionist ("I want the picture to be half an inch lower but the template doesn't allow it" or "I wish I could have navy blue text instead of just black or red"). I used HTML for the first web site I built, and, along with some outside help, it took about four weeks from start to finish. For the second one, I used a template from VeriSign/Network Solutions (www.netsol.com) and completed it in about two days. My third web site was done completely by a professional web designer.

Several recommended sites that offer templates for your web site:

www.netsol.com
www.bigstep.com
www.bcentral.com
www.yahoo.com

Search for *web site templates* to find more.

If you want a professional image and want to be taken seriously by prospects, you must have a web site, and though you don't need to spend several thousand dollars on it, at the first chance you should hire someone to build a great one for you. Several times I have been contacted by midsized to large companies and asked to bid on coaching projects based solely on the image and information they found on my company web site (www.TodaysLeadership.com).

Speaking of web site design, the most important part of your web site is your homepage. Over 60 percent of all people who visit your web site never go beyond your homepage. Here are some recommendations to help you lower that statistic on your web site.

- *Be focused.* Regardless of how much you want to be everything to everybody and attract anyone, you can't. You must target your market or you will waste your time. It must be very clear to first-time visitors who your target audience is, how you help them, and what results you achieve. You must use your homepage to draw people further into your web site. It must be inviting to your target market.

- *Be specific.* Ask yourself, "Exactly what are the visitors to my web site looking for?" When you answer that question, give them several ways to easily find that information on your web site and be specific in answering their questions.

- *Be clear.* What goals do you have for your web site? Is it merely a brochure? A place to sell your new e-book? A communication center for your existing clients? Set overall goals for your web site, then break them down into specific statements so that you can develop a web site that will clearly meet those goals.

- *Be professional.* In Chapter 7 we talked about the importance of making a positive first impression. Consistently, some of the most unprofessional web sites I come across are coaching web sites. You are asking people to trust you and pay you a lot of money—$100 to $200 an hour or more—so don't put up a web site that screams of incompetence. Either do it right or don't do it at all. Your web site enhances your credibility or it detracts from it; there is no middle ground. Be professional, because people will judge your web site by your homepage.

QUESTIONS TO ASK A HOSTING COMPANY

- What hosting packages do you offer?
- What are the hours of technical support?
- Is technical support available via phone or just e-mail?
- What are the details about the web site statistics program you use?
- If I want to move to an e-commerce web site later, what would that cost per month?
- Do you know of any particular problems with the software program I'm using? Based on my goals, which program would you recommend?
- Do you support FrontPage or Dreamweaver if I decide to use one of those programs?

HOSTING YOUR WEB SITE

Hosting a web site is the process of loading your web site files onto a server connected to the Internet, which, in turn, allows people to type in your domain name and go to your web site. The cost for doing this has dropped considerably over the past few years; it usually now costs $10 to $30 per month for a basic hosting package and $40 to $100 for one that allows e-commerce, the ability to sell items on your web site using a credit card over a secure server. When choosing a hosting company, I recommend that you go with a larger, more established company, because hundreds of hosting companies have gone out of business in the past few years, and the quality of service you receive from a larger company will be similar to that of a smaller company. You don't want to get a phone call one day from a hot prospect saying they can't find your web site, only to learn that your hosting company closed up shop the day before. Unlike domain name registration, there are many, many options hosting companies will give you, and prices can vary significantly for the same options, so shop around.

ACTION STEP

Search for *web site hosting* on your favorite search engine for a list of companies that will host your web site for a reasonable price. Hosting packages can vary greatly, so be sure to comparison shop.

MAINTAINING YOUR WEB SITE

In order for a web site to be effective at attracting new business, it must be updated and maintained:

- *It must be continually revised.* You must keep your web site up to date with new projects, new clients, new target audiences, and new speaking engagements.
- *It must be refreshing.* After looking at a couple of dozen coaching web sites, you will begin to see a lot of similarities (a lot of them make the same mistakes by copying each other). Work hard to make your web site different—not weird different, but refreshing and distinctive from the same old stuff.

- *It must be a resource.* If you want prospects to visit your web site more than once, they must perceive it as more than just a brochure or sales site, but a resource where they can learn, pick up new techniques, find ideas, and discover other aspects about coaching.

- *It must reinforce the image you want to project.* You can be the best coach in the world, with the perfect credentials, but have a web site that totally undermines your credibility or presents a confusing message (are you a personal coach, a psychotherapist, or a spiritual mentor?).

You have two choices when it comes to updating and modifying your web site: Learn to do it yourself or hire someone to do it for you. If you know you want to hire someone to do the updates for you, try to negotiate it with the person you hire to build your web site before they start, and perhaps they will give you a good deal. You can also hire college students on an hourly basis to make basic changes as needed, or even pay them to teach you how to make your own changes.

Specific Recommendations about Web Sites

Now, in addition to the preceding information, I also have some relatively strong opinions about what you should and should not include on your web site, especially if you plan to target professionals, business owners, executives, or managers. Here are some recommendations.

Web Site Dos

- Content is king—don't skimp on it or replace it with fancy pictures or graphs, but don't overdo it—a web site is *not* the place to write a dissertation on your company, so keep it clear, concise, and compelling.
- Have many, many professional colleagues and business executives review your web site before going live and publicly promoting it. No matter how good your English is, they will always catch a misspelled word, a poorly worded phrase, or a dead link. How much better to catch it before the rest of the world sees it.
- Make it easy for people to contact you by giving all your contact information (e-mail address, fax, phone, 800 number, mailing

address) on every page, not just your contact page. It is so frustrating when web site owners assume you know how to contact them. In addition, I have personally made it a point not to do business with any web site that does not offer a phone number, e-mail address, and mailing address. Remember, it's all about building trust, and not listing a phone number and mailing address does not build trust with me. I wonder how many other people feel the same way.

- Talk in terms that relate to your audience and other business professionals, not your peers. Using insider terminology may make you feel prestigious in the eyes of your peers, but it will only turn off the people who truly matter—your prospects.
- Focus on benefits and results, not features and services.
- Use your web site to advertise your services, new products, and articles of interest to your target market.
- Use the signature feature of your e-mail program to promote your web site.
- Promote your web site address on everything you have: business cards, letterhead, envelopes, newsletter, e-zine, presentation handouts, direct-mail pieces, and so on.

WEB SITE DON'TS

These are not meant as a personal affront to anyone, so please don't take them personally. They are based on my experience as a small-business owner, a marketing coach, and someone who makes money from a web site.

- Do *not* put your picture on your homepage! I believe this is one of the biggest mistakes coaches make on their web sites. If the richest person in the world, Bill Gates, does not have his picture on the Microsoft.com homepage, you shouldn't post yours, either. You are trying to get business, not get a date or win a beauty contest, and no one will hire you as their coach just because you look stunning on the homepage of your web site. From a business perspective, it is my personal opinion that this is the equivalent of opening up shop as Billy Bob's Garage—will some people go there to get their cars fixed? Yes, if they either know Billy personally and trust him or if they have no other choice. People searching the Internet for a coach don't face either issue. (There are some exceptions to this rule, mentioned later.)

- Do *not* use your personal name for your business web site (e.g., www.StephenFairley.com) unless it is the name of your business (which hopefully it is not) or you are a professional speaker or celebrity. There are a few times when this is acceptable or even required: law firms, accountants, and celebrities. Other than that, I don't recommend it.
- Do *not* use terms only the coaching industry understands ("the laws of attraction"). Speak the language of your prospects.
- Do *not* fall prey to the con artists and spammers who offer you a deal like, "Pay only $29.99 per month and we will submit your web site to 5,000 search engines." They are a scam, a complete waste of your money, and have a high potential for banning your web site from all the important search engines. The fastest way to drive traffic to your web site, other than hiring a search engine professional and promoting your site on every piece of marketing collateral, is to develop an opt-in e-mail list you continually market to.
- Do *not* expect the person or company that developed your web site to know anything about marketing it (and neither do most traditional advertising or marketing companies). If you really want to make money from your web site, hire a professional who specializes in *search engine optimization* to help you. Online marketing is *totally* different from traditional marketing. It is a specialty. Expect to spend $1,000 to $8,000 for a search engine optimization expert, depending on their level of sophistication.
- Do *not* believe that having a web site will lead to instant riches. It will take time to build your Internet presence, and even though you work hard to market the site, it will be several months before it plays a small part in growing your revenues. For the majority of coaches, having a web site is more about developing credibility than bringing in income; 63 percent of coaches making more than $75,000 have a web site, but so do 66 percent of coaches making less than $10,000 a year.

CAPTURING THE POWER OF E-ZINES

Electronic newsletters, commonly known as *e-zines*, are one of the fastest-growing marketing strategies in coaching today. An e-zine is simply a newsletter sent via e-mail, and I believe it can be a very effective way to build your coaching business. In this section I'll share with you several points to remember when writing your e-zine, but before we get into that you need to understand that developing an e-zine is a commitment over the long haul; you have to collect the e-mail addresses, you have to write the content, you have to send out the e-zine, and you have to manage the list (new people signing up, others dropping out, and people changing their e-mail addresses). However, if you are up to the challenge, a good e-zine can have many benefits, including:

- Staying in regular contact with your prospects
- Creating an image of who you are and what you stand for
- Developing credibility over time
- Building your online reputation
- Promoting your products and services

Here are some important points to remember when writing your e-zine:

Target your market.   It may come as no surprise to you by now that I believe the first and most important thing to remember when writing your e-zine is to target your market. If you target professionals who struggle with work-life balance, that's what your e-zine should focus on. If you want small-business owners as clients, your e-zine should talk about issues meaningful to them. Even if you get people to sign up, you will not keep them if your e-zine becomes the ramblings of a coach with too much time to fill and too many soapboxes to stand on. Focus on the needs of your target market. If you have more than one target market, develop a different e-zine for each one.

Name your e-zine.   The name of your e-zine should give potential subscribers an accurate picture of what to expect. In addition, when checking incoming e-mail most people first look to see who it's from, then to see what the subject is, and giving your e-zine a name can help them quickly identify it.

Keep it short.   Generally speaking, your e-zine should not be more than two to three screens of information. People do not like scrolling through pages and pages of text. In fact, studies indicate that the average user will not read more than the first couple of screen pages

Mike Jay
Founder, B-Coach
(877) 901-COACH
www.b-coach.com

Mike Jay is the founder of B-Coach, a coach-training school for business and corporate coaches, and known as a thought leader in the field. He is also the author of *Coach to the Bottom Line* (Trafford, 1999) and has over 150 different active web sites.

You have an incredible coaching practice. Tell us about it.

I have always wanted a practice with a lot of variety. My practice really started to branch out when I wrote my book, *Coach to the Bottom Line*, about five years ago. In the process, I clarified who I was and the model I wanted to use in coaching. That model still forms the basis of our coach-training program, B-Coach. Launching B-Coach in 1999 was a profound experience for me. I have always wanted to have a global practice, and I like traveling, so I started going everywhere and teaching what I was doing in my coaching practice, because I believe if you really want to learn something, find some people to teach it to.

Even today, I love working behind the scene and not being tethered to a full-time coaching practice. Over the years I have grown farther away from wanting to do straight billable hours. I now practice what I call a "just-in-time" or "just-in-case" model of coaching. There are over 125 people worldwide who have instant message access to me via live chat sessions anytime, day or night. The only rule is when I'm online, I'm available; when I'm not online, I'm not available.

Tell us a little more about your coaching model.

Our model is based on developing capabilities. We teach our clients to manage their own accountability instead of having the coach hold them accountable. There are three primary components:

- *Connection* — between the coach and client
- *Clarification* — of the client's goals and how to measure success
- *Commitment* — we inspire the commitment rather than ask for it

At B-Coach, we teach coaches how to help their clients become aligned with their core values because after they do that, everything will follow. We do not teach "gap work." We work from a strength-based approach because we believe that overcoming deficiencies is not the same thing as developing proficiencies. At its heart, coaching is a voluntary interaction where the coach has neither the responsibility, accountability, nor authority for the outcomes of the person being coached; where the person desires change, increase in performance and transformation. We also teach that coaching is very different from consulting. Take a look at the two on a continuum:

Consulting
Training or telling people what they need to do to overcome the gaps

Personal Consulting
Where most coaching is done

Coaching
Developing the person to increase their ability to cope with complexity and take increasing levels of freedom and leadership

Most coaching today is done somewhere in the middle, kind of like a personal consultant. However, we believe coaching becomes more powerful when the coach stays away from a consulting approach.

You have been able to build a very successful coaching practice while living in a town with less than 50,000 people in the middle of Montana. What's your advice to new coaches just starting out?

Understand that first and foremost you are in business. When you start up a coaching practice, you become a small-business owner. So if you are a coach, you are in business. If you are in business, you must have paying clients. If you want clients, you must go find them, because they will not come to you. Most coaches don't fail because they are a bad coach. They fail because they are a bad businessperson.

So my advice would be to find some solid training first, then look for as many ways as possible to get yourself involved: speaking, training, consulting, networking, marketing, giving things away, working with nonprofits. When you meet people you have two goals:

- Inform the other person about who you are and what you do.
- Capture their permission to market to them on a regular basis.

(Continued)

What do you believe are the future trends in coaching?

Right now coaching is a tough sell. You can sell short-term, high-impact, high-results, low-cost coaching, but you can't sell long-term development or transformational leadership development. So the first lesson to apply in the future is that you must be able to adjust what you're selling to what the market demands.

I think in the future we will see a sharp bifurcation in coaching, with coaches at the high end making a great living and coaches at the low end fighting over the scraps left over. I believe we are seeing some of that even now. At B-Coach we are already moving away from the current pop-culture coaching trend toward what I call "developmentalism," which addresses the question, "What does it take to have a person significantly increase their overall life?" This developmental coaching will become a powerful asset to the community because it teaches self-awareness, which is the linchpin of emotional competence, and emotional competence is a driving force in the business field.

Many new coaches are seeking out training. What are some critical questions they need to ask when evaluating coaching schools and making a decision on which one to attend?

Here are five good questions to ask any coaching school:

- *How much actual experience am I going to get practicing and getting feedback on my coaching?* The best way to learn coaching is to do it, not just read about it.
- *How is the school going to help me be successful in my coaching business?* Most schools only teach you their model or techniques to use, but the real struggle comes after you start coaching—how are you going to build your business?
- *Does the school have a learning theory it follows?* Is it just a bunch of techniques or does the school have a solid, comprehensive model?
- *What kinds of assessments will I learn?* Assessments can be used in a powerful way by coaches to help effect rapid change in clients.
- *How much development theory is in the program?* At its core, coaching is about developing people, so how are you going to do it unless you understand how people develop?

of anything on the Internet. Longer is not always better, but if you find yourself writing long e-zines think about sending your list a shorter version with links to the longer one on your web site or in an attached document.

Use a table of contents at the beginning. If your e-zine is more than one screen of text, think about placing a simple table of contents at the top to let readers know exactly what is in the issue and where they can quickly go to find a specific article of interest.

Provide solid content. The only reason why someone subscribes to your e-zine is that they believe you have something important to say to them. To keep subscribers you must provide them with solid, fresh content that makes a difference to them. Repeating the same information issue after issue, talking about subjects that are not important to them, or, worse, writing in a boring style are the fastest ways to kill your subscriber base. We are in the information age, and there is *nothing* you can tell anyone that they cannot find somewhere else, so don't be stingy with your knowledge. When you give away knowledge, people respect you more because they believe that if you are giving all this away, you must know a lot more about the subject that you're not telling. You have to give them a reason to join and consistently provide them with new reasons why they should stay. Your goal is to position yourself as a resource to them about the issues they care most about. This leads directly into the next point.

Minimize the promotional aspect. An e-zine is not a direct sales letter, but it can contain one. Use your e-zine to build credibility and present a pitch for your services and products, but keep it subtle. Place an ad for your new e-book at the end of your e-zine or replace your regular e-zine with a promotional pitch once a month, but don't tease your subscribers by writing about an important issue, then saying that the answers to their questions are in your new e-book, which they can purchase by clicking here. They will not respect you for that.

Keep past issues on your web site. This is a great way to both add value to your web site by giving away free information and gain new subscribers. Many web users like to know what they are getting before they give away their valuable e-mail address. Showing them a couple of your past issues is a great way to demonstrate the value of your e-zine, and it will help you to better qualify your subscribers because then they clearly understand exactly what you are offering.

Give people an easy way to opt out. Not providing a clear and easy way for subscribers to opt out is a good sign that you are spamming them. Every issue of your e-zine should clearly state exactly how sub-scribers can opt out. Not only is this good Internet etiquette (neti-quette), but it also makes good business sense. You don't want to be e-mailing people who don't want what you have to offer. Be sure to honor every request to unsubscribe.

Respect your subscribers' privacy. Be clear about your privacy policy when people subscribe. If you say you're not going to sell or give away your list, then don't do it. If you do want to do it, ask their per-mission first. Also, hide their e-mail addresses from the rest of the world by using the blind carbon copy (BCC) feature in your e-mail program. Their privacy also determines how often you send out your e-zine. The common wisdom says to start out with a quarterly e-zine then work your way up to monthly, but don't send one out more than once a week. Just because you can quickly send out an e-mail newsletter doesn't mean you should.

There are many excellent free e-zines available, but I personally like the one offered at www.MYOBforCoaches.com (probably because I write it).

DISCOVERING THE BASICS OF INTERNET MARKETING

Internet marketing is a highly specialized field. It does *not* follow the same rules or guidelines as traditional forms of marketing and advertis-ing, such as television, radio, direct mail, or print ads. Much of the extensive research done on traditional forms of marketing does not apply to the Internet.

Effective Internet marketing requires specialized knowledge of how to continuously apply 30 to 45 different techniques that constantly change as search engines modify and update how information is found on the Internet. The two primary reasons why these strategies change are that search engines are continually increasing their ability to search intelligently and that search engine companies deliberately modify the engines to keep individuals from abusing and monopolizing them. I want to be completely up front with you here, this section is not designed to answer all or even most of the questions you will have about this topic. Nor will it give you a lot of highly specific techniques and information. Why not? Because the type of information that would be specific enough to solve your current Internet marketing needs radically changes every four to six months, so by the time you actually read this book, 30 to 60 percent of it would already be out of date. If you are interested in making your web site the foundation of your marketing strategy, you are strongly advised to seek professional help from people who specialize in search engine optimization (SEO) strategies.

A COMMON PROCESS AND FOUR CRITICAL QUESTIONS

What I will share with you is that even though the specific strategies continually change, there is a common process people use to look for products or services on the Internet. Unless they are trying to locate a specific company, in which case they simply type in the web site address, most people begin by going to their favorite search engine and typing a word or phrase that describes what they are looking for. For example, if the director of human resources at a potential client company were trying to use the Internet to find an executive coach who specializes in leadership development issues, they would go to their favorite search engine and type in the phrase *leadership development* or *executive coach* or a similar phrase.

This process is clearly reflected in the statistics of Internet traffic patterns: over 85 percent of all traffic on the Internet is directed through search engines. So it is highly probable that the HR director would use a search engine. The next pattern emerges when you ask the follow-up question, "Which search engine would they use?" While there are more than 1,500 different search engines to choose from, just 8 search engines account for more than 90 percent of all the traffic. Your next question might be, "Well, which words would they use?" This is one place where getting inside the heads of your target market audience becomes critical. You need to know what their primary challenges are and how they are likely to describe them. In our example, if the HR director were to search on Google (www.google.com is one of the largest) for the phrase *leadership development,* it would return more than 3.7 million choices. When searching for *executive coach,* it would return more than 623,000 choices. That's a lot of choices! Obviously, no one will visit more than a handful to find the information they are looking for. So, the next logical question probably is, "With so many choices, which sites will the person most likely visit to find out more information?" Research strongly indicates that the vast majority of people only visit web sites found in the top 20 positions, or on the first two pages, of the resulting search. This leads you to the next question: "Of the web sites found in the first 20 positions, which ones are people more likely to read?" Answer: the ones that state in their 25-word abstract that they have the answer to the question or the solution to the problem in a clear and compelling manner.

In other words, to visit your web site potential prospects must do four things:

1. They must search for your products or services using a keyword or phrase (known as a *search term*) that distinguishes them as potential clients, such as someone searching for *leadership development, executive coach,* or *create a balanced life.*
2. They must then find your web site, using that keyword or phrase on one of the eight major search engines.
3. They must see your web site listing in one of the top 20 positions or on the first two pages of that search engine.
4. They must be interested enough by the 25-word description of your company to click on your link.

In order to be successful in marketing your web site, you must develop strategies that address all four issues. These are the strategies that constantly change, but the reason why I'm describing this process is that no matter what techniques change, the process will remain very much the same.

THE TOP 10 MISTAKES COACHES MAKE ON THE INTERNET

Just as the process of finding your web site will remain the same, the common mistakes people make will also probably remain the same for the foreseeable future. Again, I'm not sharing these mistakes with the intent of offending anyone, but as a way of helping serious professionals avoid them.

Mistake 1: Using a Free Hosting Service

You may be tempted to use a cheap or free hosting service for your coaching web site, like those offered by AOL, GeoCities, or Angelfire. I am here to say, "Resist the temptation." There are three big reasons why. First, the free servers are often overloaded, which significantly increases the amount of time needed for viewers to load and see your web site. Research indicates your web site must fully load in about seven seconds or you will start to lose viewers. Second, by agreeing to use their free hosting service you also agree to allow them to place ads on your web site. The only ad you want viewers to see on your web site is for something *you're* selling—not someone else. Third, this is a dead giveaway to savvy Web users that you are either a complete novice or someone who is not really serious about your business. You can easily find a basic hosting service for less than $20 a month, and if you're not willing to spend that on your web site, you should question whether you are really serious about building your business.

Mistake 2: Using Too Many Pictures, Graphics, or Sounds

If you think television remote controls have significantly dropped the attention span of viewers, you should try getting the attention of Internet surfers! This point goes directly back to the fact that you have only about seven seconds to capture the attention of your viewers before they go somewhere else. Since pictures, graphics, and sounds can take up to 10 times longer to load than simple text, you can ill afford to waste that precious time. Should you never use pictures, graphics, or sounds? No, but make sure they are necessary, add a lot to your site, are not used in excess, and are minimized on your homepage.

Mistake 3: Not Regularly Checking Your Web Site Links and E-Mails

You should have your entire web site's spelling and every link, navigational system, and layout triple checked by at least three different people before you go live and again every time you make any major changes (such as adding a new page). You wouldn't believe how many typos and misspelled words I find on web sites, even ones for *Fortune* 500 companies. Is it a big deal? No, but it's often the small things that undermine your credibility and lower your trust factor.

Mistake 4: Failing to Collect the E-Mail Addresses of Visitors

How many people have visited your web site since you launched it? 50? 500? 5,000? 50,000? 500,000? How much would it be worth to you to be able to contact those people and market your services directly to them? The only way to do that is to collect their e-mail addresses. Give visitors a reason to give you their e-mail addresses: let them register to win a prize or give them a white paper, a free coaching session, or a subscription to your e-zine. Do whatever you can to get them to give you their email addresses.

Mistake 5: Not Regularly Contacting Your Database

The vast majority of people will not buy coaching from you the first time they meet you. People do business with people they know, like, and trust—especially when it comes to something as personal as coaching. Trust is built over time, and the only way to build trust is to increase the number of contacts or increase the amount of time. Obviously, you want people to buy from you sooner rather than later, and the best way to do that is to maintain regular and solid contact with your prospects. An e-zine can help you do this, but it isn't the only way. Be creative, be spontaneous, but be regular.

Mistake 6: Not Giving Away Something to Your Web Site Visitors

Which person do you think is more likely to hire you as a coach: a person who stumbled across your web site and visited it one time or a person with whom you have monthly contact and who visits your web site every few weeks to read the new, free articles you post there every month on life-work balance?

Ask yourself: What are five things you could give away to your web site visitors that will not cost you much in terms of time or money? Write your ideas down for action.

Mistake 7: Damaging Your Reputation by Spamming

Technically, *spam* is any unsolicited e-mail, usually promotional, sent out to multiple recipients. Spam is a growing problem and it is generally considered to be very damaging to a Web user's reputation to be labeled a spammer. If you have had an e-mail address for longer than a month, you have probably received an unsolicited e-mail. "But," you ask, "you're telling me that I need to increase the e-mail addresses in my database so I can market to them, and since no one is visiting my web site yet or signing up for my e-zine, how do I find these e-mail addresses unless I buy them or take them off some listserv?" You may also have received a spam e-mail from a company offering to sell you thousands or even millions of e-mail addresses for your e-zine. Do not buy it!

Here are a few guidelines to spot spam instantly:

- You can't tell who the email is from.
- There is no web site to click through to, except to buy a particular product.
- There is no indication as to how they received your e-mail address.
- There is no opportunity to opt out and be removed from the list.
- It seems too good to be true (e.g., an offer to buy 1 million e-mail addresses for $29.99 when the going industry rate is $100 to $300 per 1,000).

S. Roberts, M. Feit, and R. Bly provide some guidelines for responsible e-mail marketing in their book *Internet Direct Mail* (McGraw-Hill, 2001):

- Send direct mail only to rented opt-in lists or your own client and prospect addresses.
- Give recipients an easy way to opt out of your list in every e-mail you send and be sure to honor every request.
- Do not try to deceive or fool any recipient into believing your e-mail is not promotional.
- Be ethical and straightforward in every e-mail you send.
- Do not overdo it. Just because e-mail is easy to send doesn't mean you should send it all the time. In most cases you should limit your promotional e-mails to no more than three or four a month, at the most.
- Keep your e-mail message size small. Sending graphics and pictures via e-mail can really bog down an old computer or one with a slow connection. Keep your e-mail file size to a maximum of 400 to 500 kilobytes and never more than 1 megabyte.

- Do not be misleading in your subject line. The subject line should clearly state what the person is getting.
- Keep other people's e-mail addresses hidden by using the blind carbon copy (BCC) feature included in most e-mail programs. Be respectful of people's privacy.

Mistake 8: Not Protecting Yourself against Computer Viruses

Earlier in the book I mentioned a coach who had his reputation damaged because of a self-replicating virus. A virus can ruin your day, your computer, your hard drive, and your hard-won list of prospects and clients, but most important, it can ruin your reputation. Imagine if you had worked hard over the past year to build up a strong e-mail list of 10,000 names. You regularly contacted them through your e-zine and had received many sales in the process. One day your computer is attacked by a virus that automatically sends a copy of itself to all 10,000 e-mail addresses in your database, then damages your hard drive so you are unable to do anything to stop it or even warn people not to open that e-mail. Now imagine the level of trust you have built up with these 10,000 people over the past year going right down the drain. You get the picture. Buy a good antivirus program. I personally use McAfee, but Norton is good as well. I don't really trust a free antivirus program to protect some of the most valuable information I own. Whatever program you finally go with, make sure that it is set up to automatically run in the background every time your computer is turned on and that it has an automatic update feature that periodically checks to see if new patches have come out to ward off new viruses. If you don't have a good, up-to-date antivirus program yet, put down this book and go buy one right now!

Mistake 9: Believing You Can Get Rich Quick from the Internet

I have been to several seminars, conferences, and workshops where the presenters either implied or explicitly stated that since they set up a web site they have doubled or tripled their business. I think every American wants to believe that the trip from rags to riches is as easy as setting up a web site, but this just isn't true. To make real money from your web site will take time, energy, and—guess what?—money! For the majority of coaches, you should count yourself lucky if your web site generates enough income that you break even on the cost. Having a web site is more about educating your prospects, communicating with them 24/7, providing more information than is possible in a letter or brochure, and gaining credibility in their eyes, not about striking it rich.

Mistake 10: Not Leveraging the Full Power of the Internet

It seems that not a week goes by that I don't learn about some new service, product, or web site that can make my life easier. There are web sites that help you set up and manage your e-zine, immediately send information to people who request it via e-mail, encourage visitors to tell their friends about your web site, allow you to host polls on your web site, tell you who is visiting your web site, and the list goes on and on. The mistake people often make is not exploring and leveraging the full power of the Internet to make their lives easier. Are all of these free? Absolutely not, but let me ask you: How much would it be worth to you to free up several hours of your time every week or each month? What could you do with all that free time—go to more networking events, follow up on hot prospects faster, write that book you've been procrastinating on, take that long overdue vacation, spend more time investing in your family? What is your time worth? Don't be penny wise and pound foolish. Invest in learning how to explore and leverage the full power of the Internet to automate your life, your marketing, and your business.

SUMMARY

In this chapter we have talked about the power of the Internet, your web site, and e-zines in helping you develop a dynamic marketing effort. Using Internet strategies can be an effective way to drive prospects to your business, but like any form of marketing, it takes time, energy, money, commitment, and knowledge. Many of the "tried and true" marketing techniques do not work on the Internet, especially when it comes to marketing your web site, so to be effective you have to learn new techniques. Your online presence is an extension of your business, so it should project your image in the best possible light. Following the information in this chapter will help you avoid common mistakes and obtain the best possible return on your investment.

CHAPTER 13

The Seven Secrets of Highly Successful Coaches

If you immediately jumped to this chapter instead of reading the previous chapters, you might be wondering, "What does a highly successful coach look like, and where did he get this information?" In this chapter you're going to find out! In researching this book I personally interviewed many of the top coaches in the United States and conducted an online survey of more than 300 coaches nationwide. For the purposes of this book I have defined success in coaching the easiest way I know how—by how much money they are making.

Specifically, I have defined financially successful coaches as those making more than $75,000 annually just from their coaching practice. Financially unsuccessful coaches are defined as those making less than $10,000 annually just from their coaching practice. However, for this chapter on the practices of highly successful coaches, I set the bar a little higher; unless otherwise noted, I am defining highly successful coaches as those making more than $100,000 annually just from their coaching practice. This places them in the top 8 percent of the coaching community. You may say $100,000 is not a lot, which is true in many places, but statistically speaking, that places them in the top 5 percent of all incomes in America and the top 8 percent in coaching. Furthermore, many of the coaches I talked to were making much more than the bottom cutoff limit, but did not want to openly state their incomes for obvious privacy concerns. This is not a chapter about showing off or keeping up with the Joneses, but about helping you to think outside of the box. So many coaches are taught the same things when it comes to building their businesses—many of which simply don't work in the real world.

In this chapter I'm going to give you real strategies given by real coaches and discovered using real-world research. These secrets work and I can back it up! We will talk about the following points:

- Why top coaches work so hard to get more qualified referrals
- What they really sell (and it's not coaching services)
- What top coaches do to market themselves more effectively
- How top coaches package their services for maximum profit
- Why top coaches see partnerships as invaluable to their success
- A real-world illustration of how to significantly increase your rates
- Ways top coaches multiply their outreach and profitability with products

SECRET 1: HIGHLY SUCCESSFUL COACHES GET MORE AND BETTER-QUALIFIED REFERRALS

The long-term success of any professional services firm is related to the number and quality of the referrals it receives from current and former clients and strategic referral partners (SRPs). In my research, top coaches reported finding more new clients directly from their current and former clients at twice the rate of coaches who are not financially successful. Both groups receive referrals, but top coaches receive a lot more and the leads are much better qualified.

How do they do this? Well, part of it is because they have simply been in business longer and have more satisfied clients who can refer others to them. But it's not that simple. Having a satisfied client does not guarantee referrals; you have to be informed and intentional about the whole process. I have written about this in great detail in Chapter 8, but the bottom line is that you must regularly and intentionally ask your best clients for referrals, and in order to increase the quality of those referrals, you must teach them exactly what kind of prospects you are looking for. Answer this question for them: How can they tell if the person they're talking to is a good referral for you? Don't your existing clients know what to look for simply by virtue of working with you? Yes and no. If they come across someone who has the exact same problem as they do, then that's easy. But since you certainly work with more than just one kind of client and more than one kind of problem, you need to educate them on the top two or three situations that would indicate a person is a good referral for you. The easiest way to do that is to give them a real-world example.

> Having satisfied clients does not guarantee referrals. You must be informed about how to obtain referrals from current and former clients, and you must be intentional about the process.

Perhaps you are a career coach but your client came to you for coaching as part of a recent job promotion. Tell them that a good referral source is an executive who makes over $100,000 and is looking for their next career. I even know of a top coach who puts a statement in his client intake sheet saying that he expects new clients to refer people to him—and it works.

Highly successful coaches know how to consistently overdeliver on their services, thereby making their clients their number-one fans—in effect, creating a sales force out of their current and former clients. The secret here is that when a client refers someone to you for coaching, they are already prequalified. You don't need to spend much time at all selling them on the process or benefits of your coaching, because your client has already done it for you. The question you need to address as a new coach is, "How can I build a referral system into my coaching so that I am actively seeking referrals from my current and even my former clients?

The keys to remember are these: Educate your current clients, stay in contact with your former clients, give them real-world examples of what a great referral looks like, reward them when they give you a referral, and ask for referrals on a regular basis (when they first sign up, right after a great coaching session, at least every two to four months, and again just before they end coaching).

SECRET 2: HIGHLY SUCCESSFUL COACHES DON'T SELL COACHING

Even though it may seem contradictory at first, a big secret of top coaches is that they don't sell coaching. Instead, they focus on selling the benefits they offer, the value they provide, and the results they achieve. For example, some of the benefits of your individual coaching could be:

- Increases in employee productivity
- Less conflict between team leaders
- Better communication between departments

The value you provide could be:

- You are available to your clients for quick consultations via phone and e-mail anytime between sessions.
- You are within easy driving distance and can meet with them in their office.

- You have 15 years of experience in corporate America working with managers and team leaders on improving their communication skills and interdepartmental relations.

And the results you achieve could include:

- 75 percent of your clients report increasing their productivity by more than 60 percent.
- Executive teams report significantly less conflict after just four meetings with you.
- Your average client increases their salary by more than $20,000 annually after working with you for more than three months.
- The typical sales professional you work with increases their annual revenues by 25 to 35 percent within six months.

Coaching is simply the tool or the process you use to solve problems and achieve results. Don't sell the process—sell the results, the benefits, and the value you bring to the situation.

SECRET 3: HIGHLY SUCCESSFUL COACHES KNOW HOW TO MARKET THEIR SERVICES

Highly successful coaches think strategically about marketing their coaching services:

They spend a lot more money on marketing. Among coaches making less than $10,000 annually, 69 percent report spending less than $200 monthly on any marketing-related activity, and 95 percent of them spend less than $500 monthly on marketing their services. However, 75 percent of coaches making more than $100,000 annually spend more than $200 monthly, and 58 percent spend more than $500 monthly. Now, I realize this may be a "chicken or the egg" issue; in other words, does spending a lot of money on marketing increase your income, or do coaches with more income spend more on everything, including marketing? There is also the issue that a person making less than $10,000 a year simply can't afford to spend $6,000 of that on marketing. There are no easy answers to those questions, but in my research, spending significantly more money on marketing-related activities significantly correlates with making significantly more money.

They charge a lot more per hour. The average coach charges $132 per hour. Coaches who make more than $75,000 per year charge an average of $209 per hour (with a median rate of $163), and coaches making more than $100,000 per year charge an average of $297 per hour (with a median rate of $300). How do top coaches charge these top rates? By doing two things:

- They actively find ways to significantly increase the perceived value of their services, such as increasing the quality of their marketing materials (like their web site), perfecting their sales pitch, clearly describing how their past experiences relate to helping clients with their challenges, collecting testimonials from satisfied clients, becoming more comfortable selling their services, working harder to quantify the results they achieve for clients, and seeking and obtaining more qualified referrals from former and current clients.
- They target more affluent prospects, such as small-business owners, executives, high-net-worth individuals, top salespeople, and business professionals.

They outsource areas outside of their strengths. Top coaches are much more likely to hire other professionals to help them increase their marketing effectiveness. For example, they recognize the importance of making a great first impression to prospects, so they work with other professionals to sharpen their sales and presentation skills; they hire graphic designers to create a fantastic brochure and professional-looking web sites.

They dominate a niche. The coaches who are most successful identify early on what their specific niche is and target the majority of their marketing and sales efforts toward dominating this niche. Some of the niches I have heard about are high-tech start-ups, sales professionals, family-run businesses, financial service professionals, client acquisition strategies, aspiring authors and writers, professional speaking skills, and career transition for middle managers, just to name a few. Virtually anything can be developed into a niche, but I don't recommend trying to create a niche because it takes too much time and money to educate your prospects before you can sell them your services. Instead, try to identify a niche that already exists and see where it overlaps with your skills, abilities, and expertise, then learn how to dominate the niche.

SECRET 4: HIGHLY SUCCESSFUL COACHES PACKAGE THEIR SERVICES

Highly successful coaches recognize the importance of marketing service packages, rather than just limit themselves to monthly, individual coaching. See Table 13.1 for a couple of examples.

In addition to just your coaching, what other things do you or can you offer to clients that don't cost you a lot, but have perceived value? Perhaps you regularly send existing clients e-mails to check up on them and see how things are going, or you offer to talk with them between sessions when a crisis arises. If someone was entirely unsatisfied with their coaching, would you refund their money? Most ethical people would say yes. That sounds like a 100 percent satisfaction guarantee to me. So why not make these things overt and use them in your marketing? Table 13.2 shows some revisions to a typical coaching package.

TABLE 13.1 Coaching Service Packages

Original Package	What Clients Receive	Price	Commitment
Level 1: One-on-one personal coaching	Three 45-minute coaching calls per month	$300 a month	On a month-by-month basis
Level 2: One-on-one personal coaching	Four 1-hour coaching calls per month	$500 a month	On a month-by-month basis
One-on-one small-business coaching	Four 1-hour coaching calls per month	$700 a month	On a month-by-month basis
Personal assessment	An individualized report on your personal strengths and weaknesses	$50	None

TABLE 13.2   Revised Coaching Service Packages

Revised Package	What Clients Receive	Price	Commitment
Level 1: One-on-one personal coaching	• Three 45-minute coaching calls • *Free* personal assessment using the DiSC profile • *Free* periodic e-mails between sessions • 100% satisfaction guarantee	$350 a month	3-month commitment
Level 2: One-on-one personal coaching	• Four 1-hour coaching calls • *Free* personal assessment using the DiSC profile • *Free* unlimited e-mails between sessions • *Free* short phone calls between sessions • *Free* copy of your new e-book or CD series • 100% satisfaction guarantee	$600 a month	3-month commitment
One-on-one small-business coaching	• Four 1-hour coaching calls • *Free* 2-hour initial planning session • *Free* personal assessment using the DiSC profile • *Free* periodic e-mails between sessions • *Free* short phone calls between sessions • *Free* copy of your new e-book or CD series • 100% satisfaction guarantee	$900 a month	6-month commitment

There are many different benefits to packaging your services:

- *You can increase the amount of time you work with clients.* By moving from a month-to-month model to asking for a 3-, 6-, 9-, or 12-month commitment, you start developing long-term relationships, you begin to be viewed as a trusted advisor, and you create a more even cash flow for your company (instead of receiving $100 one month and $5,000 the next month). That is a good thing when you have fixed living expenses.
- *You can increase the amount of money you charge for your services.* By adding services that don't cost you a lot or ones that you're already offering, just not overtly, you can often increase your profits significantly. How much does a simple profile or personal assessment

cost you—$30 to $60? Yet by offering this as part of your package, you have increased the perceived value and raised your fees by $50 to $200 every month, more than enough to cover the cost of the assessment.

- *You have multiple opportunities to upsell and cross sell your other services and products.* The longer you work with clients the more you get to know all their needs, and if a need arises that you can help them with, you will be the first person they turn to for advice and assistance.
- *You can offer them more value as part of the package.* If a current client called you right now in a crisis situation, would you take the call and talk to them? Of course you would. Even if you don't realize it, that is a benefit you are offering clients right now. Make all those hidden benefits obvious and clear by writing them down and advertising them in all your marketing materials.

SECRET 5: HIGHLY SUCCESSFUL COACHES PARTNER WITH OTHER COACHES

Top coaches realize the benefits of partnering with other coaches and consultants. Some of those benefits are included on the following list.

Advantages of Partnering
- You can split the cost of operating the business.
- You have more potential connections, which can lead to more business faster.
- You have the ability to effectively target more audiences.
- You can delegate responsibilities among partners to allow partners to focus on their individual strengths.
- Your partner gives you a sounding board.
- Your partnership gives you a better position to target larger contracts from larger companies that often hesitate to work with single-person businesses.
- You increase the strength of your company, which depends on the strength and depth of your management team.
- You can quickly learn from each other, thereby significantly shortening your learning curve.
- You can offer an increased number of services.

- You can provide better service to clients by specializing in your best areas and provide crisis coverage if one of the partners is away on vacation or otherwise unavailable.
- You can use the partnership to position your company more effectively.
- You gain the advantage of the *X* factor: the idea that two minds are better than one and that a partnership can multiply, not just add to, your strengths, abilities, and power.

This is not to deny that there can be some significant problems with partnerships:

Disadvantages of Partnering
- It can take more time to make decisions, thus slowing down your response time to new opportunities.
- History shows that the majority of partnerships eventually break up.
- People have different levels of risk taking.
- It can be difficult to find a true partner who has the same vision and focus as you have.
- Arguments can develop over who pays for what and when the business should bear the cost.
- There is more potential for good prospects to fall through the cracks because each of you thought the other was going to follow up with them.
- You may not be comfortable sharing your best contacts or top business secrets with someone else.
- Each of you must be willing to stand up for your point of view or the partnership can become dysfunctional.
- If both of you are new to the field, you can reinforce your lack of knowledge.
- If you offer too many different kinds of services, prospects can become confused as to what you really do.

The research I conducted indicates that there are some unexpected side benefits of partnering with other coaches that are not seen on first glance. For example, coaches with partners (CWPs) gain the following advantages:

- *They build their business faster.* CWPs are able to build their coaching clientele almost twice as fast as solo practitioners. The research shows that 31 percent of CWPs find 10 paying clients in less than 6 months, 69 percent in less than 12 months. However, less than 50 percent of solo coaches are able to find 10 clients in their first 12 months of business, and 37 percent of them do not have 10 clients at any given time (versus just 21 percent of CWPs).
- *They have more clients.* CWPs have 100 percent more clients than solo coaches, with an average of 14, while 76 percent of solo coaches have less than 10 (average of 7).
- *They work with clients longer.* CWPs tend to work with individual clients longer than solo coaches, which can significantly increase total revenues per client.
- *They charge more per hour.* CWPs find ways to significantly increase their per-hour rate compared to solo coaches, who average $147 per hour (median of $125). CWPs average $191 per hour (median of $150).
- *They make more money.* Almost half (46 percent) of solo coaches are currently making less than $10,000 a year. Only 7 percent make more than $75,000, and 4 percent are over $100,000. Yet only 20 percent of CWPs make less than $10,000 a year, almost 4 times as many make more than $75,000 annually (27 percent), and a full 4 times as many make more than $100,000 annually (16 percent versus 4 percent of solo coaches and 8 percent of all coaches).

Creating a partnership with other people is not something to take lightly. However, you shouldn't casually dismiss it if you are truly interested in becoming a top coach. Here are some good questions to start with when discussing a partnership or affiliate agreement with another coach or consultant:

- What are your goals for this business over the next two to five years?
- What stage is your personal business in and how will that affect the partnership? (Is the potential partner a new owner or a veteran?)

- What do each of you bring to the table in terms of money, property, business and life experience, marketing ability, selling skills, operations expertise, client list, contacts, and so on?
- Will your businesses operate four to six times better together than they will separately? If you cannot answer this question positively, you may want to reconsider the partnership.
- Are you looking for someone to do some cross marketing with, a cost sharing venture, or a true partnership?
- What are your individual strengths and weaknesses?
- What is the financial condition of each company (revenues, liabilities, and profits)?
- Do you get along personally?

SECRET 6: HIGHLY SUCCESSFUL COACHES TRY TO TIE THEIR FEES TO THEIR RESULTS

In traditional sales, this arrangement is a called a *commission*. In consulting, this is called *eating what you kill*—the results you achieve determine the amount you get paid. For many new coaches this is unheard of—even experienced coaches grimace and shake their heads when this idea comes up—but for top coaches who are very confident in the results they can achieve for a given client, this can bring a great windfall. This strategy is typically only used in the business world and probably is not appropriate when targeting individual clients, unless they are business owners, salespeople, or people whose salary is determined largely by commissions.

As I write this chapter, my firm, Today's Leadership Coaching, is negotiating a contract with a *Fortune* 500 company that approached us to coach their top 30 salespeople. These 30 people sold more than $45 million of services and products last year and the company wants to increase that, so they are bringing us in to work with their people both as a sales team and on an individual level. It is part of an incentive program they are offering to their top producers, the Summit Group, kind of a Million-Dollar Roundtable. Based on the actual amount of work we will have to do (there will be three of us involved), we wrote up a proposal including quarterly meetings, a teleclass, and some individual coaching for $12,000 with a bonus at the end if the program met its goals. We thought this was very reasonable, but they said it was too high for their training budget (yeah, right!). So we came back and said, "We know we do excellent work, but you've never worked with people from our company before, and we realize that we are a relatively unknown firm to you. So, suppose we eliminate all the risk for you in working with us. Instead of paying us a flat fee, we will take a percentage of any revenues your sales professionals make over and above last year's profits. So if the company made $200,000 in revenues per person last year and they make $300,000 in revenues per person this year, then we would take a percentage of the $100,000 difference. If the sales professionals don't make any more revenues for the company this year than last year, you don't pay us anything."

In this scenario, the worst the company can do is break even. They will not lose any money by using our services and will not pay us anything unless we help the company make more revenues. If we get a 10 to 20 percent cut of the revenues, that would be $10,000 to $20,000 per person (times 30 people), based on the company making $100,000 in additional revenues per person this year over last year. Is it risky? Yes, but the potential reward is incredible, and we are very confident that we can make a significant improvement in the amount of revenues these top salespeople make. As part of the offer we added that since we are taking all the risk here, we want the company's written permission to try to land each one of these sales professionals as individual coaching clients (not to hard sell them, but to offer them the opportunity to continue the coaching relationship one-on-one). The average salesperson in this group makes $300,000 to $500,000 a year—right within our target market. They said yes, no problem.

This kind of scenario isn't always possible, and many businesses are wary of splitting the profits, but if they really want your coaching, but can't seem to find a way to afford it, then offering to split the additional revenues or profits with them may be a good alternative. However, there are four things you should know in advance before you try something like this:

- In the vast majority of cases when dealing with businesses and executives, the excuse "We can't afford you" is just an excuse. It indicates that you have not done your job of convincing them of the incredible value you provide, because if you provide enough benefits and results to convince a business they can't make it without

out or that their success will be significantly greater with you, they will find a way to "afford" you.

- For this kind of situation to work, you have to be very clear about what the goals and measurements of success are. Notice that in our real-world example, we used *revenues*, not profits, because profits can easily be distorted so as to appear overinflated or nonexistent (as America has seen with the Enron, MCI WorldCom, and Tyco scandals). You have to use a simple, straightforward way to measure success, and that measurement must be agreed upon by all parties. We used revenues, because this company keeps monthly records of exactly how much revenue each salesperson makes. They know precisely how much each of them made last year. The system is already in place and is easily accessible. There will be no guesswork when it comes time to figure out the difference between last year's and this year's revenues, unless they are dishonest, which is the next point.

- You have to know and trust who you're dealing with. To make this relationship work, you have to be comfortable that the person or company you're dealing with is trustworthy and will not try to deceive you. You must have every agreement like this in writing, just to reinforce to both sides what they are agreeing to, but no amount of writing will keep a dishonest person or company from trying to find a way around paying you if that is their true intent. Here is where your intuition is valuable—listen to it.

- You must be very confident that you can help. This is not a strategy I recommend for coaches new to the field, for those who are weak of heart, or for coaches who do not have a strong, successful background in working with a particular situation. You must be 100 percent confident you can achieve the results you say you will, because your pay depends on it.

SECRET 7: HIGHLY SUCCESSFUL COACHES PRODUCTIZE THEIR SERVICES

We are quickly moving away from a postindustrial society through a service-based society toward an information-provider society in which the most valuable people will be those with access to the best information and a heightened ability to rapidly sift through that information to provide solid answers to serious questions. Being seen as a resource and information guru will be increasingly valuable in our society, and one of the best ways to do this is to productize your services—actively find ways to package and sell your information through printed books, how-to manuals, CDs, tapes, CD-ROMs, e-books, e-zines, and videos.

Creating products has several benefits, including these:

- It creates opportunities for multiple streams of revenue.
- It enhances your overall credibility.
- It encourages you to think clearly about who you are, what you do, and how you help.
- It opens up doors for speaking engagements and seminars.
- It can be sold online 24/7.
- It generates revenue that is not directly tied to your time.
- It stands as a strong advertisement for your services.
- It can be sold anywhere in the world at any time.

> Today, books are like business cards. Very few people will take the time to read your book; people just want to know if you have one.

The five keys to creating products that really work are these:

- You must really believe in it.
- It must be a quality product.
- It must subtly promote your services and other products.
- It should be easy for you to create.
- It has to tap into a real need.
- It must have a high profit margin.

Believe in your product. You must really believe in the power of your product to help people. Alan Wiess, the author of several excellent books including *Million Dollar Consultant* (McGraw-Hill, 1998), is famous for his saying, "The first sale is always to yourself." The point being that before you can effectively sell anything to someone else, you must first believe that it's really worth what you're selling it for and that it can really help them. If you believe your product is really only worth $10, there is no way you're going to be able to convince people to buy it for $100, or even $50. The same thing goes for pricing your services: If you believe your time is only worth $100 an hour, you will not find clients at $150 an hour, because you haven't sold yourself first.

Create a product that shows quality on the inside and out.   From the time prospects first see the product, to the time they touch it physically, all the way through finishing it, they must perceive that it is a quality product. For example, research indicates one of the biggest reasons people buy a book is their familiarity with the author, but since the overwhelming majority of authors are unknown to most people, the next two most important things are the title and the design of the cover. Top coaches know this and hire great graphics designers to create their self-published book covers instead of trying to do it themselves. If your product is physical (versus an e-book), it needs to have a good quality look and feel to it, because this will often determine whether someone buys it. However, once they buy it, you must have quality on the inside that exceeds the quality on the outside. You must underpromise and overdeliver on the content of your material. If you say your book will show 10 easy steps to becoming a well-paid speaker, it better!

Subtly promote your services and other products.   All of your products need to subtly cross-promote your services and other products. For example, when giving an illustration in your e-book, find a way to talk about how your coaching helped solve this person's midlife crisis or how 50 percent of your career coaching clients find jobs paying at least 20 percent more than their old jobs. You do not want to hard sell, or people will resent it. However, it is perfectly acceptable to soft sell them via illustrations, examples, coupons, special offers or follow-up e-mails. The key is to make your product of such quality that people will want to call you immediately after going through it. Always have a clear upsell or cross-sell for another service or product. Tell them what the next step is. Perhaps you wrote an e-book and sell it for $19.99—if you also do coaching you could include a 25 percent discount off the first month of coaching for readers (at $400 per month on average). Perhaps you authored a single cassette tape (selling for $9). You could also cross-sell purchasers your 10-week teleclass on the same topic (selling for $99), and in the teleclass you could upsell them on your one-on-one coaching services at $300 to $600 a month. You could also record the 10-week teleclass and burn it onto a CD, then sell the CD for $99 on your web site and through your e-zine. Where and when do you sell them? Start by mentioning your upsell in each product they purchase, and also send them follow-up e-mails and direct-mail pieces. Remember, the person who is most likely to buy from you is the person who has already bought from you.

Choose products that are relatively easy for you to create.　If you do a lot of speaking, think about creating multiple tapes on your favorite topics to sell, then perhaps pick one of your best presentations or seminars and have it videotaped. Then sell the videotape for $80. However, if you never do speaking, don't view this as your niche. If you hate writing, don't try to write a book—it will be torture, trust me; this is my third book. Find information products that are relatively easy for you to create, not ones that will sap all your time, energy, and emotional resources, because if you do finally succeed in finishing that excruciating product, you will be much less inclined to aggressively market it.

Focus on something your target market really wants and needs.　The next key to successfully productizing your services is to produce something focused on a primary need of your target market. It doesn't make much sense to produce a series of CDs on "10 Strategies for a Healthy Relationship" if your target market isn't interested in healthy relationships or if you never want to do any relationship coaching. Furthermore, it wouldn't be a good use of your time to write a book on dealing with divorces in small family businesses if that's not a primary need of your target market. It all goes back to identifying your target market audience, discovering their points of pain, then creating a straightforward product that tells them how to resolve that pain.

Choose products that have a high profit margin.　I have come across several web sites selling white papers, short reports, and small e-books for as little as $1 to less than $10 each. That strategy makes sense if you're Wal-Mart, where you can expect to sell hundreds of thousands or even millions of copies, but it does not make sense for a small-business owner, because you cannot do enough volume to overcome the low profit margin. If you're going to create a product, take the extra time to make it a great and valuable product so you can sell it for at least $20 or hopefully for a couple of hundred dollars. Part of this strategy comes from recognizing that the value of the product is not found in the form it takes (printed book or e-book, tape or CD), but in the information it provides and the severity of the problem it resolves. For example, there are many aspiring authors out there who have wanted or tried to write or finish a book for years. If you write an e-book that can show first-time authors 10 easy steps for writing their first book in less than 30 days, and your process really works, many people who have been trying to write that elusive book for years will gladly pay you for the information. Better yet, add some one-on-one coaching onto it and make it a program.

That last strategy is exactly what I did with my first book, *Selling Your Mind Without Selling Your Soul: 10 Principles for Marketing Your Professional Services* (TLC Business Press, 2002). It was designed to be a practical manual for entrepreneurs and small-business owners who are selling a service rather than a product. It helps them think strategically about their marketing. Recognizing that most people will not pay more than $40 for a book, I added two more features—a CD-ROM loaded with actual marketing materials they can use to market their service and four 30-minute business coaching sessions with me, the author. I now sell the manual only as part of the Practice Building Program. The value of the material in the manual alone is worth well over $100, the CD-ROM over $150, and the business coaching is worth $500, for a total of $750, but we currently sell the entire program for $97. The most common response I get when I tell people the price is, "What's the catch? Why is it so low?" That's a much easier question to answer than, "Wow! That's really a lot of money!" Perhaps you're asking the same thing—how can I afford to sell it so low? Call me at (888) 588-5891 and I'll tell you my secret. When people ask me how I can charge so much for my coaching, I point out that what I do helps people create significantly more wealth than what I charge them. If I help an entrepreneur making $400,000 a year to increase sales by 15 to 20 percent in six months, they will earn an extra $60,000 to $80,000—that's an incredible return on investment. It also helps that I have proven experience and solid client testimonials to back up my belief, and the products I have created enhance my credibility.

SECRET 8: OTHER SECRETS OF HIGHLY SUCCESSFUL COACHES

"Wait a minute—I thought you said there were only seven secrets of highly successful coaches?" Well, technically there are only seven (after all, thanks to Stephen Covey, everyone knows there are only seven secrets to anything, right?), but there were a few more things I found out about in my research that wouldn't fit under a simple heading, and I thought you might want to know about them. Besides, part of being a good writer is underpromising and overdelivering, and since I only promised seven secrets you should think of this as a bonus!

Top coaches actively seek out highly affluent clients and opportunities. Now this may seem rather obvious at first, but top coaches clearly recognize that very few individuals can afford to pay anyone $150 to $300 per hour for anything, much less a personal coach, so they make it part of their marketing strategy to intentionally seek out affluent people. They join networking groups that affluent people frequent. They volunteer to assist with projects and sit on boards where they can meet affluent people. They speak at networking events of affluent groups. In addition, they are open to and actively seek out business professionals, executives, and owners of companies as clients, because they recognize that such clients are used to paying high-priced consultants and often place a much higher value on their time, energy, and resources than do typical nonbusiness professionals. For example, they can quickly recognize the value of paying someone $200 a hour if that means they will increase their personal productivity by 20 percent, which results in freeing up one entire workday per week to work on other projects or spend more time with their family and still complete all their professional goals and work objectives. One reason why top coaches target business professionals is that 75 percent of them market themselves as business coaches rather than personal coaches. Even though many business coaches deal with much the same issues as personal coaches, top coaches are more likely to position themselves as business coaches.

Top coaches hire their own coach.   Research shows that 73 percent of full-time coaches make less than $10,000 their first year doing coaching. In fact, my research indicates that there are only three ways a coach will make more than $75,000 in the first year of business:

- They have already been doing consulting for a long time in some field and decided to add "coaching" to their practice.
- They were recently in a position of influence or power at a mid-sized to large company, and when they left, their former company became their first and biggest client.
- They hired an experienced, highly successful coach to work with them one-on-one.

Of these three ways, the only one most people can really influence in their favor is the third one, because either you have been doing consulting for a long time or you haven't. Either you have recently left an influential position at a large company or you haven't. But anyone can hire a successful coach. Will it guarantee your success? No. Can you be financially successful in your first year without hiring a highly successful coach? Yes. However, nothing *guarantees* success, and even 1 person in 10 million playing the lottery will be lucky enough to win. I'm not talking about a guarantee or blind luck. I'm talking about significantly increasing your odds of success. What I'm telling you is not based on my theory, but on responses of more than 300 coaches nationwide. I have already talked in depth about the various pitfalls of hiring a coach in a previous chapter, and I don't believe everyone should have a coach, but hiring an experienced, highly successful coach is one way that new coaches can immediately push themselves to the top of the financial pile. Also, don't make the mistake of hiring just any coach, because 65 percent of all coaches making less than $10,000 also hire coaches. However, when you talk to those coaches about what they discuss with their coach, it sounds more like they are receiving coaching around developing their personal life, rather than helping them build their business or find more clients. By the way, purchasing this book entitles you to free business coaching. See the last pages of this book.

Highly successful coaches do more than just one-on-one coaching.   Fully 100 percent of highly successful coaches spend some of their time speak-

Specific Action Step	Timeframe	Measure of Success

FIGURE 13.1   Action worksheet.

ing to groups, 100 percent of them spend part of their time conducting training or holding seminars, and 93 percent of them spend some of their time doing traditional consulting work. They see coaching as one of the services they offer to people, not the only service. They also use each of their services to cross-sell and upsell their other services. They use speaking to sell their coaching. They use coaching to sell their consulting. They offer coaching as a follow up to their training seminars. They work with business professionals as a team, then add on individual coaching. They are constantly looking for the next sale, even as they are completing the first one.

ACTION STEP

The real question is, how you are going to use this information to make a significant and radical difference in your practice? What are the three or four specific things you are going to do in the next 30 to 90 days can have the potential to rapidly take your business to the next level? Write them down in your notebook or copy the chart in Figure 13.1.

SUMMARY

There you have it, the eight or so secrets of highly successful coaches. In this chapter we focused on:

- How to consistently receive better referrals from your current and former clients
- Three things that sell better than coaching (they are: benefits, value, and results)

- The marketing strategies highly successful coaches use to consistently grow bigger, faster, and keep themselves in high demand
- Ways you can significantly increase your profits per client by creatively packaging your services
- The top benefits of having a partnership and how to best use one to build your company
- How to tie the results you achieve to the fee you receive
- Specific ways to productize your services and multiply the size of your effect
- How top coaches use highly successful coaches to launch them to the top of the financial pile

As we come to the end of this book I hope you have found the strategies and techniques to be helpful in creating, building, and maintaining a thriving coaching practice. For more marketing tips and business-building information, visit my web site (www.TodaysLeadership.com) and sign up for the free *Market Like a Pro!* e-zine. Here's to your never-ending success in reaching your personal and professional goals.

Index

About the Author

Stephen Fairley is an author, professional speaker, executive coach, and president of Today's Leadership Coaching (www.TodaysLeadership .com), a Chicago-based executive coaching and leadership development firm. He works with small-business owners, presidents, and executives to help them significantly increase their performance, productivity, and profitability.

Clients range from small entrepreneurial ventures to more than 20 *Fortune* 500 companies including many professional service firms, coaches, consultants, therapists, and psychologists who are looking to grow their business.

He is the author of two other books: *Selling Your Mind Without Selling Your Soul* (TLC Business Press, 2002), a self-help manual designed to help professional service providers and small-business owners discover and apply the 10 principles for effectively marketing their business, and *6 Keys for Successful Leaders* (TLC Business Press, 2003), written to help executives and business leaders strengthen their leadership skills and develop their people.

Prior to entering the field of coaching, he was a therapist at three different private practices, two community agencies, and three hospitals.

He has owned and operated four small businesses, including a consulting firm, two high-technology start-ups, and his current firm — Today's Leadership Coaching. He has two master's degrees, and is currently finishing his doctorate in clinical psychology.

He regularly speaks to groups throughout the United States on building a coaching business, small-business marketing, and developing leadership skills. For availability, call (888) 588-5891 or visit www.StephenFairley.com.

Ready to Move Forward?

By reading this book you have started on the right path to growing your business. If you're committed to building a financially successful coaching practice and you're ready to move forward, here are the next steps:

- Contact us for a 30-minute coaching session
- Ask for the Target Market Inventory (TMI)—a powerful tool to help you identify your ideal clients
- Sign up for our monthly e-zine designed to help you implement high-impact marketing on a low-impact budget
- Find out about our new MYOB for Coaches Program

To register, contact us at 1-888-588-5891 or by e-mail: Info@Getting StartedinCoaching.com.

The MYOB for Coaches Business Development Program

Since the first printing of this book, hundreds of coaches have contacted Stephen Fairley asking where to go for more help on building their practice. In response to this demand, Stephen is proud to announce the creation of the "MYOB for Coaches Business Development Program." This is an intensive, 3-month practice building program designed for coaches who are serious about increasing their revenues and creating a financially successful practice.

It will help you rapidly implement the proven techniques and real-world strategies outlined in this book. If you are one of the 50% of coaches with less than 10 paying clients and making less than $20,000 a year, then you owe it to yourself to look into the MYOB for Coaches program.

For more information or to register, contact us at 1-888-588-5891 or by e-mail: Info@MYOBforCoaches.com. Visit our web site at: www.MYOB forCoaches.com.

We Want to Hear from You!

The authors would love to hear what you think about this book! If you have a raving review about how it helped you build your coaching business, or any comments or suggestions about the contents of this book, the strategies discussed, the research conducted, or how it could be improved in the future, please take time to write them down and send them to:

Stephen Fairley
Today's Leadership Coaching
Product Department
405 East Roosevelt Road
Wheaton, IL 60187
Stephen@TodaysLeadership.com
(630) 588-0766 (fax)